Tailoring Your Tastes

Tailoring Your Tastes

Linda Omichinski, BSc, (FSc), RD
Author of **You Count, Calories Don't** *and*
creator of HUGS™ Plan for Better Health

Heather Wiebe Hildebrand, RN, BSN

To assist you in working with the techniques and tips in this book, you will find worksheets at the end of each section. Use them to write down the tips that work for you. Try your own favorite recipes and work through the process of gradual change. *Enjoy . . . .*

TAMOS Books Inc.
Winnipeg, Canada

© 1995 Linda Omichinski and Heather Wiebe Hildebrand.
For more information contact TAMOS Books Inc., 300 Wales Avenue, Winnipeg, Manitoba, Canada R2M 2S9

FIRST EDITION
3 5 7 9 10 8 6 4 2

ISBN 1-895569-34-6

Design A.O.Osen
Photography Walter Kaiser, Custom Images

PRINTED IN CANADA

Canadian Cataloguing-in-Publication Data
Omichinski, Linda, 1955–

    Tailoring your tastes

    Includes bibliographical reference and index.
    ISBN 1-895569-34-6

1. Diet. 2. Nutrition. 3. Life style.
I. Hildebrand, Heather Wiebe, 1965– II. Title.

RA784.054 1995   641.5′63   C95-920067-3

Acknowledgements

To our husbands Bernie and Mitchell, who encouraged us to pursue our goals and then supported us through the process. To our mothers and mothers-in-law, who are living the HUGS philosophy and bring many practical insights to healthy eating and living. To Heather's father-in-law for helping with the endless taste testing. To all our parents who taught us that everything can be achieved when you believe in something and work hard.

To Kathleen Harrison, MSc, RD, CDE for testing the recipes and helping us create recipes that are simple to follow and successful no matter what level of cooking experience the reader has. Also for editing the book in its initial stages.

To Monica Wiebe for her advice and counsel on the first draft of the book.

To all the HUGS class participants from Crystal City, MB, who gave us many recipes and insights on what people want to know in order to change their families' favorite foods to reflect healthier choices.

To Sandra Barsy for her insight and creativity in arranging words that capture the concepts and essence of *Tailoring Your Tastes* and for her participation in the test kitchen, tasting and giving helpful guidance.

To Florence Klassen for her inspiration and creative hand in helping prepare the food for photography; and to Lori Beattie for her expertise in creating settings for the photography.

To our publishers for believing in our ideas and using their expertise and enthusiasm to make a strong guide book for people who want to choose healthier eating patterns and enjoy the process. Our deepest thanks.

Contents

Preface

Gone are the days of reluctantly eating something healthy only because you feel it's good for you. Now health-conscious people want to learn how to acquire a taste for the textures and flavors of foods that are lower in sugar, fat, and salt and higher in fiber. To help you do this an innovative new approach is suggested here. It's a gradual three-stage process that enables you to experiment for taste comfort using the carefully modified recipes we have provided.

These delicious recipes contain a wealth of concepts and tips that demonstrate what, how, and why changes are made— cause and effect is explained. Suggestions are given on how to round out meals so that you leave the table feeling comfortably satisfied. The direction of change for fat, fiber, salt, sugar, and protein for each recipe shows you how the change is made. You benefit from a new taste experience and also from an improved nutrition profile.

The skills that you learn from following the modifications given in these recipes can be adopted to change your family's favorite recipes. Learning this step-by-step process will introduce a lifetime of healthy enjoyable eating as the preferred choice.

As co-author of *Tailoring Your Tastes*, Heather Wiebe Hildebrand brings valuable insight from her own personal experience as a dieter and a person with diabetes, a licensed HUGS facilitator, and a professional community health nurse. The introduction provides Heather's perspective on how *Tailoring Your Tastes* was developed and suggests how to use the book most effectively. Each recipe section enables you to put nondiet nutrition concepts into practice. Enjoy the experience!

Linda Omichinski, BSc, (FSc), RD
Author of *You Count, Calories Don't* and creator of
HUGS™ Plan for Better Health.

Introduction

Why another cookbook

With the glut of cookbooks on the market, why write another? When I was reviewing the cookbook world, I noticed it seemed divided into two main categories—**traditional** that leaned toward higher fat, sugar, and salt contents, and **healthy** that are wary of these ingredients. There is little between these extremes, and none that I found to help you move from traditional to healthy while still enjoying what you eat.

In my own experience, drastic changes in eating habits that I made when dieting did not permanently affect my food preferences. I made a conscious effort to make healthier food choices and dove into the "healthy" cookbook section with enthusiasm. A few recipes were wonderful and my family and I enjoyed them. However, many recipes were not tasty and my family became skeptical about my "health movement" cooking. We weren't prepared for the new flavors and textures we were experiencing. The jump was too big. We preferred the old flavors, textures, and tastes too much to sacrifice them. Disappointed with all our "health" food, I returned to old recipes and cooking techniques as soon as the diet was over.

When I started incorporating the HUGS plan for better health into my life, I stopped dieting and made the decision to strive for a healthier life-style. The book *You Count, Calories Don't* introduced me to the concept of making changes gradually. Now, as a facilitator for the HUGS program, I notice that participants often make the mistake I made. They make drastic changes too quickly. They need a step-by-step guide to show them how to introduce changes gradually.

I have been working as a community nurse for several years. I counsel individuals and groups in the area of health promotion. I found that the people who wanted to make life-style changes shared many of the dilemmas that I and my family had faced. Comments such as, "That is a great recipe but my kids would never eat that!", were common. After some discussion I found that many families had lists of the recipes that their kids would eat and these had become family favorites. Now people were asking me for ideas to help them move their family favorites toward "healthy" recipe selections. They wanted to make changes but wanted something moderate with room for movement. And that is how *Tailoring Your Tastes* began—as a tool to guide families toward healthier eating.

Why should you take the time to work through the process?

Part of the process of eating "healthy" is to learn how to nurture and feel good about yourself. Cooking satisfying meals can be relaxing, enjoyable, and rewarding. Many people do not have the confidence or the skills to know how to be creative in cooking. The easy and quick route has been eating out or buying convenience foods. The enjoyment from mealtime and family time is lost. *Tailoring Your Tastes* is a cookbook that demonstrates easy steps toward enjoyable healthier eating. It is a valuable nutrition and food preparation guide. The instructions are somewhat more detailed than the traditional cookbook so that you know what to expect as the recipes are modified. Enjoy the success it can bring to you.

Who is this book for?

- Families and individuals who want to learn to make healthier food choices
- People who have tried to change their eating patterns and have found the jump has been too big and have given up
- People who love to eat, don't want to give up the flavors and textures they enjoy, but still want to move to healthier eating
- People who have tried everything else to change their eating patterns and have been disappointed by the process
- People who don't have confidence in their cooking skills and end up eating out or using convenience foods
- People who take no enjoyment in cooking

How to use this book

Tailoring Your Tastes is meant to be a guide. Each section includes favorite recipes—all family tested and family approved. The modifications used in the modified recipes are meant as examples. Look at them. Note the change in each variation and utilize the ideas and techniques in other recipes. The changes mentioned will help you learn to adjust your own recipes gradually to reflect healthier choices. The changes made from variation to variation are highlighted in **bold** and discussed in the Notes following each variation. Also pay special attention to the Tips and Notes sections for helpful hints and suggestions on cooking techniques and options. Read these sections carefully before making the recipe so that you know what to expect. Also read the grocery list (p20) and low-fat cooking techniques (p22). These sections simplify the process of shopping and give you an overview of the new skills you will learn. As you move through the variations, the grocery list will provide you with the ingredients to stock your cupboard to reflect your new tastes and way of cooking. Since the ingredients will be used frequently throughout the book, even if there are leftovers, they will soon be used up in future recipes prior to the expiry date on the container or package. And alternate uses are sometimes given for leftovers. Have fun working with the recipes you already enjoy and start on the road to gradual change.

Some recipes may seem more complicated than others. In most cases you will want to use the recipes as indicated because they will work best the way they are written. Remember that sometimes a few extra ingredients make the difference in flavor, texture, and enjoyment. Begin with the recipes that are your favorites. The recipes chosen are from traditional family cooking. Some of the recipes make larger quantities that are great for entertaining. They will demonstrate that even when entertaining, recipes can be flavorful and enjoyable, yet still reflect your new taste and texture preferences. As you begin to experience success and enjoy homemade meals, you may find that a little extra time in the kitchen can be fun, especially if the family helps. For those days that you don't feel like cooking, there are quick-method recipes to use. Another option is to make larger recipes of those you enjoy and freeze the leftovers (we have indicated the recipes that freeze well). Remember that freezing some foods can mean a quick meal on a day that is too hectic to start from scratch. If you prefer, some of the larger recipes can be cut in half to provide less quantity. Remember, having fun during the change process is essential for healthy living!

What variation do you start with?

Look at the ingredients in the original recipe and each variation. Compare these ingredients to what you now have in your cupboard and to what you put in your current recipes. Begin with the variation that reflects those ingredients that you normally use. For some, this will mean beginning with the original version; for others, it will mean beginning at one of the variations. Be honest with yourself. If you are now on a diet, your cupboard may be filled with low-fat ingredients, but secretly you still love high-fat foods. Take this into consideration when preparing a recipe. It's important that you don't move too quickly through the variations so that you allow your taste buds to adjust to the new tastes and textures.

What will you discover as you move through the variations?

The original recipes have a richer and creamier content than the variations. The original recipes use more sauces on the main dishes, more dressing on the salads, and more icing on the desserts. You may enjoy this way of eating now. But as you move through the variations using less fat, sugar, and salt, new taste experiences will evolve. The richness supplied by fat is often replaced by protein so that you have more nutritional value plus the holding power that protein provides. And fat-rich sauces, dressing, or icing will no longer mask the natural flavor of the dish. Rather, smaller amounts used as an accent will heighten flavor. Creaminess will be replaced by a flavorful meal with more texture from increased fiber. Acquire the skill to taste and appreciate the subtle differences as you move through the variations. In time, increased flavor and texture will signify a good meal.

How quickly should you move from one variation to the next?

Each recipe has three variations. Each variation is slightly different than the one before, gradually shifting the ingredients and preparation techniques toward healthier choices. Changes are made slowly to help you and your family tailor your tastes to enjoy the new flavors and textures. Gradual change helps you to get used to and enjoy the changes rather than make you feel that the new food flavor and texture are too foreign to be repeated. If you enjoy the change you will choose it again and the new eating habits will become permanent. The flavor, taste, and textures your family prefer can slowly be altered.

We recommend that you make only one or two small changes at a time. Then continue to use that variation for a few months to a year before moving on. This will allow your family to adapt to the new flavors and textures. If you make an alteration that your family doesn't enjoy, go back to the last change or try making only half the change. The key is to enjoy your food choices so they will remain with you. When you have stayed with a variation for a while, move to the next variation. The speed and duration of each change depends on you and your family. In some recipes you may never go to the final variation and in others you may choose to make further changes.

How far should you take these ideas?

These variations are guidelines. You, along with your family, can decide how far you want to go and what changes work for you. Tailoring your tastes to enjoy new flavors and textures is a slow, enjoyable process. Over time your new choices will become preferences. You will choose cooking techniques and foods that are lower in fat, sugar, and salt and higher in fiber because you *prefer* them, not because you *should* eat them. When you prefer something, you repeat it. Repeating healthier life-style practices leads to healthier living.

The process of healthier living is an enjoyable journey. Your state of overall health does not depend only on what you eat. It depends on every part of you and your life-style including activity levels, mental health, and the ability to find balance between work and play. You can find more information regarding these areas in *You Count, Calories Don't.*

It is important to put eating and food preparation in perspective. It is only one of the many parts of your life. Don't let eating and food control you. Have fun, be adventurous. Variations in your life are limited only by your imagination, so go to it!

Why there aren't numbers (calories or fat counts) in this cookbook

We all look at numbers. What size do I wear, how much do I weigh, how many calories does that have, how many minutes have I exercised, how much cholesterol does that have? Numbers can control what we do, how we feel about ourselves, and how we cope with life.

Focusing on numbers can take the enjoyment out of life and it doesn't help us to become healthier, happier people. We exercise to lose weight or burn calories rather than to enjoy the outdoors or feel the improved energy and self-concept that activity brings. We feel good about ourselves on the days that we weigh the "right" amount and feel depressed and forlorn when we are above that number. Often we choose foods because they are lower in fat or have fewer calories rather than because we enjoy them. But when we get tired of counting we crave the familiar flavors, tastes, and activities we enjoyed before, and we return to old eating habits and patterns. None of these numbers helped us to become healthy and numbers didn't help us to learn to enjoy the flavors and textures of foods lower in fat, sugar, and salt and higher in fiber. Numbers just provided a rule book of what is good and bad to eat. So let's look at food in another way. What are the flavors and textures of the foods we enjoy? What parts of food make us enjoy it? Can we slowly change our preference for these flavors and textures to reflect healthier eating patterns without becoming obsessed with numbers? We think we can!

It isn't important to know the exact calorie or fat content of food. What is important is that you enjoy what you eat and learn to enjoy foods that are lower in fat, sugar, and salt content and higher in fiber. If you enjoy the foods, you will continue to eat them. This is considered a permanent preference change, a change that reflects healthier eating.

Each recipe variation in *Tailoring Your Tastes* includes a guide to important nutritional components. The arrows reflect a change and the direction of change. They do not reflect an amount or percentage of change. For example

VARIATION 1	VARIATION 2	VARIATION 3
Salt ▼	Salt ▼▼	Salt ▼▼▼
Sugar	Sugar	Sugar ▼
Fat ▼	Fat ▼▼	Fat ▼▼▼
Fiber	Fiber	Fiber ▲

Variation 1 changes from the original recipe as follows: salt content is decreased, sugar content remains the same, fat content is decreased, and fiber content remains the same. Variation 2 changes from Variation 1 as follows: salt is decreased, sugar remains the same, fat is decreased, and fiber remains the same. Variation 3 changes from Variation 2 as follows: salt is decreased, sugar is decreased, fat is decreased, and fiber is increased.

The goal of gradual change is not to achieve some magical percentage but rather to learn to enjoy new tastes and textures. The amount of change is not important. The point is to make small enough changes so that foods you like will still be enjoyable, while the changes will slowly reflect the healthier choices you want to incorporate into your eating patterns. By making the changes slowly, your taste buds and taste preferences will have the opportunity to gradually experience and enjoy healthier food choices and cooking techniques.

Important information about kids and their fat intake
In our zeal to eat and enjoy healthier lower fat food choices, adults may be overzealous with children's eating habits. We think that the adult belief that if some reduction in fat is good, then a large reduction is better. This is an inappropriate message for children and adolescents. Even though we are aiming for a gradual reduction in fat to develop a new taste for low-fat foods, some of the variations that are lower in fat may, in fact, be too low for a growing child. During preschool and childhood years when children are

growing, additional fat may be necessary in order to obtain the energy needed to support normal growth and development of healthy cells in the brain and body and to support growth spurts.[2,9,14]

Infants need to receive approximately 50 percent of their energy from fat. This is considered necessary for normal growth and development. Adults require less than 30 percent of their energy from fat. From the age of two until the end of linear growth (some time in adolescence) there should be only a gradual change from higher to lower fat eating patterns in order to maintain appropriate growth and development.[9]

Families striving to make healthier eating choices may want to include foods in their eating plans that emphasize a variety of complex carbohydrates including those that are lower in fat. Growing children however require foods that are higher in fat content than the adults in the family. Some higher fat foods may need to be included in children's eating plans that support this need. For example, regular cheese and peanut butter may be more appropriate choices for children than the lower fat versions. If your family enjoys lower fat versions of recipes, you may try to include higher fat choices at snack or breakfast time for your children. This will help them to acquire the extra energy and calories they need to sustain normal growth and development. A gradual shift to lower fat after adolescence can be achieved by incorporating the carbohydrate/protein balance described on p14.

Finding a healthy balance

In order to be as healthy as we can be, we need to find balance in our lives—balance between work and leisure time, rest and activity, mental stress and relaxation, and, of course, in what we eat and drink. We need to find the balance of food that will keep us satisfied, energized, nourished, and sustained. *Tailoring Your Tastes* focuses on balance in food and drink, and is a step-by-step guide to gradual change. And the book, *You Count, Calories Don't*, details how to successfully achieve a healthy balance in all areas of life.

• **EAT REGULARLY THROUGHOUT THE DAY**

When you eat regularly, you provide your body with a constant supply of nutrients and energy for active daily living. When you skip some meals and eat large amounts at other meals you confuse your body, causing it to slow down in metabolic rate when not being fed and then to feel tired, lethargic, and overfull when giving it too much food at other meals. This is because smaller, more frequent meals provide the body with a constant supply of energy.[14]

A regular energy intake actually increases your metabolic rate. You need to eat more, not less, in order to get your body working and your system revved up.

- **EAT A BALANCE OF CARBOHYDRATES AND PROTEIN FOODS AT EACH MEAL**

As a person with diabetes, I have discovered how important it is to balance my meals and snacks with carbohydrate and protein foods. If I have a snack or a meal with carbohydrate foods alone I find that I am hungry sooner and my blood glucose (sugar) jumps up very quickly and dips very low after that, leaving me feeling tired, hungry, and weak. If I include a small amount of protein food with my snack I find that I stay full longer, my blood sugars stay more consistent, and I feel energized for a longer period of time. You don't have to have diabetes to discover this benefit of balance. (*See* the diagrams and additional notes on p172 that emphasize the point.[14])

In order to understand why this is important we need to consider how carbohydrate and protein foods are used by our bodies and how they interact with each other. This will be a simplified version of the process. Carbohydrate foods create energy for the body. They include foods such as bread, bread products, cereal, pasta, rice, potatoes, crackers, dried peas, beans, and lentils, milk, starchy vegetables, and fruit. When carbohydrates are broken down in the body they become glucose. Glucose is what our body needs to have energy. *We can therefore call carbohydrate foods our energy foods.*

Protein foods contain building blocks or nutrients that help to rebuild our body. They help to build and repair tissues, hormones, and enzymes. When eaten together with carbohydrate foods, protein foods help to sustain energy. Protein foods include meats, poultry, seafood, peanut butter, eggs, cheese, dried beans, peas, and lentils. *We can call protein foods our sustaining foods.* When you include protein foods with carbohydrate foods they slow down the digestion process therefore slowing down the release of glucose into the bloodstream. This allows the energy found in carbohydrate foods to be released at a slower and steadier pace than if you eat a carbohydrate food alone.

There is one food type that crosses both the carbohydrate and protein categories—legumes (dried peas, beans, or lentils). Many legumes are not only high in carbohydrate, but also high in protein. They are also low in fat content and high in fiber.

For those people who choose a vegetarian diet, the quality, as well as the quantity, of protein is a concern. As mentioned previously, protein provides the body with building blocks. The adult body needs over 20 amino acids (protein building blocks) to maintain health. Nine of these amino acids cannot be made by the body, so they must be obtained from the foods we consume. Proteins from animal sources have these 9 amino acids in the proportions that the body needs. They are called complete proteins. Most vegetable protein sources are missing at least one of these amino acids. Therefore they are called incomplete proteins.[7] In order to complete the amino acids it is important to include a variety of foods with your vegetable protein. (They don't need to be at the same meal, just in the same day.) These add-on foods include nuts, seeds, grains, small amounts of meats, poultry, eggs, or dairy products. Adding some of these foods to your daily intake when you are using vegetable sources of protein will give you the 9 essential amino acids and help to round out the vegetable proteins into complete proteins.

Eating a combination of carbohydrate and protein foods at each meal will give you the nutrients and energy to function every day. By spreading your foods throughout the day, your evening meal will not be as top heavy in quantity and protein content. You will feel satisfied and full longer and have a more steady source of energy between eating times. This is what we all need to stay healthy and happy.

So how much can I eat?

You will notice that we have not included suggested serving sizes or the number of servings each recipe makes. We have included the *total* amount that each recipe yields. This is because the size of the serving you eat will depend on your hunger levels. Each person's hunger level varies from day to day in response to activity levels, body needs, and time of day the meal is eaten.

Many people have lost the skill of knowing how much they need to eat to feel energized and satisfied because they have spent so much of their life following regimented eating programs. Tune into your own signals of hunger and fullness. Your own body is the best guide for how much you need to eat. Become aware of how it feels to be hungry, full, or uncomfortably full. Change your eating patterns to give you a satisfied energized feeling after eating and start to eat when your body is telling you it is hungry.

A simple way to balance your meal is to look at your plate (regardless of size) and divide it up to look like this:

2/3 to 3/4 carbohydrate (i.e. vegetable, bread, potato, pasta, etc.)

and 1/3 to 1/4 protein content (i.e. meat, seafood, poultry, eggs, cheese, peanut butter, legumes).

If your meal consists of more than the main plate, *apply this concept to the entire meal*.

This simple tool allows you to quickly check what kind of balance you have in your meal and judge whether it is the balance that will leave you feeling energized and satisfied. As for the exact amounts, it is more important for you to become aware of your own hunger signals, food needs, and what will satisfy you. This is a process that may take a while, but the benefits are endless. For more information about eating patterns, learning to tune into your signals for hunger and fullness, discovering why we eat when we aren't hungry, learning balance in all areas of life, and learning how to feel good about yourself, we recommend reading *You Count, Calories Don't* and/or contacting your local HUGS facilitator who can help you learn more about living a healthier life. (*See* p176 for more details.)

- **EAT BREAKFAST REGULARLY**

People who skip breakfast actually slow down their metabolic rates and feel dragged out and without energy. When the body isn't fed regularly it slows itself down and in the end needs less energy to survive. This is because the body kicks in with a defense mechanism to protect it from starvation.

Skipping breakfast results in a sluggish mind and body. The brain requires a steady source of glucose in order to function optimally. Glucose is the breakdown product of carbohydrates. Breakfast helps to replenish these energy stores. Did you know that you actually burn more calories during and after a meal than if you skip one?

Eating infrequently by skipping breakfast can put your body into a starve/binge cycle. The insatiable hunger that builds up is your body's way of storing up food just in case you decide to return to the starvation mode.

If you aren't a breakfast eater, slowly learn to be one. Try a small amount of something you enjoy. In order to get the most from your breakfast, experiment with foods by including:

1) A carbohydrate food like bread or toast, a muffin, fruit, crackers, cereal, milk, an english muffin, a bagel, pancakes

2) A protein food like cheese, peanut butter, eggs, meat, crisp bacon, cottage cheese, quark cheese. *Notice the difference in sustained energy levels that you feel when you include a protein source in your meal.*

- **EAT SLOWLY AND TASTE, SAVOR, AND ENJOY YOUR FOOD**

When you focus on and enjoy what you eat you will find that you feel satisfied sooner and will actually need to eat less overall. Eating more slowly allows your body to feel satisfied while you are eating and slows down the release of sugar to your bloodstream. It takes about 20 minutes for your stomach to notify the brain that you are full. Eating slowly and enjoying your food will allow you to feel physically and emotionally satisfied after the eating experience. Eating is not an unproductive waste of time as many people would have us believe. It is a special time for yourself to nourish your body and mind by putting a pause in your day. Relish your food and enjoy!

- **ENJOY VARIETY IN YOUR FOOD CHOICES**

Don't eat the same thing every day. Add variety to your culinary life so that you won't get tired of the same old thing. Try mixing and matching different foods together. Enjoy the colors, flavors, and textures of food as they enhance your meal selections. Don't expect only one dish to give you balance in your eating. Add extras that give you added nutrients, colors, flavors, textures, and balance between carbohydrate and protein foods. Have fun with what you eat. This will add a new dimension to your life that will give you much satisfaction.

As you tune into the different textures and flavors of foods you will become aware of the more chewy, crunchy texture of higher fiber foods. Higher fiber foods are those that add bulk to your diet and are not digested or are only partially digested by the body. Fruits, cereals, seeds, nuts, grains, and vegetables are examples of foods that are higher in fiber content.

There are two kinds of fiber:

soluble fiber—cellulose, hemicellulose, and lignin

insoluble fiber—pectins and gums

Both fibers are important in healthy eating, the difference is where they come from and their affect on the body. Foods containing water insoluble fibers such as wheat germ, whole grains, cracked wheat, bran, bulgur, and brown rice are not digested and add bulk to the diet. They are thought to improve bowel regularity. Foods containing water soluble fibers such as seeds, legumes, oat bran, nuts, raw and dried fruits, raw and cooked vegetables, become a gel-like substance during digestion. They seem to keep blood glucose and cholesterol levels in line.[1,8,14,15,21] As well, eating patterns rich in fiber-containing foods are also thought to play a part in preventing serious bowel disorders and decreasing the risk of colorectal cancers.[10]

How you prepare your food can make a difference. Processing (i.e. cooking, pureeing, grinding) will change the size of the fibers and their effects on the body, although the total amount of fiber will be unaffected. For example, finely ground wheat bran does not have the same anti constipating effect as coarse wheat bran. For this reason, choosing a variety of high fiber foods that aren't highly processed will give you the benefits of more fiber in your diet. Include raw vegetables, legumes, beans, and coarser grains.[22]

See the introduction to Main Dishes, p94, for helpful hints on the importance of gradually increasing fiber in your diet.

Increasing fiber allows you to experience the crunchy texture of foods, rather than equating enjoyment of foods with the greasy taste and mushy texture of high-fat processed foods. As a bonus, increasing the fiber assists in decreasing fat by making you feel full more quickly. Physiologically, fiber does wonders in maintaining regularity and, depending on the type of fiber, may play a roll in lowering blood sugar or cholesterol levels.

Why is it important to increase the fiber and decrease the fat, salt, and sugar in your eating pattern? By eating in a healthier fashion, you not only have more energy and a healthier body, but you decrease the risk factors for diseases such as high blood pressure, heart disease, diabetes, and cancer.

Sugar and salt tend to be the central focus in many recipes where these ingredients may actually contribute to masking the true and natural flavors of food. When these ingredients are used in this way, they no longer serve as an accent to enhance the food. In the case of sugar, these extra empty calories have their purpose in contributing to the enjoyment and functional property of the recipe. However, in many recipes, sugar use goes way beyond the functional purpose of tenderizing and/or sweetening. Salt is also often used in excess. Physiologically, excess salt intake can cause water retention and could lead to kidney problems. When salt and sugar are used in excess, the natural flavor and texture of the recipe may be masked at the expense of a wonderful new taste experience and one's health.

Tailoring Your Tastes offers you the opportunity to experience the natural transition that occurs in appreciating healthier foods without the feeling of deprivation.

—SPECIAL NOTE—

Before you begin to apply the concepts and techniques in *Tailoring Your Tastes*, take a minute to fill out the following quiz. The questions will appear again at the end of the book. Send us a copy of both analysis responses and you will receive a free newsletter. The bonus is that you can use this analysis as a bench-mark to rate your own progress toward the enjoyment of healthier eating.

TASTE AND APPETITE ANALYSIS

1 Never
2 Rarely
3 Sometimes
4 Often
5 Very Often
6 Always

- [ ] I eat at least three meals a day.
- [ ] Foods that are good for you taste good.
- [ ] I find it easy to make changes in recipes.
- [ ] Healthy meals are easy to prepare.
- [ ] I eat fewer fatty foods.
- [ ] I eat snacks between meals if I am hungry.
- [ ] It is easy to find ingredients to make healthier meals.
- [ ] I change recipes to decrease the energy and/or fat content.
- [ ] I enjoy the taste of lower fat foods.
- [ ] I enjoy foods that have a crisp, crunchy, or chewy texture.
- [ ] I enjoy experimenting with my regular recipes.
- [ ] I start my day with breakfast.
- [ ] I eat more potatoes, rice, pasta, and legumes than meat at my meals.
- [ ] I read labels to help me make choices to suit my taste preferences.
- [ ] When I finish eating, I feel satisfied and energized.
- [ ] I use herbs to add taste to a meal.
- [ ] **TOTAL** Add **4** to the total to determine your percentage.
  (Compare this score with the same quiz at the end of the book)

Make copies of your completed Analyses (pp19 and 170) and mail to
HUGS International Inc., Box 102A, RR#3, Portage la Prairie, Manitoba,
Canada R1N 3A3. We will send you a free newsletter.

Grocery List

These items are frequently used in this recipe book. Some of these products might be new on your grocery list. We have included some helpful tips on how and why to use and buy these products.

Whole wheat or whole grain flours
• If you aren't used to using whole wheat flour, buy it in small quantities because the oil in the whole wheat flour can go rancid in your cupboard if you don't use it up quickly enough.
• Store it in an airtight container in your freezer (keeps indefinitely) or leave it in a bag tightly closed to prevent it from going rancid.
• You can often buy whole wheat flour in bulk food stores, where you can choose exactly how much you want to buy and get it at a reasonable price.

Instant flour
• These products are easy and quick to use in thickening soups, sauces, and gravies. They are slightly more expensive than using flour or cornstarch as thickeners. However, these products are quicker and easier to use and give you more successful results. If you have trouble with lumpy sauces these thickeners are a must.

Tomato paste
• Tomato paste has a somewhat harsh tomato taste and needs to be used in small amounts. It is lower in sugar and salt and higher in fiber than ketchup. Because the flavor is much stronger than ketchup, less is required when used to replace ketchup in a recipe.
• Tomato paste can be added to tomato sauce to add a zippy flavor.
• Purchase tomato paste in small cans so that you will have less excess. Seldom do you use a whole tin of tomato paste. You can store the remainder in a well sealed, labeled container in your refrigerator for about a week or in your freezer for many months. I have successfully stored it in the freezer for six months.
• To store leftover tomato paste, spoon tablespoon-size dollops onto a small cookie sheet and freeze until firm. Transfer to a plastic bag, seal, and freeze. Remove as needed and add to sauces, vegetables, soups, or stews.

Evaporated milk
• If you are used to using cream in many of your family favorite recipes, stock a few tins of whole evaporated milk in your cupboard. For those who enjoy lower fat recipes, try stocking a few tins of part-skim or skim evaporated milk. Evaporated milk has a very creamy texture that is a wonderful lower fat alternative to whole milk or cream in cream soups, gravies, sauces, and desserts.
• IMPORTANT NOTE—There is a definite flavor difference from one brand of

evaporated milk to another. If you find one has a "tinny" or "fake milk" flavor, try another! My favorite brand is Alpha.

• Extra evaporated milk can be stored in a sealed, labeled container in your refrigerator for up to a week or in your freezer for two to three months, then thawed and used in other recipes.

Plain yogurt

• Buy a small container at first. Be sure to check the expiration date before you buy the product to ensure maximum time of freshness.

• Plain yogurt is used in many of the recipes in this book, don't let our ideas limit you. Yogurt is a wonderful addition to many foods and is also a tasty treat on its own with some added fruit and honey (or sweetener of your choice). *See* p164 to make your own yogurt.

Dried or tinned lentils, chick peas (garbanzo beans), white beans, or any other legume of your choice

• Legumes are a healthy and tasty option to add to your meals. They are high in fiber and many nutrients. Many of the legume family are also high in vegetable protein and can be used as a protein source either alone or in combination with animal protein.

• If you are unfamiliar with legumes, I would suggest trying to add them in combination with animal protein.

• Tinned variations of these products are convenient because they are easy to store, easy to use (you don't have to soak and pre-prepare them); and they have a long shelf life. The drawback of tinned varieties are that they are higher in salt content and are a little more costly than buying the dried legumes and preparing them yourself.

• Dried beans or legumes are simple to prepare and the healthiest and most economical protein source available. Their only drawback is that they take a bit of forethought in preparation time.

Tips & Techniques
for Lower Fat Cooking

When you move toward lower fat foods you will find that there are some techniques and ideas that will make the move more enjoyable. Try the following suggestions. They will be repeated in many of the recipes in this book. You can use these ideas and techniques in your own recipes as well.

These techniques help to make baked and cooked foods tastier, moister, and more enjoyable when using less fat content. Some of the techniques are a little more time consuming than traditional methods of cooking. Once you begin to incorporate these skills into your way of cooking, they become a more natural quick process. The end results are worth the extra effort. Enjoy the gradual process of change. Make meal preparation a fun part of your day by including your family.

Browning ground beef
• Ground beef can be browned alone or with onion and garlic in a microwave oven. Place beef, onions, and garlic in a microwave-safe sieve. Put the sieve in a microwave-safe bowl.
• Microwave uncovered on high for 2 to 3 minutes at a time. Take the meat mixture out and stir. Return to microwave again.
• Repeat this procedure until the meat is completely browned. The sieve will allow fat to drip to the bottom of the bowl, so you aren't cooking the meat in the fat.

Sauteing vegetables
• Replace some or all of the sauteing oil with dry white wine to add moisture to vegetables. You may need a greater amount of wine than oil because the liquid cooks out of the wine faster than the oil. Adding about 1/4 cup (50 ml) white wine increases the sugar content to the equivalent of approximately 1/4 tsp (1 ml) white sugar. The increase is very small and compensates for the decrease in fat content.
• Cheaper white wine found at liquor stores is a good choice. Using a bottle with a screw top makes storage easier. Remember the alcohol content is removed during the cooking process as long as the wine boils (which is does when sauteing).
• Using wine to saute vegetables results in a lower fat food that has a lovely tangy flavor. And the aroma of vegetables cooking in white wine is very appealing.

Separate eggs and whip the whites
• Use this technique for a lighter fluffier texture, when baking lower fat cookies, puddings, cakes, or muffins.
• Separate egg whites and beat until they are white and hold their shape. Add

egg yellows to other ingredients as outlined in the recipe. Follow the recipe as instructed, leaving the egg whites until the end. Then gently fold the beaten egg whites into the remainder of the ingredients until completely blended.

Underbake cookies
• Cookies have a nicer texture if they are slightly underbaked and this is essential when the fat content is decreased.
• Never bake a lower fat cookie much longer than 8 minutes in a 375°F (191°C) oven (time will vary depending on the oven).
• When the outside of the cookies start to get firm, the middles will still look soft and unbaked. However, once the cookies have cooled they will be moister than if they are overbaked.

Tips for storing lower fat baked foods
• Most lower fat baked foods taste best fresh. If you want to store them, use an airtight container. Store them in your freezer and remove only what you want to eat at one sitting.
• Lower fat baked foods can be stored on your counter in an airtight container for a few days. However, lower fat foods don't taste as good the second day. Freezing everything not used the day it is baked is preferable.

Combining wet and dry ingredients
• Undermix wet and dry ingredients for cakes, muffins, pancakes, and quick breads. Use only a few strokes to mix dry ingredients until just moistened. The more you mix these foods the tougher the product will become.
• The more gluten protein in flour is activated (resulting from overmixing), the tougher the food will be. That is why undermixing is essential.

Using pureed cottage cheese
• Pureed cottage cheese can replace all or some of the sour cream or cream cheese in baking or cooking. Cottage cheese is lower in fat content and higher in protein content than both sour cream and cream cheese.
• It is important to puree the cottage cheese until smooth in order to prevent lumps and to ensure that the baked product has a similar texture to products baked with sour cream or cream cheese.
• Cottage cheese has a higher liquid content than cream cheese and sour cream. *If you are using it to replace these products, the cooking or baking time may need to be increased.*
• If available, skim milk quark cheese has a similar fat content to 1% cottage cheese and can be used in its place. Note that regular quark cheese is significantly higher in fat content to the skim milk version.
• A shortcut to puree cottage cheese easily and quickly—
   Mix 2 cups (500 ml) of 1% cottage cheese with 1 tbsp (15 ml) plain yogurt or milk (optional, the additional fluid allows the mixture to be pureed more easily). Puree this mixture in a blender until smooth.

Empty the blender from the bottom.
- Since the volume is equal to the weight in cottage cheese, you would purchase a 16 oz (500 g) container of cottage cheese to get 500 ml or 2 cups.
- If the recipe in which you use cottage cheese utilizes an electric mixer, the mixer rather than a blender can puree the cottage cheese. Use a spatula to scrape the sides of the bowl to ensure that the cheese is being mixed well.
- For recipes that require smaller amounts of cottage cheese, puree the cottage cheese with an electric handheld blender or mini electric chopper.
- When recipes call for smaller amounts of pureed cottage cheese, puree 2 cups (500 ml) of cottage cheese at a time and refrigerate or freeze the remainder for future use. This mixture stores in your refrigerator for the same amount of time as unpureed cottage cheese.
- Other ideas for pureed cottage cheese
  —to replace some or all of the sour cream and/or cream cheese in recipes
  —as a great dip or topping on baked potatoes sprinkled with green onions and/or bacon bits
  —added to sauces for additional flavor and body
  —added to 1 small package of lemon or lime jello at the sloppy stage (use 1/2 cup or 125 ml cottage cheese; serve set jello on a lettuce leaf as a tangy accompaniment to a meal)
  —served on toast with jam as a lower fat replacement for cheese spreads (cream cheese, quark or skyr cheese)

Using quark or skyr cheese
- Quark and skyr spreadable cheeses are found in the dairy section of the grocery store.
- Quark cheese which has a little milder flavor is more like cream cheese with a runnier texture.
- Skyr cheese has a sharper flavor and is more like sour cream.
- When adding skyr cheese in place of cream cheese or sour cream in recipes, the cooking time will increase due to the higher moisture content.
- Quark and skyr cheeses are lower in fat than sour cream and cream cheese.
- Quark cheese is slightly higher in protein than cream cheese and much higher in protein than sour cream.
- Skyr cheese is lower in fat than regular quark cheese and is higher in protein than cream cheese and sour cream.
- Skim milk quark cheese is available in some locations. It is considerably lower in fat than regular quark cheese and is also lower in fat than skyr cheese.
- Other ideas for quark or skyr cheese
  —to replace either some or all cream cheese or sour cream in recipes
  —in dips and sauces for a zippy flavor
  —in desserts, cheesecakes, and cream cheese frostings

Dilly of a Dip for Vegetables, Variation 3, p39;
Tips & Techniques for Lower Fat Cooking—
pureeing cottage cheese with an electric handheld blender
or electric mini chopper, pp23-4

Left: Sunshine Muffin, Variation 3, p63, with quark cheese;
Right: Cranberry Oat Muffin, Variation 2, p65, with peanut butter and fruit spread;
The Perfect Cup of Tea, p126

—in stroganoff, stews, and casseroles
—to serve on pancakes with a little fruit for added protein and flavor
—to serve on toast or bagels with or without other toppings such as jam or fruit spreads for a quick breakfast idea

Making lower fat gravy—The Ice Cube Technique
• Put warm drippings from meat or poultry in a saucepan.
• Add about a tray of ice cubes into the drippings (more or less, depending on how much fluid you are working with). The ice cubes cool the liquid quickly, allowing the fat to rise to the top and/or cling to the ice cubes.
• Skim the fat off.
• Reheat the liquid and add your favorite herbs and spices (if they aren't already there) and thicken with quark cheese, oat bran, and/or a lump-free thickener of your choice.
• The resulting gravy is flavorful and has less fat. Remember, gravy is an accent. Enjoy the flavors and textures of the foods underneath the gravy, don't smother them.

Using low-fat yogurt
• Plain or plain low-fat yogurt (.9% M.F. or less) can replace some of the oil, shortening, or butter/margarine in cakes, cookies, or muffins.
• Adding yogurt to a baked food replaces some of the moisture lost when fat is decreased.
• Adding yogurt to a baked food also adds a small amount of carbohydrate and protein to the food. Even though the sugar content increases due to the carbohydrate content in yogurt, the amount is small. (Adding 1/4 cup (50 ml) of yogurt to a recipe adds the equivalent of about 1/2 tsp (2 ml) of white sugar to an entire recipe.)

Using yogurt cheese
• Yogurt cheese is a low-fat option that is easy to make and a delicious substitute for higher fat ingredients. See p165 for recipe.
• The thickness of yogurt cheese can be controlled by the length of time yogurt is allowed to sit in a strainer. The longer it sits the thicker the consistency.
• Yogurt cheese has a trace of fat and some protein content.
• Use firm yogurt cheese to replace cream cheese or quark cheese in recipes. Use soft yogurt cheese to replace sour cream, mayonnaise, or whipped cream on desserts.

Using honey, corn syrup, or molasses to sweeten lower fat foods
• These products can be used in baking when you are decreasing the fat content to replace all or part of the sugar content in recipes.
• These three sweeteners replace moisture that is lost when decreasing oil and fat and add lovely flavors to foods.

• Honey, corn syrup, or molasses do not have the same sweetening capacity as table or brown sugar, so you can't replace them cup for cup in a recipe. Here are some guidelines for the same amount of sweetness:

—**Honey** about *3/4 cup (175 ml) honey to 1 cup (250 ml) sugar*
—**Corn syrup** *3/4 cup (175 ml) plus 2 tbsp (30 ml) corn syrup to 1 cup (250 ml) sugar*
—**Molasses** *1 cup (250 ml) molasses to 1 cup (250 ml) sugar*

• Honey, corn syrup, and molasses give foods an added soft texture when used in place of sugar. Molasses has a distinctive flavor and dark color.

• If you substitute honey directly for table sugars, you will actually be consuming more sugar than you were originally.

• When making changes to your recipes do so gradually. If you make changes too quickly you and your family won't enjoy the flavor changes. Slower changes last longer.

Unsweetened applesauce adds moisture to lower fat foods

• Unsweetened applesauce adds extra moisture and sweetness to recipes so you won't notice the decrease in sugar and/or fat in lower fat cooking. You may want to decrease the sugar content when using this product in baking to replace some of the fat. Otherwise you will end up increasing instead of decreasing the total sugar content due to the natural sugar in applesauce.

• Do not use unsweetened applesauce in the same recipe you are replacing the sugar content with alternate sweetening agents such as honey, molasses, or corn syrup. The end product will be too moist and won't hold together.

• Unsweetened applesauce has a much less sweet taste than table sugar. Use
1/2 cup (125 ml) unsweetened applesauce to 1 tbsp (15 ml) white sugar
for the same amount of sweetening power.

• Direct replacement of unsweetened applesauce to white sugar isn't very effective because of the quantity of applesauce you would need to equal the sugar sweetness. You would have too much moisture and applesauce flavor for the recipe. As your tastes change and you enjoy foods with less sweet tastes you can use less applesauce, and you may choose to use it to replace sugar as a sweetener.

• Unsweetened applesauce does a great job in replacing some of the fat in baking, but it does add extra sugar to a recipe. The sugar found in fruit is called fructose. It digests more slowly in the body than table sugar (sucrose).[6] This is because it first needs to be broken down into glucose before it can be used as an energy source for the body.

Use a nonstick cooking spray

• Whenever a pan needs to be greased or oiled, use a nonstick cooking spray. Your products won't stick and the amount of added fat is very low.

Use a nonstick frying pan
• When sauteing you will find that you need less or no oil to create lovely dishes if you use a nonstick pan.
• If you are adding oil to saute foods, allow the oil to get hot prior to adding the food. Foods soak up cool oil faster than hot oil.
• Use 1 tsp (5 ml) oil per person or less to prevent sticking and moisten food.
• If your pan does stick, condition your nonstick frying pan for ease of cleaning in this manner:
    —Place 2 tsp (10 ml) vegetable oil in the pan and wipe it around using a paper towel until the inside is evenly coated.
    —Place the pan over medium heat for 30 to 60 seconds. Remove from heat.
    —Wipe pan dry with paper towel and allow to cool before storing.
    —If burnt food continues to stick to the pan, a nylon scrubbing brush or pad can be used. Never use steel wool or scouring powder. This will damage the finish.

Use lower temperatures and cook lean roasts covered
• Cook lean roasts at 325°F (160°C) for tender cuts and 275°F (130°C) for medium cuts. Roasting time will need to be longer and remember to cover the roast for the most tender results.
• New slim roasts have a minimum fat covering and less marbling than roasts of the past, and cooking covered at lower temperatures will minimize shrinkage and moisture loss.
• A slow cooker or crock pot makes an easy meal. Put herbs, spices, cut-up potatoes and carrots into one pot and cook it all day (8 to 10 hours) on low heat for a tasty treat. A slow cooker or crock pot also work well for stews and meat sauces. The longer cooking time makes the meat tender and delicious. If you have less time (4 to 5 hours), you can put the slow cooker on high heat. Tougher cuts of meat become tender because of the lengthy cooking time.

Marinate lean cuts of meat
• Marinating meats help to tenderize and add flavor to lean cuts of meat.
• Marinating liquids include wine, vinegar, seasoned vinegars, soy sauce, citrus juices, beer, yogurt, and oil. The acidic ingredients soften the tough connective tissue and the oil lubricates. Often the oil can be eliminated.
• *Do not use salt in a marinade* because it draws out the moisture.

Use herbs and spices to add flavor to food
• Make creative use of seasonings to add flavor without adding extra fat, salt, or sugar.
• Use herbs such as dill, rosemary, thyme, and garlic instead of salt for flavor.
• Herbs and spices heighten the flavors of the food when fat is decreased.
• You may find that you need less herbs and spices when cooking lower fat foods because the fat often masks these flavors. Have fun experimenting with new tastes!

Cooking with Legumes

Cooking with legumes (pulses) can be a fun part of food preparation. Legumes can be added to existing dishes, used in soups, or as a puree. *Tailoring Your Tastes* gives you ideas how to incorporate legumes into recipes. This is beneficial because they are high in carbohydrates and fiber, and are an excellent form of vegetable protein. They are also very economical.

One use for cooking legumes is to puree them. You can use puree in a dip with added spices, or use instead of grated carrot, squash, or applesauce in baked goods to boost protein and fiber levels. For example, pulse (legumes) puree can be added to muffins in place of applesauce to make this snack more substantial due to the increased protein content.

How to make pulse puree
>   4 cups (1 L) pulses
>   10 cups (2.5 L) water or other liquid

Wash pulses. Cover with water. Bring to a boil and reduce heat. Cover and simmer until the pulses are very tender, (40 to 50 minutes for lentils or split peas; 1-1/2 to 2 hours for beans). Drain. Blend pulses, adding enough liquid to make a puree the consistency of canned pumpkin. As puree forms, stop and mix often until puree is smooth. *Makes 8 cups (2 L).* Freezes well.

Although many people find the preparation of legumes daunting, they are fairly simple to prepare. Here are some simple guidelines.

(Pulse puree and legume tables are printed with permission from the Saskatchewan Pulse Crop Development Board.)

Bean	Description	Soaking Method	Cooking time after soaking
Great Northern	•large oval-shaped white bean •delicate flavor •great in baked beans or salads	Quick or long	1 to 1-1/2 hours
Pink	•dusty rose color •delicate flavor •easily substituted for other beans	Quick or long	1-1/2 to 2 hours
Pinto	•sand-colored bean with brown freckles •earthy flavor •used extensively in Mexican cooking	Quick or long	1-1/2 to 2 hours
Red Mexican	•small, red oval bean •robust flavor •used in chili, bean salad, and Mexican dishes	Quick or long	1-1/2 to 2 hours
Kidney	•white, light or dark red bean •earthy flavor •used in chili and salads	Quick or long	1-1/2 to 2 hours

Bean	Description	Soaking Method	Cooking time after soaking
Navy or **White pea bean**	• small, white, round shaped bean • traditionally used in baked beans	Quick or long	1 to 1-1/2 hours
Black	• small, black oval bean • nutty flavor • turn a rich brown when cooked • traditionally used in black bean sauce	Quick or long	1 to 1-1/2 hours
Chick peas or **Garbanzo beans**	• round, bumpy, and light brown • size varies with variety • nutty flavor • often found in salad bars and East Indian cooking	Quick or long	2 to 2-1/2 hours

Lentils are circular, flat, lens-shaped seeds usually found with a green seed coat. Lentils can be used as vegetables in soups, salads, and casseroles, or pureed and added to baked products. Lentils are excellent as sprouts, too.

Lentils	Description	Soaking Method	Cooking time after soaking
Laird	• 6 mm across • light green seed coat and yellow cotyledon • nutty flavor • great in soups and purees	No soak	30 to 40 minutes (cook 45 to 50 minutes for puree)
Eston	• 4 to 4.5 mm across • light green seed coat and yellow cotyledon • nutty flavor • retain their shape after cooking • well suited to salads and soups	No soak	30 to 40 minutes (cook 45 to 50 minutes for puree)
Rose (Split)	• light green seed coat and red cotyledon • sold commercially with the seed coat removed and cotyledon split • cook quickly and are easily added to soups and tomato sauces	No soak	10 to 15 minutes
CDC Gold	• 5 mm across • thin white seed coat which becomes translucent after cooking to reveal a bright yellow cotyledon • nutty flavor • retain light color after cooking and canning	No soak	30 to 40 minutes

Field peas are usually round seeds with a translucent seed coat. Dry yellow peas, whole or split, are the main type grown, with green peas making up a small percentage of production.

Pea	Description	Soaking Method	Cooking time after soaking
Yellow	• yellow cotyledon • available whole or split • excellent in soups and salads	Whole: quick or long Split: no soak	Whole: 1 to 1-1/2 hours Split: 40 to 45 minutes For puree: 45 to 60 minutes
Green	• green cotyledon • available whole or split • traditionally used for pea soup	Whole: quick or long Split: no soak	Whole: 1-1/2 to 2 hours Split: 40 to 45 minutes For puree: 45 to 60 minutes

What about Flaxseed?

Although most flaxseed is grown for linseed oil and is generally not considered a food in Canada, it is found in many food items. Since biblical times it has been used in breads, bread products, soups, and main dish sauces. The plant has a lovely blue flower during the growth period that turns reddish brown when ready to harvest. It is one of the most attractive crops grown in the central prairies.

In the past few years flaxseed has begun to gain new status. It is becoming the "healthy" food choice of the 90s for several reasons:

1. It has the world's highest concentration of omega-3 fatty acids (linolenic acid).[3,4,5,11] Consuming omega-3 fatty acids is thought to greatly reduce the risks of heart disease and decrease the risk of some cancers.[3,4,5,13,16,17,19] Deficiencies in this fatty acid have been associated with some skin and neurological disorders.[3,5,16,17,18,19]
2. It is an excellent form of soluble fiber.
3. It has many important nutrients needed in daily living.
4. It is easy to use, easy to get, and relatively inexpensive to buy.

It is important to remember that oil in flaxseed is made available only when it is ground. Because of high-oil content, flaxseed becomes rancid quickly if it isn't used shortly after grinding. In baking it is used in place of other oils and fat in a 3:1 ratio.

NUTRITIONAL CONTENT OF FLAX[18]		
	MG/100G	% U.S. RDA
Potassium	750.00	100
Phosphate	650.00	6
Calcium	250.00	25
Magnesium	250.00	87
Iron	10.20	57
Manganese	7.00	100
Copper	.70	35
Zinc	2.00	13
B-1	.66	44
B-2	.31	18
B-3	4.40	22
Pantothenate	.70	7
Linoleic acid	6240.00	312
Linolenic acid	16920.00	846

Appetizer— a food that whets your appetite and/or begins a meal. Appetizers often stimulate the palate and delight the eye. Presented as finger foods, premeal morsels, or as party foods, appetizers are a social food— something to be enjoyed in the company of others.

Soup— a well rounded food choice that can serve as an appetizer or part of a balanced meal. Soup is often referred to as a comfort food. It is a tasty, nutritious, and economical choice for a family of any size. Soup contains many carbohydrate foods (vegetables, pasta, potatoes, rice, whole grains, etc.) with only a little protein to help sustain fullness. *Remember that the balance of carbohydrates-to-protein that we are striving for in meals is* **2/3–3/4 carbohydrates to 1/3–1/4 protein.** Making soup a part of a balanced meal may require adding more protein foods. If you don't include a balance in your meals, you will find that you get hungry soon after eating resulting in nibbling. Or you may develop a headache, or feel lethargic because you do not have sufficient energy to keep your body and mind functioning.

Appetizers and soups are fun foods. Their contents are limited only by your imagination. Try variations to create something special.

Appetizers & Soups

FOR BEST RESULTS— read through the entire recipe, each variation, and the TIPS on page 42 before preparing this soup.

This is an attractive soup with much visual appeal. Serve with hearty oatmeal bread that is topped with a favorite protein source. This soup also works as a starter for an entree with lower protein content.

Creamy Broccoli Soup

Yields 4 to 5 cups (1 to 1.25 L)

Original Recipe

6 tbsp	butter or margarine	90 ml
1	small onion, chopped	1
1 cup	chicken stock (*see* TIPS, p42)	250 ml
3 cups	broccoli, chopped	750 ml
1-1/2 cup	whole milk	325 ml
3/4 tsp	salt	3 ml
1/4 tsp	pepper	1 ml
1/2 tsp	curry powder	2 ml
dash	nutmeg	dash
1/2 cup	sour cream	125 ml
1 tsp	lemon juice (optional)	5 ml
1/3 cup	cheddar cheese, grated	75 ml

1. Melt butter in a heavy saucepan.
2. Add onions and cook until just softened.
3. Add chicken stock to onion mixture. Bring to a boil on high heat.
4. Add broccoli pieces to stock mixture. Cover tightly and simmer for 10 minutes on medium-low heat or until tender.
5. Pour from the pot into a blender, puree until smooth. Return to the pot.
6. Stir milk and spices into the pureed vegetables.
7. Heat through on medium heat.
8. Whisk sour cream and lemon juice (optional) into the hot soup.
9. Heat until hot on medium to medium-high heat, stirring frequently until the mixture is heated through. Do not boil.
10. Ladle into bowls and garnish with grated cheddar cheese and small florets of broccoli.

—NOTES—
• *Curry powder really enhances the soup flavor.*

VARIATION 1

3 tbsp	**butter or margarine**	**45 ml**
1	small onion, chopped	1
1 cup	chicken stock (p42)	250 ml
3 cups	broccoli, chopped	750 ml
1 can	**part-skim evaporated milk**	**385 ml**
3/4 tsp	salt	3 ml
1/4 tsp	pepper	1 ml
1/2 tsp	curry powder	2 ml
dash	nutmeg	dash
1/2 cup	**light sour cream**	**125 ml**
1 tsp	lemon juice (optional)	5 ml
1/3 cup	cheddar cheese, grated	75 ml

Prepare, cook, and serve as per the original recipe.

—NOTES—
• *Onions have enough moisture to adequately saute them, even with the reduction of butter.*
• *Evaporated milk has a rich texture that can replace creams and whole milk with less fat. It is condensed and therefore has a higher protein content for the same amount of liquid milk.* **Do not use condensed milk that is sweetened.**
• *Decreasing the butter, changing to part-skim evaporated milk, and light sour cream decreases the fat content without significantly changing the flavor.*

Guide to changes in salt, protein, fat, and fiber content using each variation.

	VARIATION 1	VARIATION 2	VARIATION 3
Salt		▼	▼▼
Protein	▲	▲▲	▲▲
Fat	▼	▼▼	▼▼
Fiber			▲

33

VARIATION 2

2 tbsp	**butter or margarine**	30 ml
1	small onion, chopped	1
1 cup	chicken stock (p42)	250 ml
3 cups	broccoli, chopped	750 ml
1 can	**evaporated skim milk**	**385 ml**
1/2 tsp	salt	2 ml
1/4 tsp	pepper	1 ml
1/2 tsp	curry powder	2 ml
dash	nutmeg	dash
1/2 cup	**4% cottage cheese, pureed until smooth**	**125 ml**
1 tsp	lemon juice (optional)	5 ml
1/4 cup	**cheddar cheese, grated**	**50 ml**

Prepare and cook as per the original recipe, steps 1–4.
5. Remove 1 cup (250 ml) of vegetables and set aside. Puree remaining vegetables with the chicken stock. Return pureed mixture and chunky vegetables to the soup pot.
Continue with steps 6–10; in step 8, whisk in the pureed cottage cheese.

—NOTES—

• *Using evaporated skim milk decreases the fat content in this variation.*
• *Leaving some vegetables in chunks gives this soup a coarser texture and enhances the physiological effect of the fiber. More chewing will leave you feeling full and satisfied.*
• *Pureed cottage cheese has the same texture and a similar flavor to sour cream. When added to this recipe it increases the protein content and decreases the fat content.*
• *Cheddar cheese is fairly high in fat and salt content. As an accent it is an attractive color. But you may wish to replace it with part-skim mozzarella cheese that is lower in fat and salt content.*

VARIATION 3

1 tbsp	**butter or margarine**	15 ml
1	small onion, chopped	1
1 cup	chicken stock (p42)	250 ml
3 cups	broccoli, chopped	750 ml
1 can	evaporated skim milk	385 ml
1/4 tsp	**salt**	**1 ml**
1/8 tsp	**pepper**	**.5 ml**
1/2 tsp	curry powder	2 ml
dash	nutmeg	dash
1 cup	**shredded carrots**	**250 ml**
1/2 cup	**1% cottage cheese, pureed until smooth**	**125 ml**
1 tsp	lemon juice (optional)	5 ml

1. Saute onions in butter in a non-stick pan. Continue with steps for Variation 2, adding shredded carrots just before the pureed cottage cheese.

—NOTES—

• *You may choose to add more spices to suit your family's taste preference.*
• *Carrots add a delightful change in color and texture to the soup. Carrots increase fiber, vitamins, and minerals.*
• *Moving from 4% to 1% cottage cheese decreases the fat content.*

This soup can be enjoyable as an appetizer complementing a lower protein main dish, or as a hearty meal served with a thick slice of whole grain bread.

Creamy Fish Chowder

Yields approximately 6 cups (1-1/2 L)

Original Recipe

7	strips of bacon	7
2	medium onions, chopped	2
2 cups	diced potatoes	500 ml
1/2 cup	diced carrots	125 ml
2 cups	water	500 ml
1	bay leaf	1
1/8 tsp	thyme	.5 ml
1/2 lb	cod, haddock, or halibut	250 g
2 cups	whipping cream, warmed	500 ml
1 tbsp	cornstarch	15 ml
1/2 tsp	salt	2 ml
1/8 tsp	pepper	.5 ml
	chopped fresh parsley	

1. Fry bacon until crisp in a large saucepan. Remove bacon from pan, crumble, and set aside.
2. Remove all but 2 tbsp (30 ml) of bacon fat from pan and cook onions in the fat until translucent.
3. Add potatoes, carrots, and water to pan. Cover and cook for 10 minutes.
4. Add bay leaf and thyme to mixture and stir.
5. Cut fish into bite-size pieces and place on top of the mixture in the pan.
6. Cover pan again and steam for 5–7 minutes or until the fish is opaque and flakes easily with a fork.
7. Remove bay leaf. In a small dish, mix 2 tbsp (30 ml) of warmed whipping cream with 1 tbsp (15 ml) of cornstarch until smooth. Stir this mixture into the mixture in the pan. Add the remaining cream.
8. Add salt and pepper and heat on medium-high heat, stirring constantly. When chowder begins to thicken, ladle into soup dishes.
9. Serve garnished with bacon and parsley.

VARIATION 1

6	**strips of bacon**	6
2	medium onions, chopped	2
2 cups	diced potatoes	500 ml
1/2 cup	diced carrots	125 ml
2 cups	water	500 ml
1	bay leaf	1
1/8 tsp	thyme	.5 ml
1/2 lb	cod, haddock, or halibut	250 g
1 cup	**whipping cream, warmed**	**250 ml**
1 cup	**whole milk, warmed**	**250 ml**
2 tbsp	**cornstarch**	**30 ml**
1/2 tsp	salt	2 ml
1/8 tsp	pepper	.5 ml
	chopped fresh parsley	

Prepare as outlined in the original recipe. In step 7, combine whipping cream and whole milk before adding cornstarch. Serve as per the original recipe.

—NOTES—

- *When buying bacon, choose the leanest meat available (less visible fat, more visible meat).*
- *Soaking bacon in water about 15 minutes decreases the salt content. Discard the water.*
- *Replacing some of the whipping cream with whole milk decreases the total fat content.*
- *Increasing the amount of cornstarch keeps this colorful chowder thick and creamy while decreasing the fat content.*

Guide to changes in salt, sugar, fat, and fiber content using each variation.

	VARIATION 1	VARIATION 2	VARIATION 3
Salt	▼	▼▼	▼▼▼
Sugar			
Fat	▼	▼▼	▼▼▼
Fiber			▲

35

VARIATION 2

5	strips of bacon, soaked in water	5
	(see Variation 1 Notes, Item 2)	
2	medium onions, chopped	2
2 cups	diced potatoes	500 ml
1/2 cup	diced carrots	125 ml
2 cups	water	500 ml
1	bay leaf	1
1/4 tsp	**thyme**	**1 ml**
1/2 lb	cod, haddock, or halibut	250 g
3/4 cup	**1/2 & 1/2 cream, warmed**	**175 ml**
1-1/4 cups	**2% milk, warmed**	**300 ml**
2 tbsp	cornstarch	30 ml
1/2 tsp	salt	2 ml
1/8 tsp	**lemon pepper**	**.5 ml**
	chopped fresh parsley	

1. Fry bacon in a non-stick pan until crisp. Crumble and set aside.
2. Remove all fat from the pan and wipe clean with a paper towel. Spray pan with a non-stick cooking spray. Add onions and cook until translucent.
3. Continue with steps 3–9. In step 7, combine 1/2 & 1/2 cream and milk before adding the cornstarch. In steps 7–8, it may take about 15 minutes for the chowder to thicken. Serve as per the original recipe.

—NOTES—
• *Bacon is a garnish or an accent and gives enough bacon flavor to the chowder to eliminate the need for as much bacon and the added bacon fat.*
• *Cooking onions without bacon fat and substituting 2% milk for cream decreases the fat content.*
• *Added spices give this chowder a wonderful flavor to compensate for a decrease in richness.*

VARIATION 3

1/2 cup	pearl barley	125 ml
2 cups	water	500 ml
4	strips of bacon, soaked in water	4
	(see Variation 1 Notes, Item 2)	
2	medium onions, chopped	2
2 cups	**diced potatoes, peels left on**	**500 ml**
1/2 cup	diced carrots	125 ml
2 cups	water	500 ml
1	bay leaf	1
1/4 tsp	thyme	1 ml
1/2 lb	cod, haddock, or halibut	250 g
1 cup	**part-skim evaporated milk, warmed**	**250 ml**
1 cup	**1% milk, warmed**	**250 ml**
1 tbsp	**cornstarch**	**15 ml**
1/2 tsp	salt	2 ml
1/8 tsp	lemon pepper	.5 ml
	chopped fresh parsley	

1. Cook barley in 2 cups (500 ml) boiling water for 20–30 minutes or until tender. Drain, keep warm, add to chowder when adding the milk. Chowder will thicken in 5–10 minutes.
2. Prepare and serve as outlined in Variation 2, using the above ingredients.

—NOTES—
• *Barley adds texture and increases the carbohydrate and fiber content. Barley thickens the chowder decreasing the amount of required cornstarch.*
• *Leaving the skin on potatoes adds fiber and helps to retain more nutrients. Extra fiber slows down the digestion process keeping you full longer and your blood sugar levels more constant.*

This hearty soup served with a thick slice of herbal bread can be a meal in itself. This exciting combination of vegetables is packed with vitamins and minerals. Enjoy!

Hearty Hamburger Soup

Yields 6–7 cups (1-1/2–1-3/4 L) and freezes well
Variation 3   Yields 7–8 cups (1-3/4–2 L)

Original Recipe

1 lb	hamburger	500 g
1	medium onion, chopped	1
1 cup	carrots, sliced	250 ml
1/2 cup	celery, diced	125 ml
1 cup	cabbage, shredded	250 ml
1/2 tsp	paprika	2 ml
1 tsp	dried summer savory	5 ml
1 tsp	salt	5 ml
1/4 tsp	pepper	1 ml
4 cups	hot water	1 L
2 tbsp	sugar	30 ml
2	beef bouillon, cubes or packets	2
1–19-oz can	whole tomatoes	540 ml
1–5-1/2-oz can	tomato paste	156 ml
	sour cream for garnish	

1. Brown hamburger in a heavy saucepan. Drain off fat.
2. Add browned hamburger, raw vegetables, herbs and spices, water, sugar, and bouillon to a large pot. Bring to a boil, cover, reduce heat and simmer for 55–60 minutes.
3. Add tomatoes and tomato paste. Simmer for 10 minutes more.
4. Serve in soup bowls and garnish with sour cream.

—NOTES—

• *A small bundle of fresh summer savory can be used in place of the dried variety. Remove the bundle before serving the soup.*

• *If your family prefers less tomato flavor, the tomato paste can be replaced with tomato soup.*

VARIATION 1

1 lb	**lean ground beef**	**500 g**
1	medium onion, chopped	1
1 cup	carrots, sliced	250 ml
1/2 cup	celery, diced	125 ml
1 cup	cabbage, shredded	250 ml
1/2 tsp	paprika	2 ml
1 tsp	dried summer savory	5 ml
	omit salt	
1/4 tsp	pepper	1 ml
4 cups	hot water	1 L
1 tbsp	**sugar**	**15 ml**
2	beef bouillon, cubes or packets	2
1–19-oz can	whole tomatoes	540 ml
1–5-1/2-oz can	tomato paste	156 ml
	light sour cream for garnish	

1. Place the ground beef in a microwave-safe sieve set on top of a microwave-safe bowl. Microwave on high in 2–3 minute segments. Break apart cooked meat after each time segment. Continue this process until the meat is browned. Rinse meat with hot water and discard fat under sieve in the bowl.
2. Cook and serve as outlined in steps 2–4 in the original recipe.

—NOTES—

• *Using lean ground beef increases total protein content. And microwaving the meat allows the fat to drip out, lessening fat content.*
• *Using bouillon cubes eliminates the need for added salt in the recipe.*
• *You will not notice decreasing sugar content.*
• *Using light sour cream decreases the fat content.*

Creamy Broccoli Soup, Variation 3, p33;
Honey Oatmeal Bread, Variation 1, p70

Tips & Techniques for Lower Fat Cooking—
sauteing vegetables with white wine, p22

Guide to changes in salt, protein, fat, fiber, and sugar content using each variation.

	VARIATION 1	VARIATION 2	VARIATION 3
Salt	▼	▼▼	▼▼
Protein	▲	▲▲	▲▼
Fat	▼	▼▼	▼▼▼
Fiber			▲
Sugar	▼	▼▼	▼▼

37

VARIATION 2

1 lb	extra lean ground beef	500 g
1	medium onion, chopped	1
1 cup	carrots, sliced	250 ml
1/2 cup	celery, diced	125 ml
1 cup	cabbage, shredded	250 ml
1/2 tsp	paprika	2 ml
1 tsp	dried summer savory	5 ml
1/4 tsp	pepper	1 ml
4 cups	hot water	1 L
	omit sugar	
2	low-sodium beef bouillon, cubes or packets	2
1–19-oz can	whole tomatoes	540 ml
1–5-1/2-oz can	tomato paste	156 ml
	mixture of light sour cream and plain low-fat yogurt for garnish	

1. Prepare and serve as outlined in Variation 1.
2. For the garnish, prepare a mixture of half light sour cream and half skim milk or 1% yogurt.

—NOTES—

• *Using extra lean ground beef decreases fat content and increases protein content.*
• *Low-sodium bouillon cubes or packets are available at your grocery store. The beefy flavor is retained while decreasing salt content.*
• *Sugar is added to this recipe to sweeten the tomato flavor and make it less tangy. If a tangy tomato flavor is not suitable, leave the sugar in the recipe.*
• *Replacing half of the light sour cream with skim milk or 1% yogurt decreases fat content.*

VARIATION 3

1 cup	lentils	250 ml
2 cups	water	500 ml
1	bay leaf	1
3/4 lb	extra lean ground beef	375 g
1	medium onion, chopped	1
1 cup	carrots, sliced	250 ml
1/2 cup	celery, diced	125 ml
1-1/2 cups	cabbage, shredded	325 ml
1/2 tsp	paprika	2 ml
1 tsp	dried summer savory	5 ml
1/4 tsp	pepper	1 ml
5 cups	hot water	1.25 L
2	low-sodium beef bouillon cubes or packets	2
1–19-oz can	whole tomatoes	540 ml
1–5-1/2-oz can	tomato paste	156 ml
	low-fat yogurt for garnish (optional)	

1. Add lentils and bay leaf to water. Bring to a boil and simmer for 15 minutes. Drain.
2. Prepare ground beef as outlined in Variation 1. Add legumes to the beef.
3. Cook and serve as outlined in steps 2–4 in the original recipe.

—NOTES—

• *Uncooked lentils can be added to soup. However, precooking them in separate water decreases the intestinal gas-producing effects common to most legumes.*
• *Legumes add texture, flavor, and fiber. Using legumes as a source of protein in place of meat decreases fat content and increases fiber content. Both cabbage and legumes are a good source of soluble fiber.*

FOR BEST RESULTS— read through the
entire recipe, each variation, and the TIPS on
page 43 before preparing this vegetable dip.

*A creamy dip with a distinctive tangy
flavor will accent your favorite vegetables.
The Worcestershire sauce adds the tang.
If you prefer a milder dip, omit this
ingredient.*

Dilly of a Dip for Vegetables

Yields approximately 1 cup (250 ml)

Original Recipe

3/4 cup	mayonnaise	175 ml
1/4 cup	sour cream	50 ml
1 tbsp	onion, finely chopped	30 ml
1 tsp	dried parsley	5 ml
1 tsp	Worcestershire sauce	5 ml
3/4 tsp	dried dill weed (or seed)	3 ml
1 clove	garlic, minced	1 clove
1 drop	tabasco sauce	1 drop

1. Mix all ingredients together.
2. Refrigerate for at least 6 hours to allow flavors to blend.
3. Serve with a mixture of fresh vegetables.

VARIATION 1

3/4 cup	**light mayonnaise**	**175 ml**
1/4 cup	**light sour cream**	**50 ml**
1 tbsp	onion, finely chopped	15 ml
1 tsp	dried parsley	5 ml
1 tsp	Worcestershire sauce	5 ml
3/4 tsp	dried dill weed (or seed)	3 ml
1 clove	garlic, minced	1 clove
1 drop	tabasco sauce	1 drop

Mix and serve as outlined in the original recipe.

—NOTES—

• *Worcestershire sauce is optional. It adds a
tangy flavor and gives dip a beige color. Without
the sauce the dip will have a milder more
pronounced dill flavor.*

—NOTES—

• *The texture in this variation is a little
thinner than the original.*
• *Light sour cream and light mayonnaise
decrease fat content. Remember to read the
label to discover if "light" actually means less
fat. Some light mayonnaise products contain
50% less fat and do not use egg yolks.*
• *Allow proper "sitting" time after making
this dip. Then the texture will become creamy
and the flavor will be similar to the original.*

Guide to changes in salt, protein, fat, and fiber content using each variation.

	VARIATION 1	VARIATION 2	VARIATION 3
Salt	Salt	Salt	Salt
Protein	Protein	Protein ▲	Protein ▲▲
Fat	Fat ▼	Fat ▼▼	Fat ▼▼▼
Fiber	Fiber	Fiber	Fiber

VARIATION 2

1/2 cup	**light mayonnaise**	**125 ml**
1/4 cup	light sour cream	50 ml
1/4 cup	**plain yogurt**	**50 ml**
1 tbsp	onion, finely chopped	15 ml
1 tsp	dried parsley	5 ml
1 tsp	Worcestershire sauce	5 ml
3/4 tsp	dried dill weed (or seed)	3 ml
1 clove	garlic, minced	1 clove
1 drop	tabasco sauce	1 drop

Mix and serve as outlined in the original recipe.

—NOTES—

• *The addition of yogurt makes this variation delicious and tangy. It is lower in fat content because mayonnaise is decreased.*

VARIATION 3

1/4 cup	light mayonnaise	50 ml
3/4 cup	**1% cottage cheese, pureed until smooth, OR**	**175 ml**
3/4 cup	**plain yogurt**	**175 ml**
2 tbsp	**onion, finely chopped**	**30 ml**
1 tsp	dried parsley	5 ml
1 tsp	Worcestershire sauce	5 ml
2 tsp	**dried dill weed (or seed)**	**10 ml**
1 clove	garlic, minced	1 clove
1 drop	tabasco sauce	1 drop

1. Blend the cottage cheese in a blender or with an electric hand-held blender until smooth (*see* p23). *If the cottage cheese is not pureed enough it will result in a grainy product.*
2. Mix and serve as outlined in the original recipe.

—NOTES—

• *Using an electric hand-held blender is a quick way to puree cottage cheese. Pureed cottage cheese has the same texture and a similar flavor to sour cream. Adding cottage cheese decreases fat content while increasing protein content.*

• *Increasing dill and onions adds lovely flavors and makes the decrease in fat content less noticeable.*

• *If this variation is too tangy for your tastebuds, add 1 tsp (5 ml) sugar.*

• *It is possible to decrease fat content more by using a lighter yogurt, such as .9% M.F. (milk fat).*

• *Be sure to allow the dip to set for at least 6 hours before serving to allow the flavors to blend.*

FOR BEST RESULTS— read through the entire recipe, each variation, and the TIPS on page 44 before preparing this fondue.

Fondues are "fun" foods to serve to guests. They make wonderful appetizers or an innovative evening snack. Fondues are easy to serve and allow you to enjoy great conversation while relaxing around the fondue pot.

Cheese Fondue
Yields 2–2-1/2 cups (500–750 ml) sauce

Original Recipe

1-1/3 cup	1/2 & 1/2 cream	325 ml
2 tsp	Worcestershire sauce	10 ml
1-1/2 tsp	dry mustard	7 ml
1 clove	garlic, minced	1 clove
2 tbsp	onion, finely chopped	30 ml
2 tbsp	all purpose flour	30 ml
1 lb	cheddar cheese, grated	500 g
1/4 tsp	ground pepper	1 ml
	salt to taste	

1. Heat 1 cup (250 ml) 1/2 & 1/2 cream and the Worcestershire sauce, dry mustard, garlic, and onion over medium heat in a fondue pot. Stir frequently until the mixture is hot.
2. Add flour to remaining 1/2 & 1/2 cream (1/3 cup or 75 ml) and whisk until smooth.
3. Gradually pour the flour and cream mixture into the hot mixture, whisking while pouring.
4. Add the grated cheese to this mixture.
5. Heat over medium heat, stirring constantly until the cheese is melted and the mixture is smooth and hot. If you heat it too long the mixture will separate.
6. Add salt and pepper to taste.
7. Place over a fondue heat source.
8. Serve with fresh or partially steamed cut-up vegetables and chunks of brown and white bread.

—NOTES—
• *1 lb (500 g) of grated cheddar cheese is equal to 3-3/4 cups or 925 ml. This may be a more convenient method of measure.*
• *If fondue lumps, mix with an electric handheld blender until smooth following step 6.*

VARIATION 1

2/3 cup	1/2 & 1/2 cream	150 ml
2/3 cup	whole milk	150 ml
2 tsp	Worcestershire sauce	10 ml
1-1/2 tsp	dry mustard	7 ml
1 clove	garlic, minced	1 clove
2 tbsp	onion, finely chopped	30 ml
2 tbsp	all purpose flour	30 ml
3/4 lb	cheddar cheese, grated	350 g
1/4 lb	part-skim mozzarella, grated	125 g
1/4 tsp	ground pepper	1 ml
	salt to taste	

1. Reserve 1/3 cup (75 ml) whole milk to use to mix with the flour in step 2 of the original recipe.
2. Prepare and serve as outlined in the original recipe.

—NOTES—
• *Using whole milk and part-skim mozzarella to replace the richer products decreases fat and salt content.*
• *3/4 lb (350 g) of grated cheddar cheese is equal to 2-3/4 cups or 675 ml. 1/4 lb (125 g) grated part-skim mozzarella is equal to 1 cup or 250 ml.*
• *Part-skim mozzarella may be harder to grate than cheddar cheese because it is softer in texture. Pressing the cheese firmly against the grater will make grating easier.*

Guide to changes in salt, sugar, fat, and fiber content using each variation.

	VARIATION 1	VARIATION 2	VARIATION 3
Salt	▼	▼▼	▼▼▼
Sugar			
Fat	▼	▼▼	▼▼▼
Fiber		▲	▲▲

41

VARIATION 2

1-1/3 cup	whole milk	325 ml
1-1/2 tsp	Worcestershire sauce	7 ml
1 tsp	dry mustard	5 ml
1 clove	garlic, minced	1 clove
2 tbsp	onion, finely chopped	30 ml
1 tbsp	all purpose flour	15 ml
1 tbsp	whole wheat flour	15 ml
1/2 lb	cheddar cheese, grated	250 g
1/2 lb	part-skim mozzarella, grated	250 g
1/4 tsp	ground pepper	1 ml
	omit salt	

1. Mix whole wheat flour with all purpose flour. Prepare and serve as outlined in Variation 1.

—NOTES—

• *Replacing cream with whole milk, increasing part-skim mozzarella, and decreasing cheddar cheese decreases fat and salt content.*
• *1/2 lb (250 g) grated cheese is equal to 1-3/4 cup plus 2 tbsp or 455 ml.*
• *Fat masks flavors. As the fat decreases the spices should also decrease.*
• *Because the cheeses contain enough salt and spice flavors, the salt can be omitted.*
• *Using whole wheat flour to thicken the mixture slightly increases fiber content and adds a pleasant texture.*
• *Whole wheat flour can become rancid in cupboards if it is not used quickly enough. Store whole wheat flour in the freezer to prevent this from happening.*

VARIATION 3

1-1/3 cup	2% milk	325 ml
1-1/2 tsp	Worcestershire sauce	7 ml
1/2 tsp	dry mustard	2 ml
1 clove	garlic, minced	1 clove
2 tbsp	onion, finely chopped	30 ml
1 tbsp	all purpose flour	15 ml
2 tbsp	whole wheat flour	30 ml
1/4 cup	medium or hot salsa sauce	50 ml
1/3 lb	cheddar cheese, grated	150 g
1/2 lb	part-skim mozzarella, grated	250 g
1/4 tsp	ground pepper	1 ml

Prepare and serve as outlined in Variation 1. Add the salsa when adding the cheese to the hot mixture.

—NOTES—

• *Replacing whole milk with 2% milk and decreasing the amount of cheese lowers fat content. The mixture is a bit thinner because of the addition of lower fat milk and salsa.*
• *The fat content in this variation is still quite high due to the proportion of cheese required to maintain the flavor and texture characteristic of fondues.*
• *If you prefer 1% milk or skim milk, this recipe becomes a slightly lighter version but still just as appealing in texture and flavor.*
• *Adding the salsa gives this fondue a different look, flavor, and color. It is a more spicy flavor that complements bread and vegetables nicely.*
• *Extra flour helps to thicken the mixture to compensate for decreasing fat content.*
• *Using whole wheat flour adds flecks of color to the fondue mixture.*

Tips

*The following information for the recipes given in this section
will help you make choices and add variety to your meals.*

Creamy Broccoli Soup p32

• Eating this soup as a meal allows you to become hungry sooner because it has an insufficient protein content. Including a sandwich with this soup provides an improved carbohydrate/protein balance, leaving you satisfied longer.

• Making your own soup stock is an easy task and the benefits over canned varieties are less fat, salt, and preservatives. *See* recipe in the box on this page.

• You can replace 1 cup (250 ml) of stock with 1 cup (250 ml) of boiling water and one package or cube of bouillon. Bouillon has added sodium; however, it is low in fat. Omit the salt in the recipe if you use this option.

• You can substitute 1% yogurt or skim milk yogurt for pureed cottage cheese in the recipe. Its tart flavor and texture are similar to sour cream but yogurt contains less fat. As a replacement in cooking for sour cream, it is an excellent choice.

• You may choose other vegetables along with or instead of broccoli. Celery, zucchini, cauliflower, and potatoes work well.

• If your grocery store does not carry evaporated skim or part skim milk, ask to have it brought in. These tinned goods store for long periods of time without spoiling.

• Evaporated skim or part skim milk is an excellent creamy lower fat alternative for cream or whole milk. Various brands taste differently. Choose one that satisfies you.

Soup Stock Recipe

Leftover bones and/or small pieces of meat
Water
Allspice, thyme, rosemary, summer savory

In a large pot, cover the bones/meat with water. Add 2 tsp (10 ml) each of two of the suggested herbs and spices. The amounts are dependent on your taste preferences. Simmer for 2–3 hours. Remove the bones/meat and cool the stock in the refrigerator. Once the stock has cooled, remove any scum or fat that rose to the top. This low-fat stock freezes well and can be thawed as needed. Freeze the stock in 1–2 cup (250–500 ml) portions.

Creamy Fish Chowder p34

• Fish is an excellent form of protein and contains fats that are high in omega-3 fatty acids. These fats are thought to decrease the risks of cardiac diseases and some cancers.

• If you prefer thinner chowder, add extra milk to the cream. Warm cream and milk together before adding to the chowder. This will result in a greater yield.

• Bacon, ham, and some sausages are very high in salt content. Soaking the meat in water will decrease the salt content. Soak bacon about 15 minutes, bigger pieces of meat for a few hours, and a whole ham overnight. Discard the water.

• Leaving peels on fresh vegetables with thin skin helps to retain greater amounts of nutrients. The chowder will also have more color, texture, and fiber. Increasing fiber will slow the digestion process helping you to feel full longer. Glucose will also be released more gradually into the blood stream giving you a more constant source of energy.[14]

- Adding pearl barley, buckwheat, or oat bran to soups and chowders help to thicken them and add unique flavors, textures, and fibers.
- Evaporated milk is a good substitute for cereal or whipping cream in recipes. It has a thick creamy texture with less fat content. Different brands of evaporated milk have their own unique flavor. Experiment to find the brand that suits your tastes.
- Evaporated milk is not condensed milk. Condensed milk is a sweetened milk.

Hearty Hamburger Soup p36

- Summer savory is an herb that is easily grown in your garden. To preserve it, tie it with thread into 1/8-inch (3-mm) by 3/4-inch (19-mm) bundles, and freeze in a plastic bag.
- Summer savory can be replaced with rosemary, basil, or oregano for new flavors.
- Your choice of ground beef makes a significant difference in the amount of "hidden" fat you will consume.

Ground Beef Fat Content Guide

Regular	27—30% fat
Medium	15—23% fat
Lean	11—17% fat
Extra lean	less than 10% fat

- Is your non-stick pan starting to stick or burn? Try this trick. *After cleaning, place 2 tsp (10 ml) of vegetable oil in the pan and wipe around with a paper towel until the inside is evenly coated. Place the pan over medium heat for 30–60 seconds. Remove pan from heat. Wipe pan dry and allow to cool before storing.* This should prevent sticking.
- Lentils can be replaced with other prepared legumes such as white, navy, of lima beans. *See Legume Preparation Guide, p28.*
- If adding legumes to your diet causes you abdominal discomfort, bloating, or gas, try these tips:
  1 Add legumes or other high-fiber foods *gradually* to your eating choices.
  2 Drink plenty of water. Fiber soaks water up like a sponge. Drink more water so that the fiber in the food is able to maintain anti-constipating effect.
  3 When preparing legumes, place in boiling water and cook for 3 minutes. Turn off heat, cover, and let them soak for a few hours. Discard water. Rinse raw legumes before cooking and rinse tinned and cooked legumes prior to adding to main dishes.
- Replacing meats with legumes decreases the overall protein content in the recipe. This means you can include it in a meal with other protein sources to make it a balanced food choice.

Dilly of a Dip for Vegetables p38

- Cottage cheese can be replaced with an equivalent amount of plain low-fat yogurt and 1 tsp (5 ml) sugar. This results in a yogurt-flavored dip that many people prefer.
- Pureed cottage cheese has the same shelf life as non pureed cottage cheese. When buying cottage cheese look for the latest expiry date on the container. Prepare pureed cottage cheese in bulk. It is then ready to use anywhere sour cream is used in baking, cooking, or as a topping.
- Vegetables are a healthy and delicious snack item. Remember dips are an accent to fresh vegetable flavors, tastes, and textures. Don't mask vegetables with dip, use it to highlight vegetables.
- Quark, skyr, pureed cottage cheese, or yogurt can be used to replace sour cream, cream cheese, salad and mayonnaise type dressings. These choices contain lower fat content and higher protein content.
- Remember to make substitutions gradually, combining them with the original ingredients, so you can learn to enjoy the new flavors and textures created.
- Adding extra herbs, spices, and flavorings

can also enhance flavors in dips and dressings. Try some of the following examples:

- 1 tbsp (15 ml) onion soup mix, dill weed, garlic powder, and chili powder (If using a yogurt base, add 1 tbsp (15 ml) sugar.)
- 1 tbsp (15 ml) curry powder, 1 tsp (5 ml) dry mustard, 1/2 tsp (2 ml) garlic powder, 1/2 tsp (2 ml) onion powder
- 1 tsp (5 ml) basil, 1 tsp (5 ml) oregano, 1 tsp (5 ml) crushed rosemary, 1 tbsp (15 ml) onion soup mix

Cheese Fondue p40

- This recipe characterizes a delightful, well balanced combination of carbohydrates (vegetables and breads) and protein (cheeses and milk). The process of dipping one in the other encourages you to eat more slowly and thoroughly savor your meal.
- As you change to lower fat cheeses the color of the fondue will become lighter but the sauce is still very smooth and creamy.
- Choose a variety of vegetables and breads. Include different colors, flavors, and textures to add aesthetic appeal. Our favorite combination includes vegetables such as cauliflower, broccoli, carrots, tomatoes, zucchini, and green peppers, and breads such as whole wheat, pumpernickel, and oatmeal.
- Try using different cheeses to flavor this sauce. For example, changing cheddar cheese to Swiss results in a nutty tasting white cheese sauce.
- Try different herbs and spices. For example, add caraway seeds to the first two variations; or omit the salsa and add curry powder, cumin, and coriander for another zesty option.
- Salsa in the third variation creates a lighter, chunky texture. The color changes from orange to light yellow with delightful bursts of red from the tomato. The flavor is tangier and more spicy.

Original Recipe

Here's your chance to work with these ideas and experiment with recipes that are your family favorites. Work through the process by setting up the original recipe and then choosing the changes you wish to make in each variation.

Guide to changes in salt, protein, fat, sugar, and fiber content using each variation.

VARIATION 1	VARIATION 2
Salt	Salt
Protein	Protein
Fat	Fat
Sugar	Sugar
Fiber	Fiber

VARIATION 1

VARIATION 2

—NOTES—

—NOTES—

VARIATION 3
Salt
Protein
Fat
Sugar
Fiber

VARIATION 3

WRITE DOWN THE TIPS THAT WORK FOR YOU—

—USE THESE TIPS IN YOUR FAMILY FAVORITES!

—NOTES—

Salads can be wildly exciting, extravagant, or simple and straight-forward. They add color and variety to a meal. Yet for many people, salads, especially green salads, are the ultimate diet food. They are a low-calorie, high-fiber food choice—every dieter's ideal. How often have you heard a friend say, when dining out, "I guess I *should* just have a salad because it's good for me." They don't want a salad but they feel they should have one. They choose Caesar or spinach salads that are heavy on the dressing and feel quite proud of their determination to eat only "healthy" food. But have they really chosen a healthy meal? After they have eaten the salad they may feel deprived and later become hungry. They may binge. Why does this happen? Salad ingredients are composed mainly of water, some vitamins, and if a dressing is used, a high amount of fat. Green salads do not provide enough nutrition to satisfy hunger.

But a salad created with a balance between carbohydrates and proteins such as a tuna vegetable pasta salad can be a well balanced meal. Salad components such as fresh vegetables contain essential nutrients and fiber that make them a healthy part of a meal. Salads are an exciting part, an accent, to any meal. However, with a few exceptions, *salads alone are not a well balanced, healthy meal choice.* They are a wonderful accompaniment to a meal and round off the nutritional and carbohydrate/protein balance created by other food selections.

Salads & Dressings

FOR BEST RESULTS—read through the entire recipe, each variation, and the TIPS on page 56 before preparing this salad.

Cauliflower & Broccoli Toss

This salad has a wonderful variation of textures and flavors. The "crunch" comes from fresh vegetables and crisp bacon and the "chewy" from the raisins. Take it to your potluck supper parties. It can easily be made ahead of time.

Yields 2-2/3 to 3 cups (650 to 750 ml)
Variation 1 Yields 2-1/2 to 2–2/3 cups (625 to 650 ml)

Original Recipe

	—SALAD—	
1 cup	fresh cauliflower, chopped into small florets	250 ml
1 cup	fresh broccoli, chopped into small florets	250 ml
1/3 cup	raisins	75 ml
2 tbsp	red onion, diced	30 ml
3	strips of bacon, fried & crumbled	3
1/3 cup	sunflower seeds	75 ml
	—DRESSING—	
1 tbsp + 2 tsp	sugar	25 ml
1/3 cup	mayonnaise	75 ml
2 tsp	white wine vinegar	10 ml
1/4 cup	parmesan cheese, grated	50 ml

1. Mix salad ingredients and toss.
2. Mix dressing except for parmesan cheese and blend well.
3. Pour dressing over salad. Add cheese and toss.
4. Cover and keep in refrigerator for 2 hours or more before serving to blend flavors. If you choose to let it sit longer add the sunflower seed just before serving to maintain the crunch.

—NOTES—
• *Freshly grated parmesan cheese has more flavor.*
• *Leftover salad can be stored in the refrigerator up to 2 or 3 days and served again. Double or triple the recipe if you wish to take it to a potluck or serve at a larger gathering.*

VARIATION 1

	—SALAD—	
1 cup	fresh cauliflower, chopped into small florets	250 ml
1 cup	fresh broccoli, chopped into small florets	250 ml
1/4 cup	**raisins**	**50 ml**
2 tbsp	red onion, diced	30 ml
3	strips of bacon, fried & crumbled	3
1/4 cup	**sunflower seeds**	**50 ml**
	—DRESSING—	
1 tbsp + 2 tsp	sugar	25 ml
1/4 cup	**mayonnaise**	**50 ml**
1 tbsp	**milk**	**15 ml**
2 tsp	white wine vinegar	10 ml
1/4 cup	parmesan cheese, grated	50 ml

1. Soak raisins in hot water for a few minutes and drain.
2. Fry bacon until very crisp and drain all fat and put bacon pieces on paper towel to absorb extra fat. *See* TIPS, p56, for microwave method.
3. Mix milk with mayonnaise.
4. Mix and serve as per original recipe.

—NOTES—
• *Raisins are a source of iron, fiber, and vitamins, and are high in concentrated sugar. Soaking makes them plumper so you can use less. Fiber content is lowered but because of the abundance of fresh vegetables in the salad the decrease is negligible.*
• *Frying bacon until crisp and patting with a paper towel decreases the fat content.*
• *Using less sunflower seeds, which contain soluble fiber and vegetable protein but are high in fat, decreases the fat content.*
• *Milk replaces moisture lost from the decrease in mayonnaise and the overall fat content is less.*

Left: Mom's Macaroni Salad, Variation 2, p51;
Top: Cauliflower & Broccoli Toss, Variation 1, p48;
Center: Caesar Salad Supreme, Variation 3, p55;
Right: The Milligen Toss, Variation 3, p53

Cheese Fondue, Variation 1, p40

Guide to changes in salt, sugar, fat, and fiber content using each variation.

	VARIATION 1	VARIATION 2	VARIATION 3
Salt	▼	▼	▼
Sugar	▼	▼▼	▼▼▼
Fat	▼	▼▼	▼▼▼
Fiber	▼	▼▲	▼▲▼

49

VARIATION 2

—SALAD—

1 cup	fresh cauliflower, chopped into small florets	250 ml
1 cup	fresh broccoli, chopped into small florets	250 ml
1/4 cup	raisins	50 ml
3 tbsp	**red onion, diced**	**45 ml**
2	**strips of bacon, fried & crumbled** *(see Variation 1, Item 2)*	**2**
1/4 cup	sunflower seeds	50 ml

—DRESSING—

1 tbsp	**sugar**	**15 ml**
3 tbsp	**mayonnaise**	**45 ml**
1 tbsp	milk	15 ml
2 tsp	white wine vinegar	10 ml
1/4 cup	parmesan cheese, grated	50 ml

1. Prepare and serve using original recipe and Variation 1 instructions.

—NOTES—

• *Decreasing the mayonnaise slightly and adding a little milk gives this salad a lighter flavor and adds moisture.*

• *The decrease in sugar in the dressing is not noticeable.*

• *Adding more onion increases flavor and fiber.*

VARIATION 3

—SALAD—

1 cup	fresh cauliflower, chopped into small florets	250 ml
1 cup	fresh broccoli, chopped into small florets	250 ml
3 tbsp	**raisins**	**45 ml**
3 tbsp	red onion, diced	45 ml
2	strips of bacon, fried & crumbled *(see Variation 1, Item 2)*	2
3 tbsp	**sunflower seeds**	**45 ml**

—DRESSING—

1 tbsp	sugar	15 ml
1 tbsp	**mayonnaise**	**15 ml**
2 tbsp	**plain low-fat yogurt**	**30 ml**
1 tsp	**white wine vinegar**	**5 ml**
1/8 tsp	**lemon juice**	**.5 ml**
pinch	**garlic powder**	**pinch**
3 tbsp	**parmesan cheese, grated**	**45 ml**

1. Prepare salad as per Variation 1.
2. Mix dressing ingredients except parmesan cheese and beat well. Add parmesan when tossing the salad.
3. Let salad sit at least 4 hours in the refrigerator to allow the decreased bacon flavor, garlic, and lemon juice to permeate the salad.

—NOTES—

• *Adding less bacon decreases the fat content.*

• *Increasing the onions replaces some of the crunchy texture lost by decreasing the sunflower seeds. The overall fat content is decreased.*

• *Adding yogurt and decreasing mayonnaise lowers the fat content. Yogurt adds a tangy taste so decrease the vinegar to compensate.*

• *Adding garlic and lemon juice produces a zesty flavor.*

FOR BEST RESULTS—read through the entire recipe, each variation, and the TIPS on page 56 before preparing this salad.

This recipe makes a large quantity—great for a summer picnic. Adjust the amounts for smaller families. The salad has a wonderful combination of flavors and textures. Serve as a side dish or as an entree, if you are having appetizers or dessert with a protein content.

Mom's Macaroni Salad

Yields 8 to 9 cups (approximately 2 L)

Original Recipe

2 cups	uncooked macaroni elbows	500 ml
1/2 cup	celery, diced	125 ml
1/2 cup	red onion, chopped	125 ml
1/2 cup	sliced cucumber	125 ml
1	green pepper, chopped	1
1–6-1/2 oz	tin of tuna, packed in oil	1–184 g
1 cup	cheddar cheese cut into small square chunks	250 ml
3/4 cup	mayonnaise	175 ml
1 clove	garlic, crushed	1 clove
1/4 tsp	black pepper	1 ml
1/2 tsp	salt	2 ml
2	medium tomatoes, cut into chunks	2

1. Cook macaroni as instructed on the package. Drain and rinse.
2. Place macaroni, celery, onion, cucumber, green pepper, tuna, and cheese in a bowl. Gently mix ingredients together.
3. Mix mayonnaise, garlic, pepper, and salt together.
4. Add this mixture to the macaroni mixture and toss together.
5. Refrigerate until serving time. Add tomatoes just before serving.

—NOTES—

• *Cooked pasta (any size and shape) also works well. Use 4 cups (1 L).*
• *This salad stores well for one day. Mix everything together except the tomatoes and cucumber and refrigerate. Add the tomatoes and cucumber just before serving and toss salad again.*

VARIATION 1

2 cups	uncooked macaroni elbows	500 ml
1/2 cup	celery, diced	125 ml
1/2 cup	red onion, chopped	125 ml
1/2 cup	sliced cucumber	125 ml
1	green pepper, chopped	1
1–6-1/2-oz	**tin of tuna, packed in water, drained**	**1–184 g**
1 cup	cheddar cheese cut into small square chunks	250 ml
1/4 cup	**mayonnaise, light**	**50 ml**
1/2 cup	**plain yogurt**	**125 ml**
1 clove	garlic, crushed	1 clove
1/4 tsp	black pepper	1 ml
1/2 tsp	salt	2 ml
2 tsp	**grated lemon rind (zest)**	**10 ml**
2 tbsp	**lemon juice**	**30 ml**
2	medium tomatoes, cut into chunks	2

1. Follow steps 1–2 as per the original recipe.
2. Mix mayonnaise, yogurt, garlic, lemon juice and zest, and spices together.
3. Follow steps 4–5 as per the original recipe.

—NOTES—

• *Using light mayonnaise decreases the fat content.*
• *Adding yogurt provides moisture and a tangy flavor. Lemon juice and zest combine with the yogurt and mayonnaise for added zip.*
• *Mixing light mayonnaise with yogurt makes it creamier and decreases the glue-like consistency that is sometimes associated with light mayonnaise. Some brands are creamier than others.*
• *Tuna packed in water also decreases the total amount of fat in the recipe.*

Guide to changes in salt, protein, fat, and fiber content using each variation.

	VARIATION 1	VARIATION 2	VARIATION 3
Salt		Salt ▼	Salt ▼▼
Protein		Protein	Protein ▲
Fat	▼	Fat ▼▼	Fat ▼▼▼
Fiber		Fiber ▲	Fiber ▲▲

51

VARIATION 2

1 cup	uncooked macaroni elbows	250 ml
1 cup	uncooked whole wheat macaroni	250 ml
1/2 cup	celery, diced	125 ml
1/2 cup	red onion, chopped	125 ml
1/2 cup	sliced cucumber	125 ml
1	green pepper, chopped	1
1–6-1/2-oz	tin of tuna, packed in water, drained	1–184 g
1/2 cup	cheddar cheese cut into small square chunks	125 ml
1 cup	part-skim mozzarella cheese cut into small square chunks	250 ml
2 tbsp	mayonnaise, light	30 ml
1/2 cup	plain yogurt	125 ml
1 clove	garlic, crushed	1 clove
1/4 tsp	black pepper	1 ml
1/2 tsp	salt	2 ml
2 tsp	grated lemon rind (zest)	10 ml
2 tbsp	lemon juice	30 ml
2 tsp	thyme or basil	10 ml
2	medium tomatoes, cut into chunks	2

1. Prepare and serve as per Variation 1.

—NOTES—

• *Whole wheat macaroni increases the fiber content and gives the salad a new look.*

• *Since there is less dressing the color of the salad ingredients are more noticeable. Also decreasing the mayonnaise and increasing the yogurt lowers the fat content and gives it more zip.*

• *Cheese is an accent flavor. Decreasing the amount still gives flavor and texture while lowering the salt and fat content.*

• *Thyme or basil adds flavor to the dressing and makes the decrease in mayonnaise less noticeable.*

VARIATION 3

2 cups	uncooked whole wheat macaroni	500 ml
1/2 cup	celery, diced	125 ml
1/2 cup	red onion, chopped	125 ml
1/2 cup	sliced cucumber	125 ml
1	green pepper, chopped	1
1–6-1/2-oz	tin of tuna, packed in water, drained	1–184 g
1 cup	chick peas, drained	250 ml
1 cup	part-skim mozzarella cheese cut into small square chunks	250 ml
1/2 cup	plain yogurt	125 ml
1 clove	garlic, crushed	1 clove
1/4 tsp	black pepper	1 ml
pinch	salt	pinch
2 tsp	grated lemon rind (zest)	10 ml
2 tbsp	lemon juice	30 ml
2 tsp	thyme or basil	10 ml
2	medium tomatoes, cut into chunks	2

1. Prepare as per Variation 1, adding the chick peas when adding the tuna. *It is essential to allow this salad to sit for at least an hour in the refrigerator to blend the flavors.*

—NOTES—

• *Replacing cheddar cheese with part-skim mozzarella and using yogurt instead of mayonnaise lowers the fat content.*

• *Yogurt based dressing provides a definite flavor change. The salad is more noticeably colorful, tangier, with a lighter flavor and texture.*

• *This salad contains protein, but not quite enough to keep you satisfied until the next meal. For a main dish increase the tuna and/or chick peas for protein content.*

• *Chick peas add new flavor and texture and are an excellent source of vegetable protein and fiber.*

52

The Milligen Toss

Yield varies depending on the amount of lettuce used

This aromatic side salad is irresistible. Without the lettuce it is like a Greek salad and stores well in the refrigerator. Add the lettuce just before serving. Substitute different oils and vinegars for variety.

Original Recipe

	—DRESSING—	
1 to 2	cloves garlic, crushed	1 or 2
1/3 cup	olive oil	75 ml
2 tbsp	red wine vinegar	30 ml
2 tsp	dried basil	10 ml
2 tsp	rosemary, crushed	10 ml
	—SALAD—	
1/2 cup	red onion, thinly sliced	125 ml
1/4 cup	green pepper, chopped	50 ml
1/2 cup	cucumber, cut into chunks	125 ml
1/2 cup	broccoli, chopped	125 ml
1/2 cup	cauliflower, chopped	125 ml
8	asparagus tips	8
1/2 cup	fresh mushrooms, sliced	125 ml
1/2 cup	parmesan cheese, grated	125 ml
1	large bunch of lettuce, torn into pieces	1
1	tomato, cut into wedges for garnish	1

1. Mix the dressing ingredients together in a small jar and shake well.
2. Prepare vegetables (excluding lettuce and tomato wedges) and cheese, then place in a big bowl.
3. Toss the desired amount of dressing and vegetables together. At this stage the salad stores for several days in the refrigerator. If you like it without the lettuce, garnish with tomato just before serving.
4. For a larger salad, add the lettuce to the vegetable combination and toss. Add more dressing if desired.
5. Garnish with tomato wedges and fresh basil sprigs.

—NOTES—

• *Freshly grated parmesan cheese has more flavor.*
• *Olive oil adds a distinctive flavor. Using other oils change the flavor slightly.*
• *This dressing will store covered in your refrigerator for weeks and can be used over any salad.*
• *If storing the salad, choose a bowl with a cover.*

VARIATION 1

	—DRESSING—	
1 to 2	cloves garlic, crushed	1 or 2
1/4 cup	**olive oil**	**50 ml**
3 tbsp	**red wine vinegar**	**45 ml**
2 tsp	dried basil	10 ml
2 tsp	rosemary, crushed	10 ml
	—SALAD—	
1/2 cup	red onion, thinly sliced	125 ml
1/4 cup	green pepper, chopped	50 ml
1/2 cup	cucumber, cut into chunks	125 ml
1/2 cup	broccoli, chopped	125 ml
1/2 cup	cauliflower, chopped	125 ml
8	asparagus tips	8
1/2 cup	fresh mushrooms, sliced	125 ml
1/2 cup	parmesan cheese, grated	125 ml
1	large bunch of lettuce, torn into pieces	1
1	tomato, cut into wedges for garnish	1

1. Prepare, garnish, and serve as outlined in the original recipe.

—NOTES—

• *This salad is a mix of colors, flavors, textures, and tastes and combines lots of vitamins and minerals.*
• *Reducing the oil decreases the fat content and adding extra vinegar adds zip and moisture. If you find the dressing too tangy try adding 1–2 tsp (5–10 ml) of honey.*
• *Wine slightly increases the sugar content. 3 tbsp (45 ml) of wine is about the same as 1/4 tsp (1 ml) sugar.*

Guide to changes in salt, sugar, fat, and fiber content using each variation.

	VARIATION 1	VARIATION 2	VARIATION 3
Salt		▼	▼
Sugar	▲	▼▼	▲
Fat	▼	▼▼	▼▼▼
Fiber			

VARIATION 2

—DRESSING—

1 to 2	cloves garlic, crushed	1 or 2
3 tbsp	**olive oil**	**45 ml**
3 tbsp	red wine vinegar	45 ml
1 tbsp	**water**	**15 ml**
2 tsp	**dry mustard**	**10 ml**
2 tsp	dried basil	10 ml
2 tsp	rosemary, crushed	10 ml

—SALAD—

1/2 cup	red onion, thinly sliced	125 ml
1/4 cup	green pepper, chopped	50 ml
1/2 cup	cucumber, cut into chunks	125 ml
1/2 cup	broccoli, chopped	125 ml
1/2 cup	cauliflower, chopped	125 ml
8	asparagus tips	8
1/2 cup	fresh mushrooms, sliced	125 ml
1/4 cup	**parmesan cheese, grated**	**50 ml**
1	large bunch of lettuce, torn into pieces	1
1	tomato, cut into wedges for garnish	1

1. Add mustard to dressing ingredients. Mix and serve as per the original recipe.

—NOTES—

• *This version has a sharper flavor because of the mustard and is lower in fat content because of the decrease in oil.*
• *Water is added to increase the moisture content and compensate for the decrease in oil.*
• *Parmesan cheese is an accent so you can decrease the quantity and still have the flavor, thus decreasing the fat and salt content.*

VARIATION 3

—DRESSING—

1 to 2	cloves garlic, crushed	1 or 2
2 tbsp	**olive oil**	**30 ml**
2 tbsp	**apple juice**	**30 ml**
3 tbsp	red wine vinegar	45 ml
2 tsp	dry mustard	10 ml
2-1/2 tsp	**dried basil**	**12 ml**
2 tsp	rosemary, crushed	10 ml

—SALAD—

1/2 cup	red onion, thinly sliced	125 ml
1/4 cup	green pepper, chopped	50 ml
1/2 cup	cucumber, cut into chunks	125 ml
1/2 cup	broccoli, chopped	125 ml
1/2 cup	cauliflower, chopped	125 ml
8	asparagus tips	8
1/2 cup	fresh mushrooms, sliced	125 ml
1/4 cup	parmesan cheese, grated **(optional)**	50 ml
1	large bunch of lettuce, torn into pieces	1
1	tomato, cut into wedges for garnish	1

1. Add apple juice and mustard to the dressing ingredients. Mix and serve as per the original recipe.

—NOTES—

• *The apple juice adds moisture and a slightly sweeter taste to the dressing. The added sweetness compensates for the decrease in fat content.*
• *The dressing is lower in fat because of the decrease in olive oil.*
• *Adding extra basil gives flavor and compensates for the decrease in oil.*
• *Omitting the parmesan cheese also lowers the fat and salt content. The result is a lighter more refreshing salad.*

This salad is a favorite for many. The combination of flavors and textures of the vegetables and croutons makes a lovely addition to many meals. Create the salad to reflect your flavor preference. The bacon and anchovy paste are optional.

Caesar Salad Supreme

54

Yields 5 to 6 cups (1.25 to 1.5 L)

Original Recipe

	—SALAD—	
1	bundle of romaine lettuce, torn into small pieces	1
1/3 cup	parmesan cheese, grated	75 ml
8	strips of bacon, fried crisp & crumbled	8
1 cup	croutons	250 ml
	—DRESSING—	
1 clove	garlic, crushed	1 clove
1/2 cup	olive oil or canola oil	125 ml
5 inches	anchovy paste from a tube	12 cm
1/4 tsp	black pepper	1 ml
2 drops	tabasco sauce	2 drops
1 tsp	Worcestershire sauce	5 ml
1 tsp	dijon mustard	5 ml
1 tbsp	red wine vinegar	15 ml
1 tbsp	lemon juice	15 ml
1/4 tsp	salt	1 ml
1	egg yolk	1

1. Tear the lettuce, fry the bacon until crisp, and grate the cheese. Set aside.
2. Mix dressing ingredients in a blender. Refrigerate the dressing until just before serving.
3. Just before serving, pour the dressing over the lettuce in a large bowl and toss with bacon, cheese, and croutons.

—NOTES—

• *If you don't enjoy the flavor of anchovies or do not have this in the house, you can omit it and still have a delicious salad.*

VARIATION 1

	—SALAD—	
1	bundle of romaine lettuce, torn into small pieces	1
1/3 cup	parmesan cheese, grated	75 ml
6	**strips of bacon, fried crisp & crumbled**	**6**
1 cup	croutons	250 ml
	—DRESSING—	
1 clove	garlic, crushed	1 clove
1/3 cup	**olive oil or canola oil**	**75 ml**
5 inches	anchovy paste from a tube	12 cm
1/4 tsp	black pepper	1 ml
2 drops	tabasco sauce	2 drops
1 tsp	Worcestershire sauce	5 ml
1 tsp	dijon mustard	5 ml
1 tbsp	red wine vinegar	15 ml
1 tbsp	lemon juice	15 ml
dash	**salt**	**dash**
1	**whole egg**	**1**

1. Prepare and serve as per the original recipe.

—NOTES—

• *Bacon is an accent flavor in this salad.. Decreasing the amount used decreases the overall fat and salt content while retaining the smoked flavor of bacon.*
• *Choose bacon that has more meat and less fat on each strip.*
• *Decreasing the amount of oil in the dressing makes little difference to the flavor but lowers the fat content.*
• *Adding a whole egg increases the moisture that was lost from the decrease in oil.*

Guide to changes in salt, sugar, fat, and fiber content using each variation.	VARIATION 1	VARIATION 2	VARIATION 3
Salt	▼	▼▼	▼▼▼
Sugar			
Fat	▼	▼▼	▼▼▼
Fiber		▲	▲▲

55

VARIATION 2

—SALAD—

1	bundle of romaine lettuce, torn into small pieces	1
1/2 cup	**fresh mushrooms, sliced**	**125 ml**
1/3 cup	parmesan cheese, grated	75 ml
4	strips of bacon, fried crisp & crumbled	4
3/4 cup	croutons	175 ml

—DRESSING—

1 small clove	garlic, crushed	1 small clove
3 tbsp	olive oil or canola oil	45 ml
1 tbsp	milk	15 ml
3 inches	anchovy paste from a tube	7.5 cm
1/8 tsp	black pepper	.5 ml
1 drop	tabasco sauce	1 drop
1/2 tsp	Worcestershire sauce	2 ml
1/2 tsp	dijon mustard	2 ml
2 tsp	red wine vinegar	10 ml
1 tsp	lemon juice	5 ml
1	whole egg	1

1. Prepare and serve as per the original recipe.

—NOTES—

• *This variation has less fat content because of the decrease in the amount of bacon and oil.*
• *To decrease the salt content in bacon, soak it for 15 minutes in water, discard the water, and prepare as instructed above. This is easy to do and is less costly than buying special low-salt bacon.*
• *The added milk provides moisture to compensate for the decrease in oil.*
• *This recipe makes a smaller quantity of lighter dressing but has the same flavor as the original. The decrease in dressing allows you to notice the vegetables without masking them in flavor.*
• *Including more vegetables adds flavor, texture, and fiber.*

VARIATION 3

—SALAD—

1	bundle of romaine lettuce, torn into small pieces	1
1 cup	**fresh spinach, torn into pieces**	**250 ml**
1/2 cup	fresh mushrooms, sliced	125 ml
1/4 cup	**parmesan cheese, grated**	**50 ml**
3	strips of bacon, fried crisp & crumbled	3
	(see Variation 2, Item 2)	
3/4 cup	croutons	175 ml

—DRESSING—

1 small clove	garlic, crushed	1 small clove
2 tbsp	**olive oil or canola oil**	**30 ml**
1 tbsp	milk	15 ml
3 inches	anchovy paste from a tube	7.5 cm
1/8 tsp	black pepper	.5 ml
1 drop	tabasco sauce	1 drop
1/2 tsp	Worcestershire sauce	2 ml
1 tsp	**dijon mustard**	**5 ml**
2 tsp	red wine vinegar	10 ml
1 tsp	lemon juice	5 ml
1	small whole egg	1

1. Prepare and serve as per the original recipe.
2. After blending, allow the dressing to sit in the refrigerator for at least an hour to blend flavors.

—NOTES—

• *Spinach leaves, like other dark leafy vegetables are high in vitamin A and fiber. They add color, texture, and nutritional value. You can substitute any kind of leaf lettuce for the spinach.*
• *Parmesan cheese is fairly high in fat. By slowly decreasing the amount you decrease the overall fat content without destroying the flavor.*
• *Added mustard increases the moisture in the dressing and adds color and flavor.*

Tips

The following information for the recipes given in this section will help you make choices and add variety to your meals.

Cauliflower & Broccoli Toss p48

• Variation 3 has decreased fiber content because of the lowered sunflower seed and raisin contents. This is significant because this salad is already high in fiber content and can do without the higher fat and sugar content found in sunflower seeds and raisins.

• This salad has more dressing than it requires. The dressing smothers the salad. Decreasing the mayonnaise enhances the colors and textures of this salad.

• Sometimes dressings are too thick to evenly coat the salad. Try adding a little milk to thin out the texture.

• To cook bacon in a microwave—place bacon strips on a microwave safe bacon rack in a single layer. Cover with a paper towel. Cook on high for a few minutes (check microwave instructions for exact time). If you don't have a rack, place bacon between two pieces of paper towel. Replace paper towels as they soak up the fat in the bacon during the cooking process.

• This recipe can easily be adapted for a person with diabetes. The sugar in the recipe can be replaced with spoon-for-spoon aspartame. The high level of soluble fiber found in the fresh vegetables helps to slow down the absorption of sugars into the bloodstream. Eating meals and snacks that include fiber-rich carbohydrates (like vegetables) along with food that contains protein and fat can help slow the rise in blood glucose levels that naturally occur after food is eaten. This is because fiber-rich carbohydrate foods are digested more slowly than carbohydrate foods that have little or no fiber. Foods that contain protein or fat along with carbohydrates are digested more slowly than foods that are mostly carbohydrate. Protein and fat slow down the digestion of the carbohydrates, which slows the rise in blood glucose levels after meals.[6, 12, 15]

• Broccoli is an excellent source of vitamins A and C.

• Cauliflower is high in pectin. The gel-like substance helps delay the stomach from emptying. This keeps you full longer and slows the release of sugar into the bloodstream.

• Both broccoli and cauliflower are included in the brassica or cabbage group of vegetables, which seem to have a protective effect against the risk of cancer.

• Raw vegetables in general are an excellent form of soluble fiber. They are thought to assist in lowering cholesterol levels and help to keep blood glucose levels in line.[12, 14, 15, 20]

Mom's Macaroni Salad p50

• Because of the mayonnaise you will want to keep this salad refrigerated as much as possible.

• You may choose to make this salad using 1 can (19 oz, 540 ml) of chick peas, rinsed and drained instead of using the tuna. This results in a tasty salad with lower fat, higher fiber and a good source of protein that costs less to make. If this is your main dish you may need to supplement the protein content of the salad with some extra cheese, milk, or another protein source, to keep you satisfied until the next meal.

• People with diabetes may find that including chick peas or other legumes in the diet, along with other protein sources, help maintain blood sugars at lower levels.[1, 5, 7, 12, 15] Chick peas are high in pectin and soluble fiber which become gel-like when digested. This delays the emptying of the stomach, makes you feel full longer, and slows the release of glucose into the bloodstream.

• Pastas made with whole wheat grains are higher in insoluble fiber than plain pastas. Using this kind of pasta gives this salad a wonderful mix of carbohydrates and fiber.

• If you do not enjoy the flavor and texture of "light" products, use a smaller amount of the "real" thing so that you enjoy the taste and flavor but decrease the fat content.

The Milligen Toss p52

• The dressing for this salad will store covered in your refrigerator for weeks and can be used over any salad.

• If you prefer a milkier kind of dressing, remove all the oil and add 2 tbsp (30 ml) of plain skim or 1% yogurt. This results in a dressing that is a little less "runny" and is even lower in fat.

• Have fun with the vinegars and spices. Try using a raspberry or blackberry wine vinegar instead of red wine vinegar. Add poppy seeds in place of rosemary and basil. And add softened honey in place of apple juice. This will result in a fruity dressing that is wonderful over salads that contain vegetables and fruit.

• Try tarragon vinegar and add parsley and thyme as the spices. Dressings are only limited by your imagination and cupboard contents.

• Research suggests that it isn't so much the type of fat, but rather the total amount of fat you eat that seems to affect weight and cholesterol.[14] The goal in eating healthier is to gradually decrease the **total** amount of fat you eat. So rather than using an oil or fat product that you dislike because it is healthier, use what you enjoy and begin to decrease the amounts. Gradually you will learn to enjoy the flavors and textures associated with lower-fat choices.

Caesar Salad Supreme p54

• Caesar salad is an excellent source of fiber and vitamins because it uses the darker leaves of romaine lettuce. Unfortunately the heavy dressing along with the bacon and cheese make it a high-fat salad. Making some simple modifications in the dressing, bacon, and cheese can make it a lower-fat, healthier choice.

• Fry bacon very crisp in a nonstick pan, draining the grease as it cooks. Place on paper towels to absorb additional fat.

• If you use a microwave place the bacon on a rack or between paper towels and cook on high a few minutes at a time until the bacon is crisp.

• Make your own croutons—cut bread into cubes and use a nonstick pan to fry them. Fry 1-1/2 cups (375 ml) bread cubes in 1-1/2 tsp (7 ml) margarine, 2 tsp (10 ml) water, and 1/4 tsp (1 ml) garlic and onion powder until the margarine, bread, and flavoring are well mixed. Then place the bread cubes in a single layer on a cookie sheet and bake in a slow oven (about 1 hour or more). It will look as crunchy as brown toasted bread.

Another variation is to brown the bread cubes in the oven with no oil. once crunchy, remove from oven and toss with 1 to 2 tsp (5 to 10 ml) oil and herbs of your choice. Then return to the oven to brown for a few minutes. Try using whole wheat or pumpernickel bread for added flavor, color, and texture.

• You can replace the milk in this recipe with plain yogurt for a milkier look and tangy taste. Use yogurt that has about .9% M.F. or lower. Skim milk yogurt works well and the dressing is still tangy and delicious.

A WORKSHEET FOR TRYING NEW IDEAS

Here's your chance to work with these ideas and experiment with recipes that are your family favorites. Work through the process by setting up the original recipe and then choosing the changes you wish to make in each variation.

Original Recipe

VARIATION 1

—NOTES—

Guide to changes in salt, protein, fat, sugar, and fiber content using each variation.

VARIATION 1	VARIATION 2	VARIATION 3
Salt	Salt	Salt
Protein	Protein	Protein
Fat	Fat	Fat
Sugar	Sugar	Sugar
Fiber	Fiber	Fiber

VARIATION 2

VARIATION 3

—NOTES—

—NOTES—

Carbohydrates are energy foods

The smell of fresh bread, buns, muffins, scones, pancakes, or waffles makes the mouth water in anticipation of the first bite. These carbohydrate foods along with pastas and potatoes are part of healthy eating. But at one time foods high in carbohydrates were thought to cause weight gain. When weight reduction was the goal, carbohydrate foods were restricted. Now Canada's Food Guide to Healthy Eating recommends five to twelve servings of bread and bread products a day. Carbohydrates, both simple and complex, are an essential component of a well-balanced diet.

Why is it that when you restrict your carbohydrate intake you quickly seem to lose pounds on the scale? It is because carbohydrates are stored in the body with water. As they are restricted, the result is loss of body fluids, not fat pounds. Your body is temporarily at a lower weight because it is dehydrated. And you will probably crave foods high in carbohydrates because you need them for energy.[14]

A variety of foods high in carbohydrates are needed to supply the body with the nutrients and energy it needs to function at a healthy level (see p14). Balance in your meals is important. Including a variety of carbohydrates making up 2/3 to 3/4 of your meal and a variety of proteins making up 1/3 to 1/4 will provide the ingredients to help you feel energized after eating. If your plate doesn't have this balance, slowly try to achieve it. This will result in lower fat (because of the decrease in protein intake), higher fiber, and higher nutrient content (because of the increase in whole grain and vegetable intake), and more satisfying meals.

Having fun with carbohydrates

Meals are shifting from protein-focus to carbohydrate focus as we move toward healthier eating and living. This balance helps us to feel energized after meals and keeps us satisfied for longer periods of time. Gradual change is the key. It allows our taste buds and digestive systems to adjust slowly and enjoy the process of change.

Is changing difficult? Yes. We get stuck in the rut of past eating patterns and choose the same foods and prepare them the same way. Variety is essential to keep life interesting and exciting. Trying new foods and cooking techniques is exciting. It's surprising how much better food tastes and how quickly we will feel satisfied.

Variations to include in your carbohydrate selections

Bread and cereals

Enjoy the flavors and textures of different kinds of bread and buns, such as seven-grain, pumpernickel, or rye. Try making your own bread products! The new yeasts available make bread-making much easier and quicker. You can add ingredients of your choice, such as flaxseed, cracked wheat, oatmeal, a little honey, low-fat cheese like quark or cottage cheese, and/or some fresh or dried herbs. Savor the flavors and textures of the bread. Try eating it fresh or toasting it to enjoy the crunchy textures. Avoid using too many fats on your breads that mask the flavors and textures.

Quick breads, muffins

Use oat bran, seven-grain cereal, oat or rye flour, or whole flaxseed to add color and flavor to pancakes, waffles, muffins, buns.

Rice

• Try white, brown, or other kinds of rice (or combine different rices for a colorful and flavorful option). Try white or brown basmati rice. It has a wonderful nutty flavor that complements any meal and is especially good in combination with herb flavors of curry, ginger, and/or garlic.

• When cooking rice, use converted rice to maintain vitamins and minerals. Move away from using extra fat to cook rice. Instead use half a bouillon packet or cube. It heightens flavor without adding fat or significant salt.

• Cook bulgur or couscous with your favorite herbs to accent your meals. Or mix together rice, cracked wheat, and minced vegetables like onions, garlic, and peppers to make a colorful pilaf.

Pasta

Have fun with the different shapes and textures of pasta available. Try small shell, wagon wheel, or linguini pastas, or something colorful like whole wheat, tomato, or spinach pastas.

Potatoes

Potatoes digest more quickly than many bread and cereal products. For more fiber and color try leaving the skin on the potatoes.

Legumes

Lentils and other legumes are fiber-rich carbohydrate foods. Use them in combination with or beside other

Breads & Bread Products

carbohydrate foods to add flavor, texture, and excitement.

Have fun with a variety of carbohydrates. Make them an exciting part of every meal. The benefits are endless. Balanced carbohydrate and protein intake gives you more energy, makes you feel satisfied longer, and encourages you to eat lower fat, higher fiber meals.

FOR BEST RESULTS—read through the entire recipe, each variation, and the TIPS on page 76 before preparing these muffins.

These muffins are a delightful combination of flavors and textures. The ingredients make a moist heavier muffin that is delicious. They are satisfying for lunch box or snacks.

Sunshine Muffins

Yields 14 very large muffins

Variation 2 *yields 12 to 15 large or 20 small muffins*

Original Recipe

2 cups	all purpose flour	500 ml
1-1/4 cups	sugar	300 ml
2 tbsp	baking powder	30 ml
2 tsp	cinnamon	10 ml
1/2 tsp	salt	2 ml
2 cups	shredded carrots	500 ml
1/2 cup	raisins	125 ml
1/2 cup	pecan or almond chunks	125 ml
1/2 cup	sweetened coconut	125 ml
1	apple, peeled and grated	1
3	eggs	3
1 cup	oil	250 ml
2 tsp	almond or vanilla extract	10 ml

1. Mix flour, sugar, baking powder, cinnamon, and salt together in a large bowl.
2. Add carrots, raisins, nuts, coconut, and apple to the same bowl. Stir ingredients together.
3. Beat eggs, oil, and extract in a separate bowl.
4. Add liquid mixture to the flour mixture and stir just to moisten the dry ingredients.
5. Place muffin mixture into muffin cups with paper muffin liners or spray muffin tins with a nonstick cooking spray. Fill each cup level to the top of the muffin tin.
6. Bake at 350°F (180°C) for about 20 to 25 minutes or until a toothpick comes out clean.

—NOTES—

• *You may choose to omit either the raisins, coconut, or nuts. The result is a change in flavor, texture, and decreased yield.*

VARIATION 1

2 cups	all purpose flour	500 ml
1 cup	**sugar**	**250 ml**
2 tbsp	baking powder	30 ml
2 tsp	cinnamon	10 ml
	omit salt	
2 cups	shredded carrots	500 ml
1/2 cup	raisins	125 ml
1/2 cup	pecan or almond chunks	125 ml
1/2 cup	sweetened coconut	125 ml
1	**crisp apple, grated (leave peel on)**	**1**
3	eggs	3
2/3 cup	**oil**	**150 ml**
2 tsp	almond or vanilla extract	10 ml

1. Mix and bake as per the original recipe.

—NOTES—

• *There doesn't seem to be any flavor or texture change in this variation. The carrots and apple keep the muffins moist, even with less oil and sugar.*
• *Use smaller muffin cups to make 20 to 24 smaller muffins. Smaller muffins provide the same flavor, texture, and taste, and are usually just the right amount to satisfy you.*
• *Including the apple peel adds color, texture, and fiber to the muffins. Apples should be crisp if you use the peel.*
• *We didn't notice the omission of salt from this variation.*

	VARIATION 1	VARIATION 2	VARIATION 3
Salt	▼	▼	▼
Sugar	▼	▼▼	▼▼▼
Fat	▼	▼▼	▼▼
Fiber	▲	▲▲	▲▲▲

Guide to changes in salt, sugar, fat, and fiber content using each variation.

63

VARIATION 2

1-1/2 cups	all purpose flour	375 ml
1/3 cup	whole wheat flour	75 ml
2/3 cup	sugar	150 ml
2 tbsp	baking powder	30 ml
2-1/2 tsp	cinnamon	12 ml
1/4 tsp	nutmeg	1 ml
2 cups	shredded carrots	500 ml
1/2 cup	raisins	125 ml
1/2 cup	pecan or almond chunks	125 ml
1/2 cup	unsweetened coconut	125 ml
1	crisp apple, grated (leave peel on)	1
2	eggs	2
1/2 cup	oil	125 ml
1/4 cup	plain skim or 1% yogurt	50 ml
2 tsp	almond or vanilla extract	10 ml

1. Mix and bake as per the original recipe.

—NOTES—

• *This variation makes less muffins because of the decrease in fluid and other contents.*

• *There is little change in the flavor of this version. Apples, carrots, and yogurt maintain the moisture.*

• *Decreasing sugar and increasing the "sweet spices" like cinnamon and nutmeg enhances the natural sweetness. Cinnamon has an appealing flavor and aroma.*

• *Unsweetened coconut gives a tropical flavor of coconut without adding extra sugar.*

• *Using whole wheat flour in place of all purpose flour increases the fiber content. See TIPS p78 for the formula for replacing all purpose flour with whole wheat flour.*

• *Decreasing the amount of egg decreases the fat and moisture content. However these muffins are still moist and tasty.*

VARIATION 3

1 cup	all purpose flour	250 ml
2/3 cup	whole wheat flour	150 ml
1/4 cup	sugar	50 ml
2 tbsp	baking powder	30 ml
2-1/2 tsp	cinnamon	12 ml
1/4 tsp	nutmeg	1 ml
2 cups	shredded carrots	500 ml
1/3 cup	raisins	75 ml
1/4 cup	pecan or almond chunks	50 ml
1/4 cup	unsweetened coconut, toasted	50 ml
1	crisp apple, grated (leave peel on)	1
2	eggs	2
1/4 cup	oil	50 ml
3/4 cup	plain skim or 1% yogurt	175 ml
2 tsp	almond or vanilla extract	10 ml

1. Soak the raisins in warm water for 20 minutes before adding to the mixture.
2. Put coconut and chopped nuts onto a metal pan and toast in the oven at 400°F (200°C) stirring often. Remove once browned (less than 5 minutes, watch carefully) and add to the mixture as per the original recipe.
3. Mix and bake as per the original recipe. Less batter will make only about 15 medium muffins.

—NOTES—

• *These muffins have a bread-like texture. They are still moist, but a little more crumbly.*

• *Soaking the raisins makes them plumper and juicier. You need less of them to get the chewy texture and sweet flavor.*

• *Toasting makes nut and coconut flavor more intense so you need less to get the same effect. The roasted flavors and crunch in the muffins are wonderful.*

This festive looking muffin has little bursts of tangy flavor from the orange pieces and cranberries which combines well with the sweet nutty flavor of oatmeal.

Cranberry Oat Muffins

64

Yields 12 muffins

Original Recipe

1 cup	quick cooking rolled oats	250 ml
1 cup	all purpose flour	250 ml
1 tbsp	baking powder	15 ml
1/2 tsp	baking soda	2 ml
3/4 cup	brown sugar	175 ml
	grated rind of one orange	
1/2 cup	fresh or frozen cranberries, halved	125 ml
1/3 cup	whole or 2% milk	75 ml
1	egg, beaten	1
1/4 cup	oil	50 ml
1/4 cup + 2 tbsp	sour cream	80 ml
	juice of one medium orange (about 1/4 cup or 50 ml)	

1. Combine oats, flour, baking powder, baking soda, brown sugar, orange rind, and cranberries in a bowl. Mix these ingredients together well.
2. In a separate bowl combine milk, egg, oil, sour cream, and the juice of the orange. Mix together well.
3. Add the wet ingredients to the dry ingredients and mix until the dry ingredients are just moistened. Do not overmix—15 to 20 strokes should be just about enough.
4. Fill either paper-lined or greased muffin cups to 2/3 to 3/4 full.
5. Bake at 375°F (191°C) for 20–25 minutes or until your muffins are a golden color and a toothpick comes out clean when placed in the center of a muffin. Let muffins cool in muffin tin for 5 minutes before removing.

—NOTES—
• *When you overmix the batter, the muffins become tough rather than light and airy.*

VARIATION 1

1 cup	quick cooking rolled oats	250 ml
1 cup	all purpose flour	250 ml
1 tbsp	baking powder	15 ml
1/2 tsp	baking soda	2 ml
2/3 cup	**brown sugar**	**150 ml**
	grated rind of one orange	
1/2 cup	fresh or frozen cranberries, halved	125 ml
1/3 cup	**1% milk**	**75 ml**
1	egg, beaten	1
1/4 cup	oil	50 ml
1/4 cup + 2 tbsp	**sour cream, light**	**80 ml**
	juice of one medium orange (about 1/4 cup or 50 ml)	

1. Mix and bake as per the original recipe.

—NOTES—
• *Moving from 2% or whole milk to 1% or skim decreases the overall fat content. This variation causes no flavor or texture change in the recipe.*
• *Using light sour cream decreases the overall fat content without changing flavor or texture.*
• *For most muffin, cookie, and cake recipes small decreases in sugar will not change the flavor or texture of the finished product.*
• *As the sugar content is decreased the tangy cranberry flavor is more distinctive.*

Guide to changes in protein, sugar, fat, and fiber content using each variation.

	VARIATION 1	VARIATION 2	VARIATION 3
Protein		▲	▲
Sugar	▼	▼▼	▼▼▼
Fat	▼	▼▼	▼▼
Fiber		▲	▲▲

VARIATION 2

1 cup	quick cooking rolled oats	250 ml
3/4 cup	**all purpose flour**	**175 ml**
1/4 cup	**whole wheat flour**	**50 ml**
1 tbsp	baking powder	15 ml
1/2 tsp	baking soda	2 ml
1/2 cup	**brown sugar**	**125 ml**
	grated rind of one orange	
1/2 cup	fresh or frozen cranberries, halved	125 ml
1/3 cup	**skim milk**	**75 ml**
1	egg, beaten	1
1/4 cup	oil	50 ml
1/4 cup	**light sour cream**	**50 ml**
2 tbsp	**quark or skyr cheese**	**30 ml**
	juice of one medium orange (about 1/4 cup or 50 ml)	

1. Mix sour cream and skyr or quark cheese until smooth.
2. Mix and bake as per the original recipe.

—NOTES—

• *The oatmeal plus the whole wheat flour make this a high fiber snack. But because the sugar and oil content remain the same, the extra fiber in this variation is not noticeable.*
• *The fat content in the muffins is decreased because of using skim milk in place of 1% milk.*
• *Quark and skyr are cultured cheese products. They have a sharp flavor like sour cream or cream cheese but are higher in protein content and lower in fat. Using either in place of sour cream makes these muffins substantial. Skyr is even lower in fat content than regular quark cheese.*

VARIATION 3

1 cup	quick cooking rolled oats	250 ml
1/2 cup	**all purpose flour**	**125 ml**
1/2 cup	**whole wheat flour**	**125 ml**
1 tbsp	baking powder	15 ml
1/2 tsp	baking soda	2 ml
1/4 cup	**brown sugar**	**50 ml**
	grated rind of one orange	
1/2 cup	fresh or frozen cranberries, halved	125 ml
1/4 cup	**skim milk**	**50 ml**
1	egg, beaten	1
1/4 cup	oil	50 ml
	omit light sour cream	
1/4 cup	**quark or skyr cheese**	**50 ml**
	juice of one medium orange (about 1/4 cup or 50 ml)	

1. Mix and bake as per Variation 2.

—NOTES—

• *Using whole wheat flour in place of some of the all purpose flour adds bulk and fiber. This recipe is very moist and can use the extra fiber.*
• *When decreasing a dry component in muffins such as the sugar in this recipe, decrease the accompanying liquid (skim milk) by the same amount.*

Pancakes are a wonderful quick meal. Serving them with an applesauce topping and slices of cheese on the side make an attractive tasty option that has more sustaining power than when served with syrup.

Pancakes

Yields 12 to 14 5-inch (13-cm) pancakes

Original Recipe

2 cups	all purpose flour	500 ml
1/2 tsp	salt	2 ml
1/4 cup	sugar	50 ml
2 tbsp	baking powder	30 ml
2	large eggs	2
2 cups	milk	500 ml
1/4 cup + 2 tbsp	oil	80 ml

1. Sift dry ingredients together into a bowl.
2. Make a well in the center of the dry ingredients.
3. Beat eggs in a separate bowl.
4. Add milk and oil to the eggs and whisk together.
5. Pour liquid ingredients into the well in the dry ingredients.
6. Mix until dry ingredients are just moistened.
7. Keep the mixture as lumpy as possible. Overmixing any pancake or muffin dough will cause the product to become tough rather than light and fluffy.
8. Fry on a lightly greased, hot griddle.
9. Serve immediately, topped with your favorite pancake syrup.

VARIATION 1

2 cups	all purpose flour	500 ml
1/2 tsp	salt	2 ml
1/4 cup	sugar	50 ml
2 tbsp	baking powder	30 ml
2/3 cup	**skim milk powder**	**150 ml**
2	large eggs	2
2 cups	**water**	**500 ml**
1/4 cup	**oil**	**50 ml**

1. Follow steps 1–3 from the original recipe.
2. Add skim milk powder to the dry ingredients after they have been sifted.
3. Add water to the liquid ingredients.
4. Follow steps 5–9 from the original recipe.
5. Try using a light syrup. It is lower in sugar content and a little thinner. If you don't enjoy the flavor, experiment with using less syrup or sprinkling icing sugar lightly on top of the pancakes.

—NOTES—

• *Decreasing the amount of oil and using skim milk powder instead of whole milk decreases the total amount of fat in these pancakes.*

	VARIATION 1	VARIATION 2	VARIATION 3
Salt		Salt	Salt ▼
Sugar		Sugar	Sugar ▼
Fat	▼	Fat ▼▼	Fat ▼▼▼
Fiber		Fiber ▲	Fiber ▲▲

Guide to changes in salt, sugar, fat, and fiber content using each variation.

67

VARIATION 2

1-1/2 cups	all purpose flour	325 ml
1/2 tsp	salt	2 ml
1/4 cup	sugar	50 ml
2 tbsp	baking powder	30 ml
2/3 cup	skim milk powder	150 ml
6 tbsp	whole wheat flour or other whole grain flour	90 ml
2	large eggs	2
2 cups	water	500 ml
1/4 cup	oil	50 ml

1. Follow instructions from Variation 1 except do not sift the whole wheat flour. Add it when adding powdered milk.
2. Fry in a nonstick fry pan on lower heat so you can omit oiling the pan. If you use high heat, the pancakes will burn.
3. Try topping these pancakes with some fresh fruit.

—NOTES—

• *Using whole wheat or other whole grain flour gives these pancakes added texture and flavor as well as increased fiber content.*
• *When replacing all purpose flour with whole wheat flour the total amount of flour is lessened. See TIPS p78 for the formula.*
• *The oil in this recipe has been left unchanged to allow your tastebuds to enjoy the added fiber more easily. Eliminating oil completely may cause the pancakes to stick to the bottom of the frying pan, even if it is a nonstick one. This means you need to use more oil for frying so there is no oil decrease.*
• *Using fresh fruit to top these pancakes adds extra nutrients and fiber and decreases the overall sugar content.*

VARIATION 3

1 cup	all purpose flour	250 ml
	omit salt	
2 tbsp	sugar	30 ml
2 tbsp	baking powder	30 ml
2/3 cup	skim milk powder	150 ml
2/3 cup	whole wheat flour or other whole grain flour	150 ml
2	large eggs	2
2 cups	water	500 ml
2 tbsp	oil	30 ml
1	large mashed banana	1

1. Follow instructions from Variation 2 remembering to not sift the whole wheat flour. Add it when adding powdered milk.
2. Add mashed banana at the end of the mixing process.
3. Follow the remainder of the instructions from Variation 2. Top these pancakes with quark, skyr, or ricotta cheese instead of syrup.

—NOTES—

• *This variation is higher in fiber and lower in fat because of the added whole wheat flour, banana, and decreased oil.*
• *The banana adds extra moisture and sweetness so you don't notice the decrease in sugar or oil.*
• *The tangy taste of these cheeses is a wonderful accent to the banana flavor in the pancake.*
• *Using a cheese topping improves the balance between carbohydrates and protein in this meal and makes it absorb more slowly in the digestion process.*

I remember walking into my oma's house and being greeted by the aroma of fresh buns. Those heavenly smells and the time spent visiting on these afternoons are some of my favorite memories of my oma. This is her recipe, although she never used instant yeasts.

Oma's Best Buns

Yields 3 dozen large buns

Original Recipe

2 tbsp	quick rising yeast	30 ml
8 cups	all purpose flour	2000 ml
2	eggs	2
1/2 cup	sugar	125 ml
2 tsp	salt	10 ml
1-1/2 tsp	white vinegar	7 ml
1/4 cup	margarine, melted	50 ml
2 cups	lukewarm water	500 ml

1. Mix yeast and 4 cups (1 L) flour together in a separate bowl.
2. In another large bowl beat eggs, sugar, salt, vinegar, melted margarine, and lukewarm water.
3. Add flour/yeast mixture to liquid gradually, about a cup at a time. Beat until the mixture is blended.
4. Add remaining flour and knead dough vigorously until the dough is no longer sticky and the consistency is smooth and handles well. If kneaded for 8 to 10 minutes and dough is still sticky, add a little more flour and knead some more. (This will take 10 to 12 minutes when kneading by hand.)
5. Place in a greased bowl, cover with a tea towel, and let rise in a warm place for 15 to 20 minutes or until dough doubles in bulk.
6. Punch down the dough. Cover with a tea towel again and put in a warm place. Let the dough rise again for another 15 minutes.
7. Punch dough down again and form into buns.
8. Place buns on a lightly greased pan or cookie sheet. Make sure to leave room for rising.
9. Cover buns with tea towel and put in warm place. Let rise for 1 more hour.
10. Bake at 350°F (180°C) for 15 to 20 minutes.

—NOTES—
• *The extra rising makes these buns very light and airy.*

VARIATION 1

3/4 cup	flax, freshly ground	175 ml
3 tbsp	whole flaxseed	45 ml
2 tbsp	quick rising yeast	30 ml
7-1/2 cups	all purpose flour	1875 ml
2	eggs	2
1/4 cup	sugar	50 ml
2 tsp	salt	10 ml
1-1/2 tsp	white vinegar	7 ml
	omit margarine	
2 cups	lukewarm water	500 ml

1. You can grind flax in a simple rotary coffee bean grinder.
2. Mix the ground and whole flax with the 4 cups (1000 ml) flour and yeast mixture.
3. Prepare and bake as per the original recipe.

—NOTES—
• *Flax is available in most grocery stores or try a local bulk food, health food, or specialty food store.*
• *The added flax makes these buns brown more quickly. It works best to bake them on bright shiny cooking sheets to compensate for this. Darker pans tend to make buns and cookies darker on the bottom. The finished bun has an attractive brownish flecked appearance and a wonderful new taste and texture.*
• *Adding flaxseed increases the fiber content and changes the type of fat used. Flaxseed is one of the best sources of omega-3 oils[13, 19] thought to reduce the risk of heart disease[4, 5, 11, 15].*
• *The seed coat of flax is impermeable to oil. In freshly ground flax, the omega-3 oil is available to the digestive process. See p30 for more information.*

Guide to changes in salt, sugar, fat, and fiber content using each variation.

	VARIATION 1	VARIATION 2	VARIATION 3
Salt			▼
Sugar	▼	▼	▼
Fat			▼
Fiber	▲	▲▲	▲▲▲

69

VARIATION 2

3/4 cup	flax, freshly ground	175 ml
3 tbsp	whole flaxseed	45 ml
2 tbsp	quick rising yeast	30 ml
6-1/2 cups	**all purpose flour**	**1625 ml**
2/3 cup	**whole wheat flour**	**150 ml**
2	eggs	2
1/4 cup	sugar	50 ml
2 tsp	salt	10 ml
1-1/2 tsp	white vinegar	7 ml
2 cups	lukewarm water	500 ml

1. Mix the whole wheat flour with the yeast, 3 cups (750 ml) white flour, and ground flax.
2. Mix, prepare, and bake as per Variation 1. **You may find that you need to add extra flour to keep the dough from being too sticky.**

—NOTES—
• *Adding whole wheat flour makes these buns browner in color with a heavier texture. The buns are slightly smaller than the last variation. The flavor is still wonderful.*
• *Whole wheat flour increases the fiber content. See TIPS p78 to learn the formula for substituting whole wheat flour for white flour.*
• *Leaving the amount of flax (flaxseed) the same keeps the fat content stable and allows you to enjoy the texture of the added fiber in this variation.*
• *The total flour amount is less than the formula brown-to-white flour suggests because less flour seems to be required to get the dough a soft, workable consistency. If your dough is still to sticky add another 1/2 cup (125 ml) all purpose flour.*

VARIATION 3

2/3 cup	flax, freshly ground	150 ml
1/4 cup	whole flaxseed	50 ml
2 tbsp	quick rising yeast	30 ml
5 cups	**all purpose flour**	**1250 ml**
2/3 cup	whole wheat flour	150 ml
1 cup	**oatmeal**	**250 ml**
2	eggs	2
1/4 cup	sugar	50 ml
	omit salt	
1-1/2 tsp	white vinegar	7 ml
2 cups	lukewarm water	500 ml

1. Mix the oatmeal with the whole wheat flour, yeast, 2-1/2 cups (625 ml) white flour, ground flax, and whole flax.
2. Mix, prepare, and bake as per Variation 1.

—NOTES—
• *Adding oatmeal makes these buns heavier. They have a delicious sweet/nutty flavor of oatmeal.*
• *The oatmeal adds moisture to the buns to compensate for the decrease in fat and sugar.*
• *Decreasing the amount of flaxseed decreases the total fat content.*
• *Oatmeal is a wonderful form of soluble fiber. Mixed with whole wheat and flax, these buns are an excellent form of fiber.*
• *The whole flax gives these buns more texture, color, and a look of wholesomeness.*
• *The whole flax doesn't add fat to the recipe, just fiber. Flaxseed must be ground to make the oil available for use.*
• *We did not notice the omission of salt from this variation.*

FOR BEST RESULTS—read through the entire recipe, each variation, and the TIPS on page 78 before preparing this bread.

Honey Oatmeal Bread

Yields 2 loaves

This wholesome bread has a wonderful oat flavor enhanced by the sweetness of honey. The virtues of oatmeal and whole wheat make this bread a healthy and tasty food choice.

Original Recipe

2 cups	oatmeal	500 ml
2-2/3 cup	boiling water	650 ml
4 cups	all purpose flour	1000 ml
2 cups	whole wheat flour	500 ml
2 tbsp	quick rising or fermipan yeast	30 ml
1 tbsp	salt	15 ml
1/4 cup	honey	50 ml
3 tbsp	molasses	45 ml
1/4 cup + 2 tbsp	oil	80 ml

1. In a large mixing bowl soak oatmeal in boiling water for 10 minutes.
2. In a separate bowl, mix 3 cups (750 ml) all purpose flour, the whole wheat flour, yeast, and salt.
3. Melt honey and molasses in the microwave until they are "pourable." Add to the oatmeal.
4. Add the oil to the oatmeal mixture. Allow to cool to a warm temperature. Then, slowly add the flour mixture to the oatmeal mixture. Stir and then knead until the two are combined.
5. Continue to knead the dough (about 10 to 12 minutes of vigorous kneading) adding 1 cup all purpose flour to make a dough that is easy to handle, smooth, and no longer sticky. (You may need to adjust the amount of flour added.) Knead until dough is a smooth pliable texture.
6. Place the dough into a greased bowl. Cover with a damp cloth and let rise until it is doubled in bulk (about 15 to 30 minutes).
7. Punch down and knead again. Form into 2 loaves.
8. Place in greased 9"x5"x3" (23x12.7x7.6 cm) pans.
9. Cover again with the same damp cloth, place in a warm spot, and let rise until doubled in bulk (about 40 to 45 minutes).
10. Bake at 375°F (200°C) for 40 to 45 minutes or until top is browned. Turn bread out of pans. Cool before slicing.

VARIATION 1

2 cups	oatmeal	500 ml
2-1/3 cup	**boiling water**	**575 ml**
4 cups	all purpose flour	1000 ml
2 cups	whole wheat flour	500 ml
2 tbsp	quick rising or fermipan yeast	30 ml
1 tbsp	salt	15 ml
1/4 cup	honey	50 ml
3 tbsp	molasses	45 ml
1/4 cup	**plain skim or 1% yogurt**	**50 ml**
1/2 cup	**quark cheese**	**125 ml**
1/4 cup	oil	50 ml

1. Add yogurt and quark cheese to the honey-oatmeal mixture.
2. Prepare and bake as per the original recipe.

—NOTES—
- *Decreasing the oil content and replacing it with yogurt lowers the fat content.*
- *The water is decreased because there is enough moisture from the added yogurt and quark cheese.*
- *Quark is a creamy lower fat cheese (see p24 for more information about this cheese). Adding this and yogurt gives this bread some protein content to balance the carbohydrate content. A slice of this bread gives a snack more substance.*
- *The addition of quark cheese gives this moist hearty bread an additional flavor that is absolutely delicious.*
- *Adding yogurt to replace some of the oil provides moisture as well as a small amount of carbohydrate and protein. Even though sugar content increases due to carbohydrate content of yogurt, the amount is small—equaling about 1/2 tsp (2 ml) for the entire recipe.*

Guide to changes in salt, sugar, protein, fat, and fiber content using each variation.

	VARIATION 1	VARIATION 2	VARIATION 3
Salt	▲	▼	▼▼
Sugar	▲	▼	▼▼
Protein	▲	▲	▲▲
Fat	▼	▼	▼▼
Fiber		▲	▲▲

VARIATION 2

2 cups	oatmeal	500 ml
2-1/3 cup	boiling water	575 ml
3 cups	**all purpose flour**	**750 ml**
2-1/2 cups	**whole wheat flour**	**625 ml**
2 tbsp	quick rising or fermipan yeast	30 ml
2 tsp	**salt**	**10 ml**
1/4 cup	honey	50 ml
2 tbsp	**molasses**	**30 ml**
1/4 cup	plain skim or 1% yogurt	50 ml
1/2 cup	quark cheese	125 ml
1/4 cup	oil	50 ml

1. Mix and bake as per Variation 1.
—Remember to reserve 1 cup (250 ml) all purpose flour for kneading process in step 6. This variation may make a smaller loaf due to replacement of all purpose flour with whole wheat flour.

—NOTES—
• *Adding more whole wheat to this bread gives it a heavier texture and increases the amount of insoluble fiber. We did not follow the white-to-whole-wheat-flour formula in this recipe because this dough was so moist.*
• *The added fiber helps to fill you up sooner.*
• *Decreasing the salt is not noticeable.*
• *Molasses adds lovely color and flavor that is not affected by the decreased amount.*

VARIATION 3

2 cups	oatmeal	500 ml
2-1/3 cup	boiling water	575 ml
2 cups	**all purpose flour**	**500 ml**
3-1/2 cups	**whole wheat flour**	**875 ml**
2 tbsp	quick rising or fermipan yeast	30 ml
	omit salt	
3 tbsp	**honey**	**45 ml**
2 tbsp	molasses	30 ml
1/4 cup + 1 tbsp	**yogurt**	**65 ml**
	plain, skim or 1%	
3/4 cup	**quark cheese**	**175 ml**
3 tbsp	**oil**	**45 ml**

1. Mix and bake as per Variation 1.
—Remember to reserve 1 cup (250 ml) flour for kneading process in step 6. As the moisture decreases in this variation you may need less flour to make the dough a soft, smooth, pliable consistency.

—NOTES—
• *This variation is lower in fat content and higher in fiber content. The higher quantity of whole wheat flour results in a smaller loaf.*
• *We did not follow the white-to-whole-wheat-flour formula in this recipe because this dough was so moist.*
• *Omitting the salt is not noticeable.*
• *The decrease in honey in this variation seems to make the bread a little less sweet.*
• *The yogurt was increased by 1 tbsp (15 ml) to replace the oil that was removed.*
• *Quark cheese has been increased to further promote a balance between carbohydrates and protein. It adds moisture and flavor.*

This hearty, crusty bread is a wonderful addition to any meal. It is easy and quick to make and has a yeasty aroma that is enhanced by your favorite herbs and spices.

Herb Beer Bread

Yields 1 loaf

Original Recipe

2-3/4 cups	all purpose flour	675 ml
2 tbsp	sugar	30 ml
1/4 cup	whole flaxseed	50 ml
2 tbsp	baking powder	30 ml
1 tsp	salt	5 ml
1 tsp	dried basil	5 ml
1 tsp	dried rosemary	5 ml
1 tsp	thyme	5 ml
1 tbsp	oil	15 ml
1/2 cup	unsalted sunflower seeds	125 ml
12 oz	beer, at room temperature	341 ml

1. Mix dry ingredients with the sunflower seeds, flaxseed, herbs, and spices.
2. Add oil and beer to the dry ingredients.
3. Stir until the dough is just mixed.
4. Put dough into a 9"x5"x3" (23x12.7x7.6 cm) greased loaf pan. Bake at 375°F (200°C) for 45 to 50 minutes or until the loaf is nicely browned.
5. Let the loaf stay in the pan for about 10 minutes on a cooling rack.
6. Remove loaf from pan and cool completely on cooling rack.
7. Tastes best fresh—warm or cold.

—NOTES—

• *You can use a 12-1/2 oz (355 ml) can of beer instead of the bottle. The amount of fluid changes slightly but doesn't seem to affect the outcome of the bread.*
• *When alcohol is used in cooking the alcohol content dissipates due to the heating of the alcohol.*

VARIATION 1

1-3/4 cups	all purpose flour	425 ml
2/3 cup	**whole wheat flour**	**150 ml**
2 tbsp	sugar	30 ml
1/4 cup	whole flaxseed	50 ml
2 tbsp	baking powder	30 ml
1 tsp	salt	5 ml
1 tsp	dried basil	5 ml
1 tsp	dried rosemary	5 ml
1 tsp	thyme	5 ml
1 tbsp	oil	15 ml
1/2 cup	unsalted sunflower seeds	125 ml
12 oz	beer, at room temperature	341 ml

1. Mix and prepare as per the original recipe.
2. Grease pan with a nonstick cooking spray.

—NOTES—

• *This variation results in a heavier bread with a higher fiber content.*
• *When replacing all purpose flour with whole wheat flour the amount is lessened.* **See TIPS p78 for the white-to-whole-wheat-flour formula.**
• *Whole wheat is an insoluble fiber that helps you become fuller and more satisfied when eating. This is because it slows down the digestion process, keeping you satisfied for a longer period of time.*
• *Enjoy the added texture in this bread.*
• *The oil content is left constant in this variation so that the transition to a higher fiber texture is more palatable.*

Pancakes, Variation 2, p67, with fruit & quark cheese;
Favorite Fruit Drink (orange), Variation 3, p123

Crab-filled Crepes, Variation 1, p104;
Herb Beer Bread, Variation 3, p73; Favorite Fruit Drink (white grape), Variation 3, p123

Guide to changes in salt, sugar, fat, and fiber content using each variation.

	VARIATION 1	VARIATION 2	VARIATION 3
Salt		▼	▼▼
Sugar		▼	▼
Fat		▼	▼▼
Fiber	▲	▲▲	▲▲▲

73

VARIATION 2

1-3/4 cups	all purpose flour	425 ml
2/3 cup	whole wheat flour	150 ml
2 tbsp	sugar	30 ml
1/3 cup	**whole flaxseed**	**75 ml**
2 tbsp	baking powder	30 ml
1/2 tsp	**salt**	**2 ml**
1 tsp	dried basil	5 ml
1 tsp	dried rosemary	5 ml
1 tsp	thyme	5 ml
2 tsp	**oil**	**10 ml**
1/4 cup	**unsalted sunflower seeds**	**50 ml**
12 oz	**light beer,**	**341 ml**
	at room temperature	

1. Mix as per the original recipe. Add flaxseed when adding sunflower seeds.
2. Grease pan with a nonstick cooking spray.

—NOTES—

• *Decreasing the oil and sunflower seeds in this variation lowers the overall fat content.*
• *Using light beer gives this recipe a lighter beer flavor and decreases the sugar content in the recipe.*
• *Sunflower seeds are an accent in this bread. Although they are a fairly good source of fiber and vegetable protein, they are also high in fat content. Using less retains the flavor and texture while decreasing the fat content.*
• *Flaxseed is an excellent form of soluble fiber with no added fat unless it is crushed. For more information about flaxseed see p30.*

VARIATION 3

1 cup	**all purpose flour**	**250 ml**
1-1/4 cup	**whole wheat flour**	**300 ml**
2 tbsp	sugar	30 ml
1/3 cup	whole flaxseed	75 ml
2 tbsp	baking powder	30 ml
	omit salt	
1 tsp	dried basil	5 ml
1 tsp	dried rosemary	5 ml
1 tsp	thyme	5 ml
1 tsp	**oil**	**5 ml**
1/4 cup	unsalted sunflower seeds	50 ml
12 oz	light beer,	341 ml
	at room temperature	

1. Mix as per the original recipe. Add flaxseed when adding sunflower seeds.
2. Grease pan with a nonstick cooking spray.

—NOTES—

• *Decreasing the oil lowers the fat content. The beer gives the dough enough moisture.*
• *Using more whole wheat flour than white flour makes this a high fiber choice. However, the bread doesn't seem to rise as high and is denser in texture.*
• *This bread smells and tastes wonderful. It is a heavy crusty bread that adds flavors and texture to any meal.*
• *There are enough other flavors in this bread that you do not miss the salt flavor.*

FOR BEST RESULTS—read through the entire recipe, each variation, and the TIPS on page 78 before preparing this recipe.

These crepes are delicious filled with meat mixtures, vegetables, or fruit. They freeze well so they are handy to make ahead of time. Thaw just before using.

Crepes
Yields 18 to 20 crepes

Original Recipe

2-1/2 cup	whole milk	625 ml
2	eggs	2
2 tbsp	melted butter or margarine	30 ml
2 cups	all purpose flour	500 ml
1/4 tsp	salt	1 ml

1. Put milk and eggs into a blender and blend together until frothy. (If you do not have a blender, mix dry and wet ingredients in separate bowls. Add wet to dry ingredients alternately in a separate bowl and whisk until smooth. Then follow steps 4 to 10.)
2. Add melted butter to blended milk and eggs.
3. Add flour and salt to the blender mixture and blend together until mixture is smooth.
4. Lightly grease a heavy 8-inch (20-cm) skillet pan.
5. Pour about 1/4 cup (50 ml) of batter in the pan (less if your skillet is smaller—just enough to coat the bottom of the pan) rotating the skillet until the bottom is coated with the batter.
6. Cook on medium high to high heat until the top appears firm.
7. Flip to other side and cook until the crepe is light brown. You may need to add more fat to the pan if the crepes begin to stick.
8. Stack crepes and cover so they do not dry out.

—NOTES—
• *You can prepare crepes ahead of time. Just stack them with wax paper between crepes.*
• *Crepes can be stored for 2 days in the refrigerator and 2 to 3 months in the freezer. They take about 3 hours to thaw to room temperature.*
• *The yield will vary depending on the size of your pan and how thin you make them.*

VARIATION 1

2-1/2 cup	2% milk	625 ml
2	eggs	2
2 tbsp	melted butter or margarine	30 ml
1-1/2 cups	all purpose flour	375 ml
1/3 cup	whole wheat flour or other whole grain flour	75 ml
1/4 tsp	salt	1 ml

1. Mix as per the original recipe.
2. Fry on medium-high heat in a nonstick pan. You will need little or no oil or nonstick cooking spray to keep the crepes from sticking.

—NOTES—
• *This variation is higher in fiber content because of the added whole wheat or another whole grain flour. The taste remains the same.*
• *Whole wheat flour gives these crepes a flecked appearance and a slightly denser texture.*
• *Using a nonstick pan allows you to decrease the additional fat used to cook these crepes.*

Guide to changes in salt, sugar, fat, and fiber content using each variation.

VARIATION 1	VARIATION 2	VARIATION 3
Salt	Salt	Salt
Sugar	Sugar	Sugar
Fat	Fat	Fat
Fiber	Fiber	Fiber

75

VARIATION 2

2-1/2 cup	1% milk	625 ml
2	eggs	2
2 tbsp	melted butter or margarine	30 ml
1 cup	**all purpose flour**	**250 ml**
2/3 cup	**whole wheat flour**	**150 ml**
	or other whole grain flour	
1/4 tsp	salt	1 ml

1. Mix and prepare as per original recipe.
2. Cook as per Variation 1.

VARIATION 3

2-1/2 cup	skim milk	625 ml
2	eggs	2
1 tbsp	**melted butter or margarine**	**15 ml**
1 cup	all purpose flour	250 ml
2/3 cup	whole wheat flour	150 ml
	or other whole grain flour	
1/4 tsp	salt	1 ml

1. Mix and prepare as per original recipe.
2. Cook as per Variation 1.

—NOTES—

• *Using more whole wheat flour increases the fiber content in this recipe.*

• *Using 1% milk in this recipe lowers the overall fat content with no flavor or texture change.*

—NOTES—

• *This version is lower in fat because of the move to skim milk and lower butter content.*

• *The crepe is still moist and tasty, but has a heavier texture than the original.*

Tips
The following information for the recipes given in this section will help you make choices and add variety to your meals.

Sunshine Muffins p62

• Plain yogurt can be used in baking to replace moisture in muffins and cakes when decreasing the fat content.

• Nuts, coconut, and raisins in this recipe are accents both in flavor and texture. You can decrease their amounts and still get the satisfying crunch, chew, and flavor.

• Muffins with decreased fat and sugar content don't stay fresh as long. Freezing them in an airtight container helps to preserve moisture and flavor. Remove from freezer just before serving and thaw in microwave.

• Many people are concerned about their egg intake because of the cholesterol in egg yolks. However, the amount of egg per muffin is so insignificant that decreasing eggs is not necessary.

• People with diabetes can replace sugar or other sweetening agents spoon for spoon with aspartame or liquid sugar replacement plus 2 tbsp (30 ml) sugar to help coagulate eggs. The texture is a little drier but the flavor is great!

Cranberry Oat Muffins p64

• In Variations 2 and 3 you will get less overall batter so you will either get fewer muffins or smaller muffins. In order to make a dozen, put less batter in each muffin cup.

• We did not use the white-to-whole-wheat-flour formula when replacing all purpose flour with whole wheat flour in this recipe because this recipe is so moist. It can use the extra bulk of the added fiber in the whole wheat.

• Skyr or quark cheese can be replaced with unsweetened applesauce or plain yogurt, if desired. For more information about these cheeses, *see* p24.

• When muffin mix is too liquid, muffins do not hold their shape. Therefore when lowering the quantity of dry ingredients, lower the accompanying liquid ingredient.

• You can use yogurt to replace some or all of the oil and cream cheese in cake and muffin recipes. Yogurt has a tangy taste that can also be substituted for sour cream. Plain yogurt is a lower fat choice.

• You can use applesauce in a recipe to replace some of the fat content. Applesauce adds moisture and a natural sweetness. If you use applesauce along with or in place of fats the sugar content in the recipe will be increased.

• Adding crushed pineapple or applesauce to cake, muffin, and cookie recipes to replace some of the fat provides sweetness and moisture. These ingredients also increase the liquid content in the recipe, so you must offset the increased moisture by decreasing the oil content in recipes. This technique can be used in muffins, cookies, cakes, breads, and loaves. As you remove fat from recipes, they will taste best the same day they are baked. If you store them, do so in the freezer and thaw only the amount you will immediately eat.

• The saying, "Eat oatmeal, it will stick to you," has more truth than you think. Oatmeal contains oat bran which is a soluble fiber. During digestion it becomes a gel-like substance that slows down the digestion process of sugars to the bloodstream.[21] This keeps the blood sugar levels more constant and makes you stay full longer. Foods containing soluble fiber are thought to aid in decreasing cholesterol levels.[8]

• Whole wheat flour is a form of insoluble fiber. Other examples include bran cereals, whole grain cereals, cracked wheat, bulgur, etc. These give the body more roughage and help to improve regularity. It is thought that including this kind of fiber in your diet can decrease the risk of some cancers.

• Increasing both kinds of dietary fiber is a healthy choice. A side effect can be stomach distress and bloating. This can be avoided by increasing your fiber intake slowly and drinking plenty of water.

Pancakes p66

• When you use skim milk powder you can mix up the dry ingredients ahead of time and store in an airtight container until you are ready to mix the pancakes. This is excellent for camping or for an easy quick meal on a busy day. Remember to add some protein to the meal, perhaps cheese of peanut butter, to give it the "staying full" power from the combination of carbohydrates and protein. *See* p14 for a discussion on the balance of carbohydrates and proteins.

• Fructose is the name of sugar found in fruit. Syrup contains sucrose, a simpler form of sugar that digests very quickly. Topping the pancakes with fruit instead of syrup adds extra fiber which slows the digestion process while adding color and nutrients.

• Added protein slows digestion resulting in a slower release of sugar (the glucose that is the body's energy source) into the bloodstream. The result is more sustained energy levels or "staying full" power.

• Some people do not like the flavor of banana. Here is a tasty option to replace the banana in Variation 3:

    1. Using a nonstick fry pan, cook 1 cup (250 ml) unsweetened fresh or frozen apple chunks with the skins left on with 2 tbsp (30 ml) water, 1/2 tsp (2 ml) cinnamon, and a sprinkling of sugar or aspartame.

    3. Prepare pancakes as usual omitting the banana. Top with a small amount of quark, ricotta, or skyr cheese and the apple mixture.

Or try this variation:

    1. Omit the banana.

    2. Cut up some of your favorite fruit, mix it with quark cheese, and place it on top of your pancakes. The result is delightfully refreshing and satisfying.

Or try this variation:

    1. Mix quark cheese and jam, or peanut butter on banana or plain pancakes. This is a favorite with kids and gives these pancakes a nutty flavor while still adding protein.

• If you do not like bananas, use 1/2 cup (125 ml) of your favorite berries in the pancakes.

• If you find that your pancakes are sticking to the nonstick fry pan, make sure the heat is not too high and try a quick spray of nonstick cooking spray. Or try the pan preparation technique outlined on p27.

Oma's Best Buns p68

• This recipe was altered from Oma's original recipe to use fast-rising yeasts so these buns can be ready to serve in 2 hours.

• As you move through the variations, don't go too quickly. If you need to add butter or margarine to your bun to satisfy your tastebuds, this is a signal that you may be moving too quickly. Go back to the variation you enjoyed without any added toppings.

• For best results, grind flaxseed just before you use it. Flax grown now does not have a long shelf life after it is ground (it will go rancid). It can be refrigerated in an airtight container for a few days before use.

• When making buns or bread use liquid ingredients at room temperature. Yeast products need to be warm (not hot or cold) to rise effectively.

• Ground flaxseed can be used in place of any oil or fat in any bread or bread product recipe. The formula is: **amount of oil X 3 = flaxseed** For a recipe that calls for 1/4 cup (50 ml) of oil, margarine, or shortening, use 3 X 1/4 = 3/4 cup (175 ml) of flaxseed.

• Whole wheat flour can be used in place of all purpose flour in any bread or bread product recipe.
The formula is: **1 cup (250 ml) all purpose flour = 2/3 cup (150 ml) whole wheat flour.**
For a recipe that calls for 4 cups (1000 ml) all purpose flour use 2 cups (500 ml) all purpose flour and 1-1/3 cup (325 ml or g) of whole wheat flour.
• Remember that when you are increasing the fiber in your diet it is essential to do it slowly. This will prevent the bloating and stomach discomfort that can come from adding too much fiber too quickly. Water keeps you well hydrated and helps your digestive system cope with the extra bulk.

Honey Oatmeal Bread p70

• After you have baked the loaves of bread and turned them out of the pans, if the sides of the loaves aren't crusty, put them back in the oven without the pan for another 10 minutes.
• This bread will store for a short time (about 1 week) in an airtight bag or container on the counter. It will store for several months in airtight containers in the freezer.
• Oatmeal is an excellent form of soluble fiber. When digested this fiber becomes a gel-like substance and slows the digestion process. This in turn slows the release of sugars into the bloodstream. It is also thought to keep cholesterol and blood sugar levels in line.
• Bread is a healthy food choice. Including a variety of whole wheat, rye, and oatmeal breads in your eating choices can add excitement and variety to your diet.
• Pay attention to the flavors and textures of whole grain breads. Enjoy the extra chewing and textures in your mouth.
• You may omit the molasses altogether in this recipe. The result is a bread that is less sweet with less caramel color and flavor.
• Have fun experimenting with different types of flour. Instead of the 4 cups (1000 ml) whole wheat flour add 3 cups (750 ml) whole wheat flour and 1 cup (250 ml) rye flour. This gives a bread with a rye flavor.
• Experiment with nuts and seeds. Add 1/2 cup (125 ml) sesame, 1/4 cup (50 ml) poppy, flax, and/or sunflower seeds to the bread dough. These add texture and interest to the final bread loaf. If you choose to use these, brush the loaf with milk and sprinkle some of these seeds on top of the loaf before baking. The result is an attractive multigrain loaf that looks as good as it tastes!

Herb Beer Bread p72

• Try making this bread by omitting all of the added oil. This results in a low-fat bread that seems to get enough moisture from the beer used in the recipe.
• Each variation adds to the insoluble fiber content. Insoluble fiber is thought to improve bowel regularity and makes you feel satisfied sooner and longer when included in a meal.
• Have fun with spices. Try these combinations:
    –oregano, fennel seeds, freshly ground pepper
    –dill, parsley, lemon rind
    –coriander, cumin, ginger, orange rind with sesame seeds instead of sunflower seeds
• If you aren't planning to eat this bread fresh, freeze it and thaw just before serving. This will keep it fresher and more moist in flavor and texture. We have found that heating bread up very briefly in the microwave helps to restore the freshness. This bread is fast and easy to make. It tastes best fresh.

Crepes p74

• These crepes are wonderful filled with meat, vegetables, or fruit. They freeze well so are handy to use for a main dish or dessert.
• If your nonstick pan sticks, use the hints suggested on p27.
• *See* Sunshine Muffins, Tip 4, p76, if you are concerned about the egg content in this recipe. It is fairly insignificant, only 2 eggs for 20 crepes.

A WORKSHEET FOR TRYING NEW IDEAS

Here's your chance to work with these ideas and experiment with recipes that are your family favorites. Work through the process by setting up the original recipe and then choosing the changes you wish to make in each variation.

Original Recipe

VARIATION 1

—NOTES—

Guide to changes in salt, protein, fat, sugar, and fiber content using each variation.

VARIATION 1	VARIATION 2	VARIATION 3
Salt	Salt	Salt
Protein	Protein	Protein
Fat	Fat	Fat
Sugar	Sugar	Sugar
Fiber	Fiber	Fiber

VARIATION 2

VARIATION 3

—NOTES—

—NOTES—

Vegetables

Vegetables are colorful, multi textured, nutritious, and versatile. They are high in fiber and vitamins, low in fat, and many are an excellent form of complex carbohydrates. Healthy eating means including more vegetables in your diet. Unfortunately, many people view vegetables as a necessary food that you "should" eat. Because this label is hard to shake, vegetables are often approached with little enthusiasm.

Yet, vegetables are exciting, colorful, and tasty food choices. Even if you dislike them, you can learn to enjoy them! Begin gradually to include them in your eating patterns. Start with vegetables that you like and try preparing them in different ways. Add vegetables to your favorite soups or meat sauces. As you progress you will begin to acquire a taste for them. Prepare them in a variety of ways—raw or cooked. Try to find the textures and flavors you enjoy. If you like crispy foods, eat your vegetables raw or steamed so they retain their crunch. If you like softer foods, choose to steam your vegetables longer and/or try vegetables that have a creamier texture such as mashed potatoes, turnips, or peas.

If you enjoy vegetables in sauces remember to *use the sauce as an accent.* Tune into the flavor and texture of the vegetable rather than the sauce. Try not to take a healthy, tasty, low-fat ingredient like vegetables and turn them into a high-fat food by masking their flavor and texture with the sauce poured over them. Try steaming vegetables with your favorite herbs until they are just done. Steaming vegetables retains the nutrients and color

and allows you to control how tender you want the vegetables to be (*see* p87). The color, flavor, and texture of vegetables cooked in this way are exceptional. You will be surprised how enticing a vegetable dish can be.

When people start to view vegetables as an exciting part of a meal, to be enjoyed and prepared in many different ways, they begin to crave them and choose them.

Cheese Sauce for Vegetables

Yields 1-1/2 cups (375 ml)

This cheesy sauce is a wonderful accent for any steamed vegetable. It is also delicious over omelets and pasta. For a tasty meal, cook pasta, steam vegetables, and place both on a plate. Pour cheese sauce over this combination.

Original Recipe

3 tbsp	butter	45 ml
1/4 cup	Spanish onion, minced	50 ml
1 clove	garlic, minced	1 clove
2 tbsp	all purpose flour	30 ml
1 cup	whole milk	250 ml
1 tbsp	white wine	15 ml
2 tsp	caraway seed	10 ml
1/8 tsp	pepper	.5 ml
3/4 cup	cheddar or Swiss cheese	175 ml

1. Heat butter in a heavy saucepan.
2. Add onions and garlic and saute until softened.
3. Sprinkle flour over the hot onions, garlic, and butter, stirring constantly. Cook for about 1 minute.
4. Add milk to hot ingredients in pan and whisk ingredients together. Cook until it starts to thicken, stirring frequently.
5. Add wine, spices, and grated cheese to the milk mixture.
6. Continue to heat until the mixture is hot.
7. Serve immediately over steamed vegetables.

—NOTES—

• *Use your favorite wine to add flavor. For tips on cooking with wine, see p22.*
• *Try replacing caraway seeds with other herbs, such as dill. Use 1 to 2 tsp (5 to 10 ml) depending on the flavor and strength you enjoy in a sauce. We recommend you use less with stronger spices.*
• *Cheddar or Swiss cheese can be replaced with other kinds of cheese if you prefer. Use white cheese over darker colored vegetables and yellow cheese over lighter vegetables for an attractive contrast.*

VARIATION 1

2 tbsp	butter	30 ml
2 tbsp	white wine	30 ml
1/4 cup	Spanish onion, minced	50 ml
1 clove	garlic, minced	1 clove
2 tbsp	all purpose flour	30 ml
1 cup	2% milk	250 ml
2 tsp	caraway seed	10 ml
1/8 tsp	pepper	.5 ml
3/4 cup	cheddar or Swiss cheese	175 ml

1. Saute onions and garlic in the melted butter and the white wine in a nonstick pan.
2. Continue following steps 3–7 in the original recipe.

—NOTES—

• *Decreasing the butter and changing to 2% milk lowers the fat content of this recipe without greatly altering the flavor or texture.*
• *The added white wine replaces the fat and gives a bit more moisture for the onion and garlic to be sauteed in. It also slightly increases the sugar content. 1 tbsp (15 ml) wine increases the sugar content to the same degree as about 1/10 of a tsp (1/10 of 5 ml) of sugar.*
• *The all purpose flour is used as a thickener in this recipe. You may wish to use convenience products for thickening such as Veloutine or Robin Hood Easy Blend Flour. The amounts may vary, see instructions on package. These products are a little more costly than flour; however, they are easier to use and can be added directly to the heating liquid.*

Guide to changes in salt, sugar, fat, and fiber content using each variation.

	VARIATION 1	VARIATION 2	VARIATION 3
Salt			▼
Sugar	▲	▲▲	▲▲▲
Fat	▼	▼▼	▼▼
Fiber		▲	▲

83

VARIATION 2

2 tsp	**butter**	10 ml
3 tbsp	**white wine**	45 ml
1/4 cup	Spanish onion, minced	50 ml
1 clove	garlic, minced	1 clove
2 tbsp	**whole wheat flour**	30 ml
1 cup	**1% milk**	250 ml
1-1/2 tsp	**caraway seed**	7 ml
1/8 tsp	pepper	.5 ml
3/4 cup	cheddar or Swiss cheese	175 ml

1. Prepare and serve as per Variation 1.

—NOTES—
• *The fat is lowered by decreasing the butter and changing to 1% milk.*
• *Some people do not enjoy sauces with texture. In this case omit the whole wheat flour option and continue using all purpose flour. Note—instant flours for thickening are not available in whole wheat versions.*
• *Using whole wheat flour to thicken this sauce gives a heartier flavor with added texture.*
• *Whole wheat flour increases the insoluble fiber content of this sauce.*
• *Fat masks flavors so when lowering the fat content in this variation you need to decrease the spices so they won't overpower the flavor of the sauce.*
• *The sugar content is increased because of the added wine.* See Variation 1, note 2.

VARIATION 3

	omit butter	
1/4 cup	**white wine**	50 ml
1/4 cup	Spanish onion, minced	50 ml
1 clove	garlic, minced	1 clove
2 tbsp	whole wheat flour	30 ml
1 cup	1% milk	250 ml
1 tsp	**caraway seed**	5 ml
1/8 tsp	pepper	.5 ml
1/2 cup	**cheddar or Swiss cheese**	125 ml
1/4 cup	**part-skim mozzarella cheese**	50 ml

1. Prepare and serve as per Variation 1, using the white wine to saute the onions and garlic.

—NOTES—
• *Using wine to saute the vegetables gives this sauce a lovely flavor and allows you to omit the butter.*
• *This variation is lower in fat because of the omission of butter and the replacement of some of the regular cheese with part-skim mozzarella cheese.*
• *Using part-skim mozzarella cheese lowers the overall fat and salt content of this recipe.*
• *This variation is less rich than the last variation but is still creamy and cheesy.*
• *The sugar content is increased because of the added wine.* See Variation 1, note 2.
• *The Swiss/mozzarella mix with dill is very attractive served on whole wheat spaghetti. Add a tossed salad for a satisfying meal.*

FOR BEST RESULTS—read through the entire recipe, each variation, and the TIPS on page 90 before preparing this dish.

Green beans have lovely color and texture when they are prepared properly. When overcooked they lose their vibrant color and crisp texture. This side dish along with small boiled potatoes with skins intact is a wonderful complement to roast beef or roast chicken.

Swiss Green Beans

Yields about 3-1/2 cups (650 ml)

Original Recipe

3 cups	green beans	750 ml
2 tbsp	oil	30 ml
1 tbsp	onion, minced	15 ml
1 tbsp + 1 tsp	all purpose flour	20 ml
3/4 tsp	salt	3 ml
1/4 tsp	pepper	1 ml
3/4 tsp	sugar	3 ml
1/2 cup	sour cream	125 ml
3 tbsp	whole milk	45 ml
3/4 cup	crushed cracker crumbs	175 ml
3/4 cup	Swiss cheese, grated	175 ml

1. Cook green beans in a small amount of water until tender. Drain off the water.
2. Heat oil in a skillet and when hot, add the onions. Cook until they are translucent.
3. Sprinkle flour over the onions, stirring frequently for 1 minute.
4. Whisk spices, sugar, sour cream, and milk into the hot onion mixture over the heat.
5. Continue to heat until the mixture starts to thicken.
6. Mix sauce with cooked beans and place in a medium-sized casserole dish.
7. Mix crushed cracker crumbs and swiss cheese and sprinkle over the bean mixture.
8. Bake covered at 350°F (175°C) for about 15 minutes and then uncovered for 5 minutes until the cheese is slightly browned.

VARIATION 1

3 cups	green beans	750 ml
1 tbsp	**oil**	**15 ml**
1 tbsp	onion, minced	15 ml
1 tbsp + 1 tsp	all purpose flour	20 ml
1/2 tsp	**salt**	**2 ml**
1/8 tsp	**pepper**	**.5 ml**
3/4 tsp	sugar	3 ml
1/3 cup	**sour cream**	**75 ml**
3 tbsp	**2% milk**	**45 ml**
3/4 cup	crushed cracker crumbs	175 ml
2/3 cup	**Swiss cheese, grated**	**150 ml**

1. Using a steamer basket in the saucepan, steam green beans until just crunchy. *See* p87 for steaming tips for vegetables.
2. Prepare sauce and remainder of dish as per the original recipe.

—NOTES—

• *Green beans will stay a more vibrant color and retain more nutrients when steamed.*
• *You need less salt and pepper because decreased fat allows you to taste these condiments better.*
• *Using light sour cream and 2% milk decreases the overall fat content in this recipe with little or no flavor or texture change.*
• *Swiss cheese is an accent in this dish. Using less still gives the distinctive nutty flavor while decreasing the fat and salt content.*
• *This variation uses less sauce. Slowly we learn to enjoy the beans with an accent sauce rather than smothering the taste of the vegetables with sauce.*

Guide to changes in salt, protein, fat, and fiber content using each variation.

	VARIATION 1	VARIATION 2	VARIATION 3
Salt	▼	▼▼	▼▼▼
Protein	▼	▼▼	▼▼▼
Fat	▼	▼▼	▼▼▼
Fiber		▲	▲▲

85

VARIATION 2

3 cups	green beans	750 ml
2 tsp	oil	10 ml
2 tbsp	onion, minced	30 ml
1 tbsp + 1 tsp	all purpose flour	20 ml
3/4 tsp	thyme or oregano	3 ml
1/4 tsp	salt	1 ml
1/8 tsp	pepper	.5 ml
3/4 tsp	sugar	3 ml
2 tbsp	light sour cream	30 ml
3 tbsp	plain yogurt	45 ml
3 tbsp	1% milk	45 ml
3/4 cup	crushed cracker crumbs	175 ml
1/2 cup	Swiss cheese, grated	125 ml

1. Prepare as per Variation 1, using thyme or oregano to replace some of the salt.

—NOTES—

• *Decreased fat and increased spices enhance the flavors of a recipe. Increasing the onion content and adding thyme or oregano gives a lovely flavor to this dish. I use them to replace salt. These spices complement beans and give the dish additional flavor and aroma so the salt isn't missed.*

• *Yogurt is lower in fat and has a similar texture and appearance to sour cream but gives a lighter, tangier flavor to the recipe.*

• *Low-fat or yogurt Swiss cheese is sometimes available. Using these in place of regular Swiss cheese further decreases the fat content in this dish. When low-fat cheese are heated they are stringier in texture, therefore holding the sauce together more effectively while using less cheese.*

• *This variation uses less sauce.*

VARIATION 3

3 cups	green beans	750 ml
	omit oil	
3 tbsp	onion, minced	45 ml
1 tbsp + 1 tsp	all purpose flour	20 ml
1/2 tsp	thyme or oregano	2 ml
	omit salt	
1/4 tsp	pepper	1 ml
3/4 tsp	sugar	3 ml
	omit sour cream	
1/4 cup	plain yogurt	50 ml
3 tbsp	1% milk	45 ml
1/4 cup	crushed cracker crumbs	50 ml
1/4 cup	crushed bran flakes	50 ml
1/4 cup	Swiss cheese, grated	50 ml

1. Prepare a nonstick pan with nonstick cooking spray. Saute the onions in the pan, stirring constantly.
2. Prepare remainder of dish as per Variation 2, mixing **raw** beans with white sauce.
3. Mix the crushed bran flakes, crushed cracker crumbs, and cheese. Sprinkle over the bean mixture. Cook as per the original recipe.

—NOTES—

• *Using more onion adds flavor, texture, and fiber.*

• *Using a nonstick pan allows you to omit oil, decreasing the fat content.*

• *Using less sour cream, cracker crumbs, and Swiss cheese decreases the overall fat and salt content on this variation.*

• *Bran flakes are a good source of fiber and add more texture to this dish.*

• *There is less sauce in this variation which makes the flavor, crunchy texture, and color of the beans more noticeable.*

FOR BEST RESULTS—read through the entire recipe, each variation, and the TIPS on page 91 before preparing this dish.

Carrots are an excellent source of vitamin A and are high in fiber. This colorful dish is a delicious addition to any meal.

Basil Garlic Carrots

Yields 1-1/2 to 2 cups (375 to 500 ml)

Original Recipe

6	medium carrots	6
2 tbsp	butter or margarine	30 ml
1/2 tsp	garlic salt	2 ml
1 tbsp	lemon juice	15 ml
1 tbsp	chopped fresh basil, or 1 tsp (5 ml) dried basil	15 ml
1/8 tsp	white pepper	.5 ml

1. Slice carrots diagonally into 1/8-inch (3 mm) slices.
2. Melt butter in a heavy skillet.
3. Add all other ingredients to the heated butter in the skillet and cover.
4. Simmer gently over low heat for 14 to 16 minutes or until carrots are tender.

—NOTES—
• It is a good idea to use a heavy skillet in this recipe. If you don't you may have trouble with burning. Add a little water if a heavy skillet is unavailable to you.

VARIATION 1

6	medium carrots	6
1 tbsp	**butter or margarine**	**15 ml**
1-1/2 tbsp	**water**	**25 ml**
1/2 tsp	garlic salt, or	2 ml
	1 clove garlic minced and a dash of salt	
1 tbsp	lemon juice	15 ml
2-1/2 tsp	**chopped fresh basil, or** 3/4 tsp (3 ml) dried basil	**12 ml**
1/8 tsp	white pepper	.5 ml

1. Prepare as per the original recipe, cooking the carrots for no more than 8 to 9 minutes.

—NOTES—
• It is essential to use a heavy skillet in this variation. If you don't you may have trouble with burning. Add more water if a heavy skillet is unavailable to you.
• The vibrant orange color of the carrots stays brighter and the texture remains crisper when cooked for less time.
• As fat is decreased you will find the herbs and spices have a stronger flavor. For this reason the basil was decreased in this variation.
• Fresh minced garlic is often preferred to the taste of garlic salt. It has a fresher flavor and then you can adjust the amount of salt to add.
• Fresh basil should be used within 10 to 30 minutes of picking. If not used almost immediately, much of the flavor is lost.

	VARIATION 1	VARIATION 2
Guide to changes in salt, sugar, fat, and fiber content using each variation.	Salt	Salt ▼
	Sugar	Sugar
	Fat ▼	Fat ▼▼
	Fiber	Fiber

87

VARIATION 2

6	medium carrots	6
1 tsp	**butter or margarine**	**5 ml**
3 tbsp	**water**	**45 ml**
1/2 tsp	garlic salt, or	2 ml
	1 clove garlic minced and a dash of salt	
1 tbsp	lemon juice	15 ml
2-1/2 tsp	chopped fresh basil, or	12 ml
	3/4 tsp (3 ml) dried basil	
1/8 tsp	white pepper	.5 ml

1. Cut the carrots as per the original recipe. Steam them over boiling water for 3 to 5 minutes or until just tender.
2. Heat the remainder of the ingredients in the microwave until they are hot and mix together well.
3. Pour warmed spice liquid mixture over tender warm carrots and toss.
4. Serve immediately.

—NOTES—

• *The decrease in butter is compensated by the increase in water. This gives enough moisture to coat the carrots after they are steamed.*
• *Steaming is a method of cooking that means cooking over, not in, water. This method of cooking preserves colors, textures, and nutrients.*
• *The butter and herbs give flavor to the dish so we didn't notice the omitted salt.*
• *We prefer this variation because the vegetables were crisper and the color was more vibrant.*

YOU CAN STEAM VEGETABLES BY VARIOUS METHODS.

1) Over boiling water on your stove top— You need a strainer or other perforated container to put the vegetables in so they sit in the pot out of the water. The pot needs a lid to seal in the steam. Put the vegetables over the water only after it is boiling so you can control the time they are cooking.

2) In the microwave oven— This is done by adding about 1 tbsp (15 ml) of water to the raw, cut vegetables. Put the water and vegetables in a vented, microwave-safe bowl. Cook on high for a few minutes. Check your microwave instruction book to determine times as each microwave is different. Remember to allow for "sitting time" because food cooked in the microwave continues to cook even after it has turned off.

3) On your barbecue or in your oven— Wrap the vegetables (or fish) in foil, shiny side in. Place this on a barbecue at medium heat. The water in the vegetables (or fish) will create the steam needed to cook them.

These delicious potatoes are well complimented when served with pork and red cabbage.

Herbed Scalloped Potatoes

Yields 3 to 4 cups (750 to 1000 ml)

Original Recipe

1 cup	whole milk	250 ml
3	large potatoes, sliced thin	3
1-1/2 tbsp	all purpose flour	22 ml
1 tsp	salt	5 ml
1	medium onion, chopped	1
1/4 tsp	dried oregano	1 ml
1/4 tsp	dried rosemary	1 ml
1/4 tsp	dried basil	1 ml
1-1/2 tbsp	butter or margarine	22 ml
	garnish with paprika	

1. Place milk in a microwave-safe bowl and heat on high for about 2 minutes, until hot.
2. Grease a 1-1/2 quart (1-1/2 L) casserole with butter or margarine.
3. Mix flour, salt, and spices in a small bowl. Layer potatoes and onions, in the greased baking dish, sprinkling a little flour/spice/salt mixture on each layer.
4. Dot the top of the potato/onion mixture with butter or margarine. Sprinkle with paprika.
5. Pour the hot milk over the entire casserole.
6. Cook uncovered for 15 to 20 minutes in the microwave oven on high, stopping very 5 minutes to stir the potatoes. Or cook in a conventional oven at 35o°F (175°C) for 50 minutes covered or until potatoes are tender. If too much sauce remains, cook uncovered for about 10 minutes more or until liquid evaporates.
7. When using the microwave, cover and let sit for 10 minutes before serving.

—NOTES—
• *Be sure the all flour mixture gets mixed with the liquid.*

VARIATION 1

1 cup	**2% milk**	**250 ml**
3	**large unpeeled potatoes, sliced thin**	**3**
1-1/2 tbsp	all purpose flour	22 ml
1 tsp	salt	5 ml
1	medium onion, chopped	1
1/4 tsp	dried oregano	1 ml
1/4 tsp	dried rosemary	1 ml
1/4 tsp	dried basil	1 ml
1-1/2 tbsp	butter or margarine	22 ml
	garnish with paprika	

1. Before slicing potatoes, wash them very well and leave the peel on. Then slice.
2. Prepare as per the original recipe.

—NOTES—
• *Moving from whole to 2% milk decreases the fat content without changing the texture.*
• *Leaving the peel on the potatoes adds color and texture to this dish and gives it some extra fiber so that it will digest a little slower. Much of the vitamin C found in potatoes is found directly under the peel. When peeled, this is removed. If the peel remains, so do more of the vitamins.*

Guide to changes in salt, sugar, fat, and fiber content using each variation.

	VARIATION 1	VARIATION 2	VARIATION 3
Salt			▼
Sugar			
Fat	▼▲	▼▼	▼▼▼
Fiber	▲	▲▲	▲▲

VARIATION 2

1 cup	1% milk	250 ml
3	large unpeeled potatoes, sliced thin	3
2 tbsp	all purpose flour	30 ml
1 tsp	salt	5 ml
1	medium onion, chopped	1
1/4 tsp	dried oregano	1 ml
1/4 tsp	dried rosemary	1 ml
1/4 tsp	dried basil	1 ml
1 tbsp	butter or margarine	15 ml
	garnish with paprika	

1. Mix and prepare as per Variation 1 with the following exceptions:

Cook in microwave covered for the first 15 minutes and uncovered 5 minutes.

Prepare casserole dish with a nonstick cooking spray.

—NOTES—
• *Using 1% milk and less butter decreases the amount of fat in this variation.*
• *The sauce is lighter but still is creamy and flavorful.*
• *As fat is decreased, which serves as a thickener, the amount of flour is increased.*

VARIATION 3

1 cup	skim milk	250 ml
3	large unpeeled potatoes, sliced thin	3
3 tbsp	whole wheat flour	45 ml
pinch	salt	pinch
1	medium onion, chopped	1
1/8 tsp	dried oregano	.5 ml
1/8 tsp	dried rosemary	.5 ml
1/8 tsp	dried basil	.5 ml
1 tbsp	butter or margarine	15 ml
	garnish with paprika	

1. Mix and prepare as per Variation 2.

—NOTES—
• *Skim milk is lower in fat content than 1% milk, decreasing the overall fat content in this recipe.*
• *Using whole wheat flour to thicken the sauce on the potatoes adds extra texture and color to this dish and increases the fiber content.*
• *There is insufficient protein content in this dish to be considered a balanced meal. If you choose to make this dish a focus of your meal it is important to add another protein source to make the meal balanced. See p14.*
• *As the fat content decreases, the flavor of the herbs and spices increases. In this variation, some of these have been decreased to prevent them from becoming overpowering.*

Tips

*The following information for the recipes given in this section
will help you make choices and add variety to your meals.*

Cheese Sauce for Vegetables p82

• For a satisfying meal, add pureed cottage cheese to the cheese sauce to improve the carbohydrate/protein balance in the meal. Another option—use some vegetable protein such as chick peas in an accompanying salad.

• This sauce can be altered into a cream sauce by removing the cheese and replacing the milk with part-skim or skim evaporated milk. A cream sauce can be served over vegetables and pasta for a tasty alternative.

• If you are using this sauce as your protein source (because you are having a vegetarian meal and want to complete your protein intake), increasing the cheese content by adding 1 cup (250 ml) of 1% pureed cottage cheese will lower the overall fat content in the meal, and adds a tangy flavor to the sauce.

• Consider steamed broccoli, asparagus, brussels sprouts, cauliflower, and cabbage with this sauce.

• When preparing vegetables steam them covered with boiling water for 2 to 3 minutes. This will retain the color and nutrients in the vegetables that is lost when they are cooked in water. *See* p87 for more information on steaming vegetables.

• Steamed vegetables have lovely color and a crisp tender texture. They are colorful and tasty when served alone. If you choose to use a sauce over them, use it as an accent. Remember that sauces are an accent for vegetables not a mask!

Swiss Green Beans p84

• If you prefer a less crunchy texture, cut the beans smaller.

• In Variation 3 the beans have enough cooking time during the baking process to provide a crunchy texture and vibrant green color. If you prefer the beans a little more tender, steam them for 2 to 3 minutes before baking them in the sauce.

• The Swiss cheese and crumbs are accents. You can use less than outlined in the original recipe and still keep the look and flavors you enjoy while decreasing fat, protein, and salt content.

• If you would like to decrease the fat content even more, try using light yogurt. Look for yogurt that has about .9% M.F. or less or prepare your own skim milk yogurt (p164) for a delicious tangy flavor.

• Vegetables usually accompany a main dish that contains protein, such as meat, fish, or poultry. Therefore, the protein content in this recipe could be gradually lowered by decreasing the amount of cheese in the sauce.

• Steaming vegetables helps to maintain their vitamins and color. When steaming, bring the water to a boil first before adding the vegetables. This helps control the cooking time. Try steaming for just a minute or two.

• Mixing plain skim or 1% yogurt with sour cream is an excellent way of changing the fat content in recipes without making big flavor changes.

• Try steaming onions, beans, and herbs or spices such as **nutmeg, garlic, thyme, basil, oregano, marjoram, or lemon or orange rind,** and serve as a delicious and colorful side dish without the sauce. The flavors of vegetables are enhanced with different herbs and spices decreasing the need for added salt or fat.

Basil Garlic Carrots p86

• Margarine and butter are interchangeable in this recipe. One in not "healthier" or "better" than the other. Remember it is the TOTAL amount of fat that you are trying to decrease while still enjoying the flavor of the food. If you don't like the flavor of margarine, don't use it. Use what you enjoy and try to gradually decrease the overall amount of fat you use. Focus on the texture and flavor of your foods and how they are changed when you use less fat. Enjoy the process.

Herbed Scalloped Potatoes p88

• Some families don't enjoy or are unable to tolerate heavily spiced and herbed foods. This dish can be made without the added oregano, rosemary, and basil. The result is a creamy sauce with a more bland flavor. As a sauce becomes less rich you can taste the herbs more easily, so decrease the amounts used according to your taste.

• If your family doesn't enjoy onion pieces in food, try pureeing the onions until they are almost liquid. Then add them. This gives the flavor of onions without the added texture.

• If your potatoes stick to the casserole dish, cover the casserole for the final 5 minutes of cooking time, as well as the 10 minutes of sitting time.

• Microwave cooking often involves sitting time. It is important to allow for the sitting time because microwaves continue to cook the food even after the oven has stopped. If you don't let your food have the sitting time outlined, your food may not be completely cooked.

WRITE DOWN THE TIPS THAT WORK FOR YOU—

—USE THESE TIPS IN YOUR FAMILY FAVORITES!

WRITE DOWN THE TIPS THAT WORK FOR YOU—

—USE THESE TIPS IN YOUR FAMILY FAVORITES!

THE BIG DECISION
"I've decided that our whole family is going to move to healthier eating."

	THE BIG JUMP	THE SMOOTH SLIDE
First action on decision	BRACE YOURSELF. Quickly eat all of your favorite foods because they won't be part of your diet tomorrow.	LOOK AT YOURSELF AND FEEL GOOD ABOUT YOU! Feel good that you have made the conscious decision to start making slow changes that will reflect a healthier life-style.
First shopping trip for healthy food	Stock up on foods that say "light," "low fat," and/or "diet" on the labels regardless of whether you enjoy them. Your family likes whole milk but now that you've made the decision to "eat healthy," you buy skim milk.	Stock up on a wide variety of foods that you and your family enjoy, paying more attention to moving towards more carbohydrate foods and less protein. Buy a few herbs to highlight the flavors of your foods. Your family likes whole milk, so now you buy some 2% milk and plan to serve it to your family. If they don't like it at first, you can mix it half and half with whole milk till they prefer the lighter mouth feel.
Feelings of cook after 1 week	Frustrated and overwhelmed. Food is drier than the family enjoys. You still have a strong resolve to eat healthy, even if rest of family isn't as enthusiastic.	Encouraged by how easy it has been to make small changes to the foods, cooking techniques, and carbohydrate/protein balance that the family already enjoy. Surprised that the family hasn't complained or even really noticed the changes. Notices that the foods have a nicer color and texture yet the taste they had before.
Reaction of family after 1 week	Concerned that the food will never be "tasty" anymore. Tired of the new chewier, drier tastes and textures of these new foods. Longing for last week's menu. Quite agile at slipping food to grateful canine under table. Wishing that the budget allowed more order in or eat out foods for next week. Snacking and eating away from home as much as possible.	Surprised that even though the decision to "go healthy" was made, they still get to eat the foods they love! Notice that the foods they loved have more color and just as much, if not more, flavor than before. Feel more energized after they eat rather than tired and overfull.
Feelings of cook at 1 month	Almost ready to give up because no one (including the cook) is enjoying the food that is prepared. Disappointed and feeling deprived. Misses cooking and eating all the foods that the family used to eat. Wishes that cooking wouldn't be such an overwhelming chore. Sneaking "favorites" more and more often.	Excited that the process is still so enjoyable; not even thinking about quitting; having more and more fun experimenting with old and new recipes; pleased with the results, flavors, and textures.
Feelings of family at 1 month	Ready to move to the neighbors during the meal time. Wishing the "health kick" that hit the house would stop kicking. Eating out or ordering in as much as possible and when eating foods they enjoy, really eating lots. Snacking and sneaking foods that they love on a more frequent basis.	Still enjoying the food that is on the table. Asking for certain favorites more often, "When are you going to make that great bread again?" Noticing that they aren't hungry between meals as often.
Situation after 3 months	Disillusioned with the "health movement." Feeling disappointed and a little guilty, they give up and return to the old ways of eating and cooking again. Some of the family only feels "joy" because they finally get to eat what they love!	Feel good about themselves and their new ways of eating and preparing foods. Energized by the successes, the whole family wants to keep moving on the smooth slide toward healthier eating. They are surprised and pleased to find that they actually like the new ways better. They prefer the new flavors, textures, and tastes and don't want to go back.

Tailoring Your Tastes—go for the smooth slide

Carbohydrate/protein balance

Main dishes are usually the focus of the meal that the other dishes revolve around. The main dish offers a good opportunity to practise balance—balance of color, flavor, texture, and nutritional components. A satisfying ratio of carbohydrates to protein is 2/3 to 3/4 carbohydrates to 1/3 to 1/4 protein (*see* p14). Using the main dishes as a focus of your balancing act is a fun part of meal planning.

The trend today of increasing fiber and carbohydrate intake and decreasing fat has made vegetarian eating more popular. It is important to remember that animal proteins are not "bad" or "unhealthy." They play an important part in daily nutritional needs. Meat, fish, and poultry contain the nine essential amino acids that need to be provided by food. They are complete proteins that help the body build and rebuild tissues, hormones, enzymes, and maintain energy stores (they slow down the breakdown of carbohydrates, helping to give a sustained energy release from them). Canadian beef and pork are much leaner than they were fifteen years ago—as much as 35% leaner.[14] In fact, some cuts of beef and pork are leaner than chicken and some seafood selections. The leanest cuts of beef include round steaks, roasts, sirloin tips, eye of round, flank steak, and stewing beef. The leanest cuts of pork include tenderloin, leg, and loin. The leaner cuts of lamb include tenderloin, boneless loin, and leg cuts.

With the shift in eating styles and preferences (eating higher fiber, higher carbohydrate foods) many people are moving toward incorporating more vegetable protein into their eating patterns. This results in eating meals that are higher in fiber and nutrient levels and lower in fat. But it is important to remember that vegetable proteins are not complete on their own. They need to be supplemented with other food sources to provide the 9 essential amino acids an adult body requires for health and energy.[7,14] Some examples of supplemental foods include nuts, seeds, whole grains, small amounts of animal proteins, or dairy products. You don't have to consume these combinations in the same meal (although you may choose to) in order to complete the protein sources. *See* p14 for additional information about including legumes, dried beans, or peas in your diet.

Meat is an excellent source of iron. There are also plant sources of iron, but these are not as easy for the body to use. If you choose to get your iron from plant sources (legumes, whole or enriched grains, green leafy vegetables, dried fruit, etc.), you may need to increase your vitamin C intake, which helps to make a greater amount of iron available for the body's use. Foods that are high in vitamin C include citrus fruits, tomatoes, broccoli, berries, green peppers, etc. If plant foods are your main source of iron it is important to remember also that you should avoid drinking tea or coffee with your meals. Tea decreases iron absorption (especially from plant sources) by over 60 percent.

If you have never included vegetable proteins in your meals, it may be fun to start. Vegetable proteins add fiber, texture, and nutrients. They will also help to reduce the cost and fat content in your meals. Here are some tips on how to begin:

1) Add legumes or dried beans or higher fiber products to your meals gradually.
This will allow you to enjoy the flavors and textures of all the added foods without losing the flavors and textures of the foods that you enjoy. Start off with Spaghetti Meat Sauce Pie, p102.

2) Use easy preparation techniques to prevent dried peas and beans from causing gastrointestinal discomfort.
Drop the legumes into boiling water and cook them for 3 minutes. Turn heat off, cover, and soak for 2 to 3 hours (can be longer). Pour the water out. The legumes are ready to use in your favorite recipe.

3) Drink lots of fluids.
Additional fiber (legumes) causes your intestines to have a greater quantity of contents. Increasing fluid improves the regularity of bowel movements.

4) Keep eating eggs and dairy products.
Vitamin D and B_{12} are only found in animal products. Plants do not contain vitamin B_{12}. If you don't eat these foods you will need to drink soy products that have been enriched with these nutrients.

5) Don't be surprised if you get hungry sooner.
Vegetable proteins served along with a variety of carbohydrates are lower in fat content than a similar meal served with an animal protein and you may feel hungry sooner. Meals containing animal proteins with more fat digest more slowly and keep you full longer.

As you begin to include more vegetable protein (either by replacing animal proteins with vegetable proteins in some of our weekly meals or supplementing animal

Main Dishes

proteins with the vegetable proteins) it may be difficult to meet total daily protein needs in three main meals. You may need to include more snacks. Including a carbohydrate and protein combination for snacks can assist you in meeting your daily protein requirements. This will also help you to stay full between meals and help to regulate the release of sugar into your bloodstream so that you will have a more constant supply of energy. Eating smaller, balanced meals throughout the day gives you the optimal amount of energy for daily living.

The healthiest way of eating demonstrates balance—balancing carbohydrates with proteins as well as balancing a variety of carbohydrate and protein sources. To maintain adequate nutrition it is important to include variety in your weekly meals. Experiment to find the balance that makes you feel satisfied and energized.

FOR BEST RESULTS—read through the
entire recipe, each variation, and the TIPS
on page 114 before preparing this dish.

*This tangy recipe is a colorful mix of
protein and carbohydrates. Cabbage is
packed with surprises. It is a brassica
vegetable—thought to have a protective
effect against cancer. It is also a good
source of vitamin C and fiber.*

Cabbage Rolls

Yields about 2 dozen

Original Recipe

1	small cabbage	1
1-1/4 cup	long grain rice, uncooked	300 ml
1/2 lb	ground beef	250 g
1	medium onion, finely chopped	1
	salt and pepper to taste	
1 tbsp	catsup	15 ml
1 tbsp + 1-1/2 tsp	vinegar	22 ml
24.5 oz	can of tomato sauce	725 ml
1 cup	water	250 ml
2 tbsp	cereal cream (optional)	30 ml

1. Remove core from 1 small cabbage.
2. Cover the cabbage with boiling hot water for 30 minutes or until leaves can be taken apart (*see* p14).
3. Pull leaves off the head. If leaves are larger than approximately 5 inches (12.5 cm) square, cut to size. Cut out the thick stem parts.
4. Mix rice, beef, onion, and spices together in a bowl.
5. Put about 2 tbsp (30 ml) of meat mixture into each leaf and wrap together. Each pocket of meat is called a cabbage roll.
6. Put the cabbage rolls in the roaster. You can place them very close together.
7. Mix catsup, vinegar, tomato sauce, water, and cereal cream (optional) together. Pour sauce over the cabbage rolls.
8. Bake covered at 350°F (180°C) for 1-1/2 hours, basting cabbage rolls with sauce 3 to 4 times while cooking.

—NOTES—

• *People from different ethnic backgrounds prepare cabbage rolls in different ways. If you prefer, the cream can be omitted.*
• *Cabbage rolls freeze well. Freeze them without the sauce. Add sauce just before baking and serving.*

VARIATION 1

1	small cabbage	1
1-1/4 cup	long grain rice, uncooked	300 ml
1/2 lb	**lean ground beef**	**250 g**
1	medium onion, finely chopped	1
1/4 cup	**green pepper, finely chopped**	**50 ml**
	pepper to taste, **omit salt**	
1 tbsp	**tomato paste**	**15 ml**
1 tbsp + 1-1/2 tsp	vinegar	22 ml
24.5 oz	can of tomato sauce	725 ml
1 cup	water	250 ml
2 tbsp	**whole milk (optional)**	**30 ml**

1. Prepare and bake as per original recipe with the following exceptions: add green pepper when adding onions to the meat mixture, add tomato paste and whole milk instead of catsup and cream (optional) to the sauce.

—NOTES—

• *Using lean or extra lean ground beef in this recipe decreases the fat content without changing the flavor or texture.*
• *Adding green pepper gives an added flavor and texture to the cabbage rolls while also increasing vitamins, minerals, and fiber.*
• *Changing from catsup to tomato paste decreases the sugar, salt, and preservatives in this sauce while still keeping the rich tomato taste and color.*
• *When you use 1 lb (500 g) lean or extra lean ground beef instead of regular ground beef, you are increasing the amount of protein in your meal. Lean ground beef has more meat and less fat than an equal amount of regular ground beef so it is a better protein source.*

Tasty Pot Roast, Variation 2, p99;
Basil Garlic Carrots, Variation 2, p87;
Herbed Scalloped Potatoes, Variation 3, p89;
Caesar Salad Supreme, Variation 3, p55;
Oma's Best Buns, Variation 3, p69;
Favorite Fruit Drink (red grape), Variation 3, p123

Tomato Sauce Lentils, Variation 2, p101;
served on Honey Oatmeal Bread, Variation 1, p70, in pita pockets, and on basmati rice

Guide to changes in salt, sugar, protein, fat, and fiber content using each variation.

	VARIATION 1	VARIATION 2	VARIATION 3
Salt	▼	▼▼	▼▼▼
Sugar	▼	▼▼	▼▼▼
Protein	▲	▲	▲▲
Fat	▼	▼▼	▼▼▼
Fiber	▲	▲▲	▲▲▲

97

VARIATION 2

1	small cabbage	1
1-1/4 cup	**converted rice, uncooked**	**300 ml**
1/2 lb	lean ground beef	250 g
1	medium onion, finely chopped	1
1/4 cup	green pepper, finely chopped	50 ml
1/2 cup	**shredded carrots**	**125 ml**
	pepper to taste	
1 tbsp	tomato paste	15 ml
1 tbsp + 1-1/2 tsp	vinegar	22 ml
14 oz	**can of tomato sauce**	**398 ml**
19 oz	**can of whole tomatoes**	**540 ml**
1/2 cup	**water**	**125 ml**
2 tbsp	whole milk (optional)	30 ml

1. Prepare and bake as per original recipe with the following exceptions: add shredded carrots when adding onions to meat mixture; cut whole tomatoes into small chunks and add them along with the liquid from the can to the tomato sauce and water when making the sauce.

—NOTES—

• *Converted rice has undergone a process in which the nutrients are pushed back into the rice grain resulting in a higher retention of minerals and vitamins in cooked grain.*
• *Converted rice breaks down into glucose more slowly in your bloodstream giving you a longer time of fullness and less fluctuation in blood glucose.*
• *Adding the shredded carrots increases the fiber content in this variation. It also adds extra color, texture, and moisture to this dish.*
• *Adding canned whole tomatoes instead of tomato sauce decreases the sugar, salt, and preservatives in this recipe and increases the fiber content. Less water is needed because the whole tomatoes and the fluid create enough moisture.*

VARIATION 3

1	small cabbage	1
2/3 cup	**converted white rice, uncooked**	**150 ml**
2/3 cup	**converted brown rice, uncooked**	**150 ml**
1/2 lb	**extra lean ground beef**	**250 g**
1	medium onion, finely chopped	1
1/4 cup	green pepper, finely chopped	50 ml
1/2 cup	shredded carrots	125 ml
	pepper to taste	
1 tbsp + 1-1/2 tsp	vinegar	22 ml
	omit tomato sauce	
28 oz	**can of whole tomatoes**	**796 ml**
5.5 oz	**tin of tomato paste**	**156 ml**
1/2 cup	**water**	**125 ml**
2 tbsp	**2% milk (optional)**	**30 ml**
1 clove	**garlic, minced**	**1 clove**

1. Prepare and bake as per original recipe with the following exceptions: cut whole tomatoes into small chunks and add them along with the liquid from the can to the tomato paste and water when making the sauce. Add garlic to tomato mixture also.

—NOTES—

• *Brown rice has a higher fiber content and breaks down into glucose a little slower than white rice. This flattens the glucose response in your body giving a more consistent release of energy.*
• *The less a vegetable is processed and pureed the greater the value it has in adding useable fiber. The tomato chunks also give the sauce more texture.*
• *Adding garlic makes the decrease in fat content unnoticeable.*
• *Extra tomato paste and water give the sauce a richer flavor.*

Roast is a familiar family favorite! This recipe creates a tasty moist roast combined with soups, herbs, and spices.

Tasty Pot Roast

Yields 4 servings

Original Recipe

3 to 4 lb	brisket or less tender cut of beef	1.5 to 2 kg
2–10 oz	cans cream of mushroom soup	2–284 ml
1 pkg	onion soup mix	1 pkg

1. Place roast in a large crock pot, slow cooker, or medium-sized covered casserole dish.
2. Combine mushroom soup and onion soup mix.
3. Pour mixture over roast.
4. Bake covered at 325°F (170°C) for 3 to 4 hours or until roast is well done.
5. No need for thickener as the soup and fat in this recipe give the gravy substance.

—NOTES—
• *Tougher cuts of beef will become more tender if they are cooked for a longer period of time at a lower heat. (See TIPS p114.)*

VARIATION 1

3 to 4 lb	brisket or less tender cut of beef	1.5 to 2 kg
10 oz	**can cream of mushroom soup**	**284 ml**
1 pkg	onion soup mix	1 pkg

1. Trim all visible fat off roast. Then place roast in a covered casserole dish.
2. Combine mushroom soup and onion soup mix and pour over roast.
3. Bake covered at 325°F (170°C) for 2 to 3 hours or until roast is tender.

—NOTES—
• *Decreasing the amount of mushroom soup decreases the overall fat and salt content in this recipe. Using one can gives the mushroom flavor.*
• *The longer a tougher cut of meat is cooked the more tender it becomes. This remains true until the gravy and fluids produced during cooking are completely absorbed, then it will eventually dry out.*

Guide to changes in salt, sugar, fat, and fiber content using each variation.	VARIATION 1	VARIATION 2	VARIATION 3
	Salt ▼	Salt ▼▼	Salt ▼▼▼
	Sugar	Sugar	Sugar
	Fat ▼	Fat ▼	Fat ▼▼
	Fiber	Fiber	Fiber ▲

99

VARIATION 2

3 to 4 lb	brisket	1.5 to 2 kg
	or less tender cut of beef	
10 oz	can cream of mushroom soup	284 ml
1/2 pkg	onion soup mix	1/2 pkg
1 tsp	oregano	5 ml
1 tsp	marjoram	5 ml
1 tsp	sage	5 ml

1. Prepare, cook, and serve as per Variation 1. Add spices to the onion soup mix.

—NOTES—

• *Adding herbs to the roast gives a lovely new flavor to this meal. The herbs allow you to decrease the amount of onion soup mix used to add flavor and pizzazz. Therefore you don't notice the decrease in salt from the soup mix.*

VARIATION 3

3 to 4 lb	brisket	1.5 to 2 kg
	or less tender cut of beef	
10 oz	can "Healthy Request" cream of mushroom soup	284 ml
1	medium onion, chopped	1
1 tbsp	onion soup mix	15 ml
1/2 tsp	oregano	2 ml
1/2 tsp	marjoram	2 ml
1/2 tsp	sage	2 ml

1. Prepare, cook, and serve as per Variation 1. Add spices and onion to the soup mixture before pouring over the roast.

—NOTES—

• *Adding fresh onion to the roast gives the gravy more substance and adds a lovely flavor to the roast. The added onion gives this dish more substance and fiber.*

• *The addition of fresh onions and herbs allows you to decrease the amount of onion soup mix used in this recipe. You can use just a little to add the flavor you enjoy when adding soup mixes. The flavor outcome is delicious. The aroma of roast cooking with fresh onions is unbeatable. You do not notice the decrease in salt content in this variation.*

• *Healthy Request soups are lower in salt, fat, and sometimes sugar contents. If they are not available at your grocery store you can ask your grocer to order them.*

Tomato Sauce Lentils

Yields 5 to 6 cups (1.25 to 1.5 L)

The spicy flavor of this dish can be enjoyed either hot or cold. Lentils can be part of any traditional meat sauce recipe and are an excellent source of protein and fiber and low in fat.

Original Recipe

1 cup	lentils, rinsed	250 ml
	or another prepared dried bean (*see* p118)	
2	beef bouillon cubes	2
1/2 tsp	salt	2 ml
2-1/2 cup	water	625 ml
1	bay leaf	1
2 tbsp	lemon juice	30 ml
1 tbsp	chopped parsley	15 ml
1/4 cup	butter or margarine	50 ml
1	large onion, chopped	1
1	large clove garlic, minced	1
10 oz	can tomato soup	284 ml
10 oz	can water	284 ml
1–2 tbsp	curry powder	15–30 ml
	sour cream for garnish	

1. Combine the first 7 ingredients in a saucepan and bring to a boil. Simmer covered for 20 minutes.
2. Saute onions and garlic in butter in a heavy saucepan until the onions are translucent.
3. Drain lentils. Add them to the saucepan containing the onion mixture along with the remaining ingredients.
4. Simmer for about 10 minutes or until moisture evaporates enough to achieve the desired consistency.
5. Serve over rice or in a pita pocket. Garnish with sour cream.

—NOTES—
• *If you do not like the flavor of curry powder substitute 1 tsp (5 ml) each basil, oregano, and rosemary.*
• *Cook longer for a thicker sauce to serve in a pita pocket, cook less for a thinner sauce to serve over rice.*

VARIATION 1

1 cup	lentils, rinsed	250 ml
	or another prepared dried bean (*see* p28)	
2	beef bouillon cubes	2
1/4 tsp	**salt**	**1 ml**
2-1/2 cup	water	625 ml
1	bay leaf	1
2 tbsp	lemon juice	30 ml
1 tbsp	chopped parsley	15 ml
2 tbsp	**butter or margarine**	**30 ml**
1	large onion, chopped	1
1	large clove garlic, minced	1
10 oz	**can "Healthy Request" tomato soup**	**284 ml**
10 oz	can water	284 ml
1–2 tbsp	curry powder	15–30 ml
	light sour cream for garnish	

1. Prepare, cook, and serve as per original recipe.

—NOTES—
• *Beef bouillon has a salty flavor so the decrease in salt is not noticed.*
• *Using light products in cooking can often decrease the total amount of fat/salt/sugar in a recipe without altering flavor or texture. If you enjoy the regular products more than light products, use them and learn to enjoy them in smaller quantities. Gradually lessen the amounts you use in your foods so that you can taste the true flavors and textures of the meals you eat.*
• *"Healthy Request" soups are lower in salt, fat, and sometimes sugar contents. If they are not available at your grocery store, ask your grocer to order them.*

Guide to changes in salt, sugar, fat, and fiber content using each variation.

	VARIATION 1	VARIATION 2	VARIATION 3
Salt	▼	▼	▼
Sugar		▲	▲▲
Fat	▼	▼▼	▼▼▼
Fiber		▲	▲▲

VARIATION 2

1 cup	lentils, rinsed	250 ml
2	beef bouillon cubes	2
	omit salt	
2-1/2 cup	water	625 ml
1	bay leaf	1
2 tbsp	lemon juice	30 ml
1 tbsp	chopped parsley	15 ml
2 tbsp	**white wine**	**30 ml**
1 tbsp	**oil**	**15 ml**
1	large onion, chopped	1
1	large clove garlic, minced	1
10 oz	can "Healthy Request" tomato soup	284 ml
1/2 cup	**chopped or crushed tomatoes**	**125 ml**
10 oz	can water	284 ml
1–2 tbsp	curry powder	15–30 ml
	light sour cream and plain low-fat yogurt for garnish	

1. Prepare, cook, and serve as per original recipe with the following exceptions: use wine and oil to saute onions, add only the first 6 ingredients in step 1 because salt is omitted. For garnish make a half-and-half mixture of sour cream and yogurt.

—NOTES—

• *Adding wine increases the sugar content to the equivalent of approximately 1/8 tsp (.5 ml) white sugar. The increase is very small and compensates for the decrease in fat content.*

• *Using wine to saute onions decreases the oil needed. The wine gives this dish an extra tangy flavor that complements the curry.*

• *Because of the added tomatoes the finished dish is a little brighter red in color, has a more pronounced tomato flavor, and has more fiber content.*

VARIATION 3

1 cup	lentils, rinsed	250 ml
2	beef bouillon cubes	2
2-1/2 cup	water	625 ml
1	bay leaf	1
2 tbsp	lemon juice	30 ml
1 tbsp	chopped parsley	15 ml
1/4 cup	**white wine**	**50 ml**
1	large onion, chopped	1
1	large clove garlic, minced	1
10 oz	can "Healthy Request" tomato soup	284 ml
14 oz	**tin of tomatoes, chopped or crushed**	**389 ml**
	omit water	
1–2 tbsp	curry powder	15–30 ml
	plain low-fat yogurt for garnish (optional)	

1. Prepare lentils as per Variation 2.
2. Using a nonstick pan saute the onions and garlic in the wine on medium heat (high heat causes sticking).
3. Continue as per original recipe.

—NOTES—

• *We didn't notice the decrease in fat used to prepare the onion/garlic mixture.*

• *If you do not like the texture of chopped whole tomatoes, puree them before adding to the recipe.*

• *The wine content is increased in this variation and replaces the oil content. This increase raises the sugar level slightly. The increase from Variation 2 is equivalent to about 1/8 tsp (.5 ml) white sugar.*

This easy-to-make main dish is a favorite and has similar flavors to lasagna. It can be prepared ahead of time except for the baking and kept frozen in a covered container for several weeks. The fennel seed adds a distinctive Italian flavor.

Spaghetti Meat Sauce Pie

Yields 1—10 inch (25 cm) pie

Original Recipe

—CRUST—		
2-1/2 cups	cooked spaghetti	625 ml
1/4 cup	fresh parmesan cheese, grated	50 ml
1	egg, beaten	1
2 tbsp	oil	30 ml
—TOPPING—		
1-1/4 cup	ricotta cheese	300 ml
3/4 lb	regular ground beef	375 g
1/2 cup	onion, chopped	125 ml
1	clove garlic, minced	1
1/4 cup	green pepper, chopped	50 ml
14 oz	can of tomato sauce	398 ml
1–2 tsp	dried basil (to desired taste)	5–10 ml
1/8 tsp	crushed hot red pepper (optional)	.5 ml
1/2 tsp	fennel seed	2 ml
1/2 tsp	salt	2 ml
1 cup	mozzarella cheese, grated	250 ml

1. Combine the first 4 ingredients in a bowl.
2. Grease or spray a 10-inch (25-cm) pie plate.
3. Spread the crust mixture over the bottom of the plate.
4. Spread ricotta cheese over the crust and set aside.
5. Brown meat in a large heavy saucepan. Add onion and garlic and saute until onion is translucent.
6. Add green peppers, tomato sauce, herbs and spices.
7. Bring mixture to a boil on medium high heat. Then reduce heat to low and cook uncovered for about 10 minutes.
8. Spread tomato beef mixture over entire crust so spaghetti crust won't dry out. Sprinkle mozzarella over the entire pie.
9. Bake the pie at 350°F (180°C) for 30 minutes. Remove from oven. Allow mixture to set 10 minutes before cutting.

VARIATION 1

—CRUST—		
2-1/2 cups	cooked spaghetti	625 ml
1/4 cup	fresh parmesan cheese, grated	50 ml
1	egg, beaten	1
1 tbsp	**oil**	**15 ml**
—TOPPING—		
1-1/4 cup	ricotta cheese	300 ml
3/4 lb	**lean ground beef**	**375 g**
1/2 cup	onion, chopped	125 ml
1	clove garlic, minced	1
1/4 cup	green pepper, chopped	50 ml
14 oz	can of tomato sauce	398 ml
1–2 tsp	dried basil (to desired taste)	5–10 ml
1/8 tsp	crushed hot red pepper (optional)	.5 ml
1/2 tsp	fennel seed	2 ml
1/4 tsp	**salt**	**1 ml**
1 cup	mozzarella cheese, grated	250 ml

1. Follow steps 1 to 4 in original recipe.
2. Put ground beef, onion, and garlic in a microwave-safe sieve placed over a bowl. Microwave on high for 2 to 3 minutes at a time. Take meat mixture out and stir. Return to microwave and repeat procedure until meat is cooked. Strainer allows fat to drip to bottom of bowl.
3. Add cooked meat to green pepper, tomato sauce, and spice mixture in a heavy saucepan.
4. Follow steps 7 to 9 in original recipe.

—NOTES—

• *Using lean ground beef and the microwave preparation decreases the overall fat content.*
• *Moving to lean ground beef increases the amount of protein in your meal because lean ground beef has more meat and less fat than an equivalent amount of regular ground beef.*

Guide to changes in salt, protein, fat, and fiber content using each variation.

	VARIATION 1	VARIATION 2	VARIATION 3
Salt	▼	▼▼	▼▼▼
Protein	▲	▲▲	▲▲▲
Fat	▼	▼▼	▼▼▼
Fiber		▲	▲▲

VARIATION 2

—CRUST—

2-1/2 cups	cooked spaghetti	625 ml
1/4 cup	fresh parmesan cheese, grated	50 ml
1	egg, beaten	1
1 tbsp	oil	15 ml

—TOPPING—

1-1/4 cup	**part-skim ricotta cheese**	**300 ml**
1/2 cup	onion, chopped	125 ml
1	clove garlic, minced	1
3/4 lb	**extra lean ground beef**	**375 g**
1/2 cup	**green pepper, chopped**	**125 ml**
14 oz	can of tomato sauce	398 ml
1-1/2 tsp	**dried basil**	**7 ml**
1/8 tsp	crushed hot red pepper (optional)	.5 ml
1/4 tsp	**fennel seed**	**1 ml**
	omit salt	
1/2 cup	**mozzarella cheese, grated**	**125 ml**
1/2 cup	**part-skim mozzarella, grated**	**125 ml**

1. Prepare, cook, and serve as per Variation 1.

—NOTES—

• *This variation has decreased fat content because of extra lean beef, part-skim ricotta and part-skim mozzarella cheeses. The flavor and texture is not altered.*

• *Part-skim mozzarella cheese is stickier and has a more rubbery texture and is harder to grate.*

• *Overall salt content is decreased in this variation.*

• *Using extra lean ground beef increases the protein content in this recipe.*

• *Because of the lower fat content in this variation, you will need less basil and fennel to give this dish flavor. You may prefer even less herbs than suggested.*

VARIATION 3

1 cup	**lentils**	**250 ml**
2 cups	**water**	**500 ml**

—CRUST—

2-1/2 cups	**cooked whole wheat spaghetti**	**625 ml**
1/4 cup	fresh parmesan cheese, grated	50 ml
1	egg, beaten	1
1 tbsp	oil	15 ml

—TOPPING—

1-1/4 cup	part-skim ricotta cheese	300 ml
1/2 cup	onion, chopped	125 ml
1	clove garlic, minced	1
3/4 lb	extra lean ground beef	375 g
1/2 cup	green pepper, chopped	125 ml
14 oz	can of tomato sauce	398 ml
1 tsp	**dried basil**	**5 ml**
1/8 tsp	crushed hot red pepper (optional)	.5 ml
1/4 tsp	fennel seed	1 ml
1 cup	**part-skim mozzarella, grated**	**250 ml**

1. Cook lentils in water for 30 minutes. Drain and add to tomato mixture.
2. Continue preparation, cooking, and serving as per Variation 1.

—NOTES—

• *Start cooking lentils before beginning to make the rest of the recipe. This allows them to be ready when making the sauce. Do not cook them until they are soggy.*

• *Using whole wheat noodles increases the fiber content in this recipe. The color of the base is darker but the flavor stays the same.*

• *Adding lentils as a vegetable protein increases the overall protein as well as the fiber content.*

The original recipe produces a very rich and creamy dish. Gradually moving through the variations provides a less creamy, tasty alternative with more pronounced flavors.

Crab-filled Crepes

Yields about 20 small crepes

Original Recipe

3 tbsp	margarine	45 ml
1/4 cup	shallots or onions, diced	50 ml
2 cups	cooked crab meat, chopped	500 ml
1-1/2 cups	softened cream cheese	375 ml
2 tbsp	sherry	30 ml
1/3 cup	1/2 & 1/2 cream	75 ml
1/4 tsp	cumin	1 ml
2 tsp	lemon juice	10 ml
3 tbsp	fresh parsley, chopped	45 ml
1 cup	Swiss cheese, grated	250 ml
2 tbsp	green onion, chopped	30 ml
1/2 cup	toasted almonds	125 ml
20	crepes (p74)	20

1. Melt margarine in a hot skillet, add onions or shallots and saute until translucent.
2. Mix together in a bowl the cream cheese, cream, sherry, cumin, lemon juice, parsley, crab meat, and hot onion.
3. Place about 2 tbsp (30 ml) of this mixture into each crepe and roll.
4. Place crepes in a casserole dish, leaning up against each other. Top with Swiss cheese.
5. Bake at 350°F (180°C) for 15 minutes covered and 5 to 10 minutes uncovered or until the tops start to brown.
6. Let crepes sit in cooking dish out of the oven for about 5 minutes before serving to allow the filling to set. If you don't they may fall apart when removing from the pan.
7. Garnish with green onions and toasted almonds.

—NOTES—
- *Crab flavored pollock is an excellent substitute for crab meat.*
- *You can fill crepes with mixture and freeze prior to baking.*

VARIATION 1

2 tbsp	**margarine**	**30 ml**
1/4 cup	shallots or onions, diced	50 ml
2 cups	cooked crab meat, chopped	500 ml
1-1/2 cups	**light cream cheese**	**375 ml**
1/3 cup	**whole milk**	**75 ml**
1/4 tsp	cumin	1 ml
2 tsp	lemon juice	10 ml
3 tbsp	fresh parsley, chopped	45 ml
2 tbsp	sherry	30 ml
1 cup	Swiss cheese, grated	250 ml
2 tbsp	green onion, chopped	30 ml
1/2 cup	toasted almonds	125 ml
20	crepes (p74)	20

1. Saute onions in a nonstick pan with margarine. Prepare, bake, and serve as per the original recipe.

—NOTES—
- *A nonstick pan allows you to use less margarine to saute the onions or shallots.*
- *Decreasing the margarine, changing to light cream cheese, and replacing the 1/2 & 1/2 cream with whole milk lowers the overall fat content in this recipe.*
- *This variation produces little flavor change yet the total fat content has been decreased.*

Guide to changes in salt, sugar, protein, fat, and fiber content using each variation.

	VARIATION 1	VARIATION 2	VARIATION 3
Salt			▼
Sugar		▲	▲
Protein	▲	▲▲	▲▲
Fat	▼	▼▼	▼▼▼
Fiber		▲	▲▲

VARIATION 2

1 tbsp	margarine	15 ml
1 tbsp	white wine	15 ml
1/4 cup	shallots or onions, diced	50 ml
2 cups	cooked crab meat, chopped	500 ml
1/2 cup	carrots or broccoli, chopped very fine	125 ml
3/4 cup	light cream cheese	175 ml
3/4 cup	quark cheese	175 ml
1/3 cup	2% milk	75 ml
1/4 tsp	cumin	1 ml
2 tsp	lemon juice	10 ml
3 tbsp	fresh parsley, chopped	45 ml
2 tbsp	sherry	30 ml
1 cup	Swiss cheese, grated	250 ml
2 tbsp	green onion, chopped	30 ml
1/2 cup	toasted almonds	125 ml
20	crepes (p74)	20

1. Saute onion with margarine and wine in a nonstick pan.
2. Add quark cheese to the cream cheese. Add crab and chopped broccoli or carrots to this mixture.
3. Prepare, bake, and serve as per the original recipe.

—NOTES—

• *The protein level is increased in this variation because of replacing some of the cream cheese with quark cheese. The fat is being replaced with protein.*
• *Increasing the vegetable content increases the vitamin, mineral, and fiber content.*
• *This variation is still creamy but lighter in texture. The flavors are more pronounced due to lower fat content.*
• *Adding 1 tbsp (15 ml) white wine increases the sugar in this variation very slightly. The increase is equivalent to 1/10 of 1 tsp (1/10 of 5 ml) white sugar.*

VARIATION 3

	omit margarine	
1 tbsp	white wine	15 ml
1/4 cup	shallots or onions, diced	50 ml
2 cups	cooked crab meat, chopped	500 ml
3/4 cup	carrots or broccoli, chopped very fine	175 ml
	omit light cream cheese	
1-1/2 cup	quark cheese	375 ml
1/3 cup	1% milk	75 ml
1/2 tsp	cumin	2 ml
2 tsp	lemon juice	10 ml
3 tbsp	fresh parsley, chopped	45 ml
2 tbsp	sherry	30 ml
3/4 cup	Swiss cheese, grated fine	175 ml
2 tbsp	green onion, chopped	30 ml
1/2 cup	toasted almonds	125 ml
20	crepes (p74)	20

1. Place onions and wine in microwave-safe bowl. Cover with a vented lid or plastic wrap and cook on high for 1 minute. Then let sit for 1 minute.
2. Prepare, bake, and serve as per Variation 2.

—NOTES—

• *Crepes will not be as creamy and will provide a lighter meal. The sauce is still tangy and tasty.*
• *Cooking onions in this manner keeps them juicy without adding fat.*
• *The overall fat content is lower because of decreasing the Swiss cheese, replacing 2% milk with 1%, and replacing cream cheese with quark cheese. The protein remains about the same.*
• *The Swiss cheese is an accent. Grating it finely allows you to distribute a smaller amount more evenly over the entire dish.*

FOR BEST RESULTS—read through the entire recipe, each variation, and the TIPS on page 116 before preparing this sauce.

Vegetable Alfredo is delicious but is it a healthy choice? Recipes are often high in fat ingredients and low in protein ingredients. Protein needs to be part of your meal to keep you full longer. In order to make Vegetable Alfredo a more balanced meal, increase protein and decrease fat content. You will notice this shift through the variations.

Vegetable Alfredo Sauce

Yields 3 to 4 cups (750 to 1000 ml) sauce

Original Recipe

1 cup	broccoli florets	250 ml
1 cup	diced carrots	250 ml
1 cup	fresh mushrooms, sliced	250 ml
1–2	cloves garlic, minced	1–2
4 tbsp	butter or margarine	60 ml
1-1/2 cup	whipping cream	375 ml
1/8 tsp	pepper	.5 ml
1/2 tsp	salt	2 ml
1/4 cup	fresh parsley, chopped	50 ml
1 cup	parmesan cheese, grated	250 ml

1. Steam broccoli and carrots until tender but still crisp.
2. Saute mushrooms and garlic in 2 tbsp (30 ml) butter until tender in a heavy saucepan. Set vegetables aside.
3. Using the same saucepan, melt 2 tbsp (30 ml) butter, add cream, and heat until very hot but not boiling (it may curdle if boiled).
4. Add salt, pepper, parsley, parmesan cheese, mushrooms, garlic, broccoli, and carrots to the cream mixture.
5. Heat on medium high heat, stirring constantly, until the sauce is heated through and is the desired consistency.
6. Serve over your favorite pasta.

—NOTES—

• *If you prefer, fresh basil can replace the parsley.*
• *If you prefer a thinner sauce, add more milk once the sauce is cooked. If you prefer a thicker sauce, whisk in instant thickener.*

VARIATION 1

1 cup	broccoli florets	250 ml
1 cup	diced carrots	250 ml
1 cup	fresh mushrooms, sliced	250 ml
1–2	cloves garlic, minced	1–2
3 tbsp	**butter or margarine**	**45 ml**
1 cup	**1/2 & 1/2 cream**	**250 ml**
1 cup	**2% cottage cheese, pureed until smooth**	**250 ml**
1/8 tsp	pepper	.5 ml
	omit salt	
1/4 cup	fresh parsley, chopped	50 ml
1 cup	parmesan cheese, grated	250 ml

1. Prepare as per the original recipe with the following exceptions: saute mushrooms and garlic in 1 tbsp (15 ml) butter; and mix together cream and cottage cheese, then use a whisk to prevent lumping when heating with butter.
2. Serve as per the original recipe.

—NOTES—

• *This variation is lower in fat because of the change to 1/2 & 1/2 cream and decrease in butter.*
• *Adding cottage cheese lowers the overall fat content and increases the protein content giving this meal a healthier carbohydrate/protein balance, and adds a wonderful tangy flavor.*
• *Mushrooms have enough water in them to need only 1 tbsp (15 ml) of butter for sauteing.*
• *The parmesan cheese is the thickener in this alfredo. Stirring it in in step 4 (original recipe) gives this sauce its lovely consistency.*
• *Cottage cheese contains salt and give this dish enough salt flavor so you don't miss the table salt.*
• *There is very little protein in this dish until the cottage cheese is added.*

Guide to changes in salt, sugar, protein, fat, and fiber content using each variation.

	VARIATION 1	VARIATION 2	VARIATION 3
Salt			▲
Sugar			
Protein	▲	▲▲	▲▲▲
Fat	▼	▼▼	▼▼▼
Fiber			

107

VARIATION 2

1 cup	broccoli florets	250 ml
1 cup	diced carrots	250 ml
1 cup	fresh mushrooms, sliced	250 ml
1–2	cloves garlic, minced	1–2
2 tbsp	**butter or margarine**	**30 ml**
1 cup	**evaporated milk**	**250 ml**
1 cup	2% cottage cheese, pureed until smooth	250 ml
1/8 tsp	pepper	.5 ml
1/4 cup	fresh parsley, chopped	50 ml
1 cup	parmesan cheese, grated	250 ml

1. Prepare as per Variation 1 with the following exceptions: reduce the butter in sauce to 1 tbsp (15 ml), and replace cream with evaporated milk.

—NOTES—
• *Evaporated milk has a similar creamy texture to cream and is lower in fat and higher in protein.*
• *This variation is lower in fat because of the decrease in butter and cream.*
• *The sauce has a lighter texture but is still creamy and has all the flavor of the original recipe.*

VARIATION 3

1 cup	broccoli florets	250 ml
1 cup	diced carrots	250 ml
1 cup	fresh mushrooms, sliced	250 ml
1–2	cloves garlic, minced	1–2
1 tbsp	**butter or margarine**	**15 ml**
1 cup	**part-skim evaporated milk**	**250 ml**
1-2/3 cup	**1% cottage cheese, pureed until smooth**	**400 ml**
1	egg	1
1/8 tsp	pepper	.5 ml
1/4 cup	fresh parsley, chopped	50 ml
1 cup	parmesan cheese, grated	250 ml

1. Prepare as per Variation 2 with the following exceptions: use half the butter for sauteing the mushrooms and garlic and half for the sauce; puree the cottage cheese with the egg until smooth; add cottage cheese/egg mixture to milk mixture, then prepare and serve as per the original recipe.

—NOTES—
• *This variation is lower in fat because of the decrease in butter and the elimination of cream.*
• *This sauce has a wonderful light texture that doesn't leave you feeling so full and bloated when you are finished.*
• *The egg and parmesan cheese thicken this variation. Usually when decreasing fat you may need to add some additional thickening agents like flour or cornstarch. This variation is the right consistency without these additions.*
• *The added cottage cheese and egg increase the protein content in this recipe so that there is a better balance between carbohydrates and proteins.*

FOR BEST RESULTS—read through the entire recipe, each variation, and the TIPS on page 116 before preparing this dish.

This spicy, tangy stroganoff is a delicious dinner selection for family or company. Serve it over fettuccine noodles with steamed carrots and a fresh salad. There are many ingredients that add to the overall flavor. If you have your own favorite recipe, you may want to try some of these ideas.

Beef Stroganoff

Yields 6 to 7 cups (1.5 to 1.75 L)

Original Recipe

1/4 cup	oil	50 ml
2	medium onions, sliced	2
1	clove garlic, minced	1
1-1/2 lb	beef tenderloin or rib eye steak	750 g
1/4 tsp	pepper	1 ml
10 oz	can of beef broth	284 ml
1/2 cup	water	125 ml
1 cup	whole milk	250 ml
1 tsp	Worcestershire sauce	5 ml
1 tbsp	tomato paste	15 ml
1/2 tsp	salt	2 ml
1 cup	fresh mushrooms, chopped	250 ml
1/4 cup	flour	50 ml
1 cup	sour cream	250 ml

1. Using a heavy saucepan with lid, heat oil and saute onions and garlic until translucent.
2. Slice the steak into thin strips and sprinkle with pepper.
3. Add meat to saucepan with onions and garlic and stir fry on medium high heat quickly until just browned (if you stir fry too long the meat will become tough).
4. Add remaining ingredients, **except** sour cream and flour, whisking until sauce is smooth.
5. Heat mixture on high until boiling. Reduce heat, cover and cook slowly for 40 minutes or until meat is tender (when poked with a fork the meat pierces easily). Stir occasionally.
6. Stir flour into sour cream until smooth, and whisk into beef mixture. Cook, stirring constantly, until thickened.
7. Serve hot over fettuccine noodles.

VARIATION 1

3 tbsp	oil	45 ml
2	medium onions, sliced	2
1	clove garlic, minced	1
1-1/2 lb	beef tenderloin or rib eye steak	750 g
1/4 tsp	pepper	1 ml
10 oz	can "Healthy Request"	284 ml
	beef broth, or 1 low-salt bouillon cube in 1-1/4 cup (300 ml) hot water	
1/2 cup	water	125 ml
1 cup	2% milk	250 ml
1 tsp	Worcestershire sauce	5 ml
1 tbsp	tomato paste	15 ml
1/2 tsp	salt	2 ml
1 cup	fresh mushrooms, chopped	250 ml
1/4 cup	flour	50 ml
1 cup	light sour cream	250 ml

1. Use a large nonstick pot to brown meat, onion, and garlic. Prepare, cook, and serve per the original recipe.

—NOTES—

• *Using less oil, 2% milk, and light sour cream decreases the fat content in this recipe.*
• *Using a nonstick pan allows you to use less oil when frying the meat and vegetables.*
• *When buying "light" products, read the label carefully. Look for B.F. or M.F. percentages or grams of fat per serving to discover if the product actually has less fat content.*
• *Some people do not like the flavor of light products. For cooking, however, there is no difference in flavor or texture when using light sour cream.*

Peach Spice Chicken, Variation 2, p111; The Milligen Toss, Variation 3, p53,
Herb Beer Bread, Variation 3, p73; Marble Cheesecake, Variation 3, p141

Top and clockwise: Wine Sangria, Variation 1, p126;
Hot Apple Cider, Variation 1, p128; Milk & International Coffee, Variation 1, p132;
Tropical Refresher, Variation 2, p125

Guide to changes in salt, protein, fat, and fiber content using each variation.

	VARIATION 1	VARIATION 2	VARIATION 3
Salt	▼	▼	▼▼
Protein		▲	▲
Fat	▼	▼▼	▼▼▼
Fiber		▲	▲

VARIATION 2

2 tbsp	oil	30 ml
2	medium onions, sliced	2
1	clove garlic, minced	1
1-1/2 lb	bccf tenderloin or rib eye steak	750 g
1/4 tsp	pepper	1 ml
10 oz	can "Healthy Request"	284 ml
	beef broth, or 1 low-salt bouillon cube	
	in 1-1/4 cup (300 ml) hot water	
1/2 cup	water	125 ml
1 cup	2% milk	250 ml
1 tsp	Worcestershire sauce	5 ml
1 tbsp	tomato paste	15 ml
1/2 tsp	salt	2 ml
1 cup	fresh mushrooms, chopped	250 ml
1/4 cup	**whole wheat flour**	**50 ml**
1/2 cup	**light sour cream**	**125 ml**
1/2 cup	**1% cottage cheese**	**125 ml**

1. Prepare as per Variation 1 with the following exception: combine the cottage cheese, sour cream, and flour and puree until the mixture is smooth. Whisk this mixture into the sauce and continue following the original recipe.

—NOTES—

• *Adding cottage cheese to dishes lowers the overall fat content and increases the protein content making the meal a healthier choice. See p23 for more information about cottage cheese.*
• *Moving to whole wheat flour to thicken this sauce increases the insoluble fiber content in this dish. The sauce has a bit more texture.*
• *Low-fat cottage cheese has a tangy taste and similar texture to sour cream. Combining the two ingredients makes this sauce lighter.*
• *Decreasing the oil lowers the overall fat content in this recipe.*

VARIATION 3

1 tbsp	oil	15 ml
2	medium onions, sliced	2
1	clove garlic, minced	1
1-1/2 lb	beef tenderloin or rib eye steak	750 g
1/4 tsp	pepper	1 ml
10 oz	can "Healthy Request"	284 ml
	beef broth, or 1 low-salt bouillon cube	
	in 1-1/4 cup (300 ml) hot water	
	omit water	
1 cup	1% or skim milk	250 ml
1 tsp	Worcestershire sauce	5 ml
1 tbsp	tomato paste	15 ml
	omit salt	
1 cup	fresh mushrooms, chopped	250 ml
1/4 cup	whole wheat flour	50 ml
1 cup	**1% cottage cheese**	**250 ml**
1 tbsp	**1% or skim milk**	**15 ml**

1. Prepare as per Variation 2 with the following exception: mix cottage cheese, flour, and 1 tbsp (15 ml) milk, then puree until smooth.

—NOTES—

• *Because we are using a tender cut of meat, browning the meat quickly seals in moisture and keeps the meat tender.*
• *This variation is lower in fat because of the move to 1% or skim milk and using cottage cheese to replace the sour cream. The flavor is zesty and delicious because of the added cottage cheese. The decrease in fat content makes the sauce thinner.*

This aromatic dish is as tasty as it is attractive. It is well complemented by cooked white or brown basmati rice, steamed beans or broccoli, and a side salad of fresh vegetables.

Peach Spice Chicken

Yields 4 pieces of chicken

Original Recipe

1/2 cup	fine dry bread crumbs	125 ml
1 tbsp	grated orange rind	15 ml
4	medium chicken breasts	4
1/4 cup	milk	50 ml
1	chicken bouillon cube or packet	1
3/4 cup	water	175 ml
1 tsp	mace	5 ml
1 tsp	coriander	5 ml
1/2 tsp	cinnamon	2 ml
1/4 tsp	ginger	1 ml
1 tbsp	soya sauce	15 ml
1/4 cup	butter or margarine, melted	50 ml
1/2 cup	peach or apricot jam	125 ml
1	large onion, sliced	1
1	large peach, sliced, or	1
	8 canned peach slices, or 2 halves	
1	green pepper, sliced	1

1. Combine bread crumbs and orange rind in a shallow bowl. Dip chicken pieces in milk, then in the bread crumb mixture.
2. Place pieces in a medium-sized casserole dish, cover, and bake at 350°F (180°C) for 30 minutes.
3. Mix bouillon in 3/4 cup (175 ml) boiling water. Stir until dissolved. Add spices, soya sauce, jam, and melted butter.
4. Place onion slices on top of the chicken. Pour bouillon mixture over the hot chicken and onions.
5. Cover and bake another 35 minutes, basting frequently.
6. Put green pepper and peach slices on top of chicken pieces and baste again.
7. Bake uncovered for another 10 minutes or until chicken is tender, basting twice in this time.
8. Serve immediately with cooked rice or linguini. Pour extra sauce over rice or linguini.

VARIATION 1

1/2 cup	fine dry bread crumbs	125 ml
1 tbsp	grated orange rind	15 ml
4	medium chicken breasts	4
1/4 cup	**skim milk**	**50 ml**
1	chicken bouillon cube or packet	1
3/4 cup	water	175 ml
1 tsp	mace	5 ml
1 tsp	coriander	5 ml
1/2 tsp	cinnamon	2 ml
1/4 tsp	ginger	1 ml
1 tbsp	soya sauce	15 ml
2 tbsp	**butter or margarine, melted**	**30 ml**
1/2 cup	peach or apricot jam	125 ml
1	large onion, sliced	1
1	large peach, sliced, or	1
	8 canned peach slices, or 2 halves	
1	green pepper, sliced	1

1. Mix and bake as per the original recipe with the following exceptions: remove and discard the skin and fat under the skin of the chicken before dipping in milk and crumb mixture.

—NOTES—

• *Much of the fat in chicken is in or just under the skin. By removing it, you are left with a leaner piece of meat.*
• *Decreasing the butter in the sauce seems to make no difference to the flavor and texture of this dish, but lowers the fat content.*
• *Using skim milk to moisten the meat before rolling in crumbs works well and is lower in fat than any other milk.*

Guide to changes in salt, sugar, protein, fat, and fiber content using each variation.

VARIATION 1	VARIATION 2	VARIATION 3
Salt	Salt	Salt
Sugar	Sugar ▲	Sugar ▲▼
Protein	Protein	Protein
Fat ▼	Fat ▼▼	Fat ▼▼▼
Fiber	Fiber	Fiber ▲

111

VARIATION 2

1/2 cup	fine dry bread crumbs	125 ml
1 tbsp	grated orange rind	15 ml
4	medium chicken breasts	4
1/4 cup	**orange juice**	**50 ml**
1	chicken bouillon cube or packet	1
3/4 cup	water	175 ml
1 tsp	mace	5 ml
1 tsp	coriander	5 ml
1/2 tsp	cinnamon	2 ml
1/4 tsp	ginger	1 ml
1 tbsp	soya sauce	15 ml
1/2 cup	**peach or apricot spread,**	**125 ml**
	that contains more fruit and less sugar	
2 tbsp	**peach or apricot nectar**	**30 ml**
2 tsp	**butter or margarine, melted**	**10 ml**
1	large onion, sliced	1
1	large peach, sliced, or	1
	8 canned peach slices, or 2 halves	
1	green pepper, sliced	1

1. Mix and bake as per Variation 1 with the following exceptions: Use orange juice instead of milk to dip the chicken; add the nectar to the bouillon mixture.

—NOTES—

• *Moving from milk to orange juice adds a wonderful tangy orange flavor to the chicken and removes all milk fats but increases the sugar quantity slightly.*

• *Choose spreads that have more fruit and less sugar. These spreads have a more fruity flavor. Less added sugar in jams and spreads result in a delicious product because fruit has enough natural sweetness.*

• *Using nectar in the sauce decreases the need for added butter and lowers the overall fat content.*

VARIATION 3

1/2 cup	fine dry whole wheat	125 ml
	bread crumbs	
1 tbsp	grated orange rind	15 ml
4	medium chicken breasts	4
1/4 cup	orange juice	50 ml
14 oz	**can peaches in pear juice**	**398 ml**
	(reserve 2 peach halves for garnish)	
2 tbsp	**peach juice from can**	**30 ml**
1 tbsp	**cornstarch**	**15 ml**
1	chicken bouillon cube or packet	1
3/4 cup	water	175 ml
1 tsp	mace	5 ml
1 tsp	coriander	5 ml
1/2 tsp	cinnamon	2 ml
1/4 tsp	ginger	1 ml
1 tbsp	soya sauce	15 ml
	omit peach or apricot spread and nectar	
	omit butter or margarine	
1/4 cup	**juice from can of peaches**	**50 ml**
2	**large onions, sliced**	**2**
1	large peach, sliced, or	1
	8 canned peach slices	
1	green pepper, sliced	1

1. Mix and bake as outlined in Variation 1 with the following exceptions: use a blender to mash the peaches with 2 tbsp (30 ml) juice and the cornstarch. Add to bouillon mixture and whisk until smooth.

—NOTES—

• *Using whole wheat bread crumbs increases the fiber content and is still a tasty coating.*

• *Crushed peaches increases the fiber content.*

• *Replacing butter with peach juice lowers the overall fat content in the recipe.*

• *Extra onion adds more flavor and more fiber.*

There are many sweet and sour recipes with varying flavors, colors, and tastes. We love the pineapple and vegetable combination in this one. If you like, you can use these ideas in your own favorite recipe.

Sweet & Sour Pork

Yields 5 to 6 cups (1.25 to 1.5 L)

Original Recipe

1 lb	boneless tenderloin pork	500 g
1 tsp	salt	5 ml
1/4 tsp	pepper	1 ml
2 tbsp	oil	30 ml
1/4 cup	onions, diced	50 ml
1	large clove garlic, minced	1
14 oz	can chunk pineapple in light syrup	398 ml
1/4 cup	vinegar	50 ml
1/2 cup	brown sugar	125 ml
2 tbsp	soya sauce	30 ml
1/2 cup	catsup	125 ml
1 tbsp	cornstarch	15 ml
1/4 cup	green pepper, diced	50 ml

1. Cut pork meat into 1-inch (2.5-cm) cubes and season with salt and pepper.
2. Heat oil in a heavy skillet and saute meat, onions, and garlic until browned. Remove meat chunks and place them in a casserole dish.
3. Drain the pineapple, saving the juice.
4. Add vinegar, brown sugar, soya sauce, catsup, and half the pineapple juice to the onions in the skillet and heat over medium heat stirring frequently until just boiling.
5. In a separate bowl whisk the cornstarch and remaining pineapple juice together until smooth. Add this to the skillet and cook for a few minutes stirring constantly until the mixture starts to thicken.
6. Pour over pork pieces, cover, and bake at 350°F (180°C) for about 1 hour or until meat is tender. (If meat needs to be cooked longer, add about 1/2 cup (125 ml) water to the sauce to keep it from drying out.
7. Add the green pepper and pineapple chunks, cover, and bake another 10 minutes. Serve over rice.

VARIATION 1

1 lb	boneless tenderloin pork, all fat trimmed off	500 g
1 tsp	salt	5 ml
1/4 tsp	pepper	1 ml
1 tbsp	oil	15 ml
1/4 cup	onions, diced	50 ml
1	large clove garlic, minced	1
14 oz	can chunk pineapple, in its own juice	398 ml
1/4 cup	vinegar	50 ml
1/2 cup	brown sugar	125 ml
2 tbsp	soya sauce	30 ml
1/2 cup	catsup	125 ml
1 tbsp	cornstarch	15 ml
1/2 cup	carrots, sliced thin	125 ml
1/4 cup	green pepper, diced	50 ml

1. Use a nonstick pan to saute meat, garlic, and onions. Add carrots when adding cornstarch and pineapple juice. Prepare and cook as per original recipe.

—NOTES—

• *Whenever using any meat or poultry be sure to trim off any excess fat before cooking. This gives you a leaner protein choice.*
• *Carrots add color, flavor, fiber, and vitamin A to this recipe. They enhance the overall appearance of this dish.*
• *Using pineapple canned in its own juice decreases the amount of added sugar. Pineapple has enough natural sweetness for this recipe.*

Guide to changes in salt, sugar, protein, fat, and fiber content using each variation.

	VARIATION 1	VARIATION 2	VARIATION 3
Salt		▼	▼▼
Sugar	▼	▼▼	▼▼
Protein			▲
Fat	▼	▼▼	▼▼▼
Fiber	▲	▲▲	▲▲▲

VARIATION 2

1 lb	boneless tenderloin pork, all fat trimmed off	500 g
1/2 tsp	**salt**	**2 ml**
1/4 tsp	pepper	1 ml
2 tsp	**oil**	**10 ml**
1/4 cup	onions, diced	50 ml
1	large clove garlic, minced	1
14 oz	can chunk pineapple, in its own juice	398 ml
1/4 cup	vinegar	50 ml
1/2 cup	brown sugar	125 ml
2 tbsp	soya sauce	30 ml
1/4 cup	**catsup**	**50 ml**
3 tbsp	**tomato paste**	**45 ml**
2 tbsp	**water**	**30 ml**
1 tbsp	cornstarch	15 ml
1/2 cup	carrots, sliced thin	125 ml
1/2 cup	**green pepper, diced**	**125 ml**

1. Brown the meat, garlic, and onions over medium heat, stirring constantly to prevent burning.
2. Add tomato paste and water when adding catsup. Cook and prepare as outlined in Variation 1.

—NOTES—

• *The amounts of fat used to cook the meat and onions is slowly decreasing. There is enough moisture in the meat and onions to brown them without extra oil which lowers the overall fat content in the recipe.*
• *Moving from catsup to tomato paste decreases the sugar, salt, and preservatives in this dish.*
• *Increasing the vegetable content gives this dish added texture, flavor, and fiber. Increased soluble fiber slows the digestion process and keeps you full longer.*

VARIATION 3

1 lb	boneless tenderloin pork, all fat trimmed off	500 g
	a pinch of salt	
1/4 tsp	pepper	1 ml
1 cup	**garbonzo beans, drained, rinsed**	**250 ml**
omit oil		
1/2 cup	**onions, diced**	**125 ml**
1	large clove garlic, minced	1
14 oz	can chunk pineapple, in its own juice	398 ml
1/4 cup	vinegar	50 ml
1/3 cup	**honey**	**75 ml**
2 tbsp	soya sauce	30 ml
	omit catsup	
5 tbsp	**tomato paste**	**75 ml**
1/2 cup	**water**	**125 ml**
1 tbsp	cornstarch	15 ml
1/2 cup	carrots, sliced thin	125 ml
1/2 cup	green pepper, diced	125 ml

1. Boil pork chunks in water for 50 minutes. Drain well and rinse with hot water. Then salt and pepper meat.
2. In a nonstick pan sprayed with nonstick spray, saute onions and garlic until starting to brown. Add pork chunks and brown quickly.
3. Prepare as per Variation 2, adding honey, tomato paste, and water when adding soya sauce and vinegar.
4. Place pork, garbonzo beans in casserole dish and continue as per the original recipe, steps 3–7.

—NOTES—

• *Boiling the pork removes some fat during the cooking process that can be drained off in the water. The pork is more tender, color is lighter, but there is no flavor change from previous versions.*

Tips

The following information for the recipes given in this section
will help you make choices and add variety to your meals.

Cabbage Rolls p96

• Choose a cabbage head whose leaves feel loose and thin. To remove cabbage leaves easily place head in a plastic bag and freeze overnight. Thaw the next day; leaves will be pliable and pull off without breaking. If you are still having difficulty, soak head in boiling water and leaves will come off easier.

• Adding vegetables to main dishes as fillers or toppings can make a dull dish exciting and colorful. Health benefits include more vitamins, minerals, and fiber.

• Including brassica vegetables (cabbage, broccoli, turnip, cauliflower, and brussels sprouts) in your meals may help to reduce the incidence of some cancers.[10]

• People with diabetes will find that their blood sugars will remain more consistent if they include food choices that are higher in different forms of fiber-rich carbohydrates. Eating meals and snacks that include fiber-rich carbohydrate foods along with foods that contain protein and fat can help slow the rise in blood glucose levels that occurs naturally after food is eaten because a) fiber-rich carbohydrate foods are digested more slowly than carbohydrate foods that have little or no fiber, and b) food that contain protein or fat are digested more slowly than foods that are mostly carbohydrate. Combining some protein or fat with carbohydrate food sources helps to slow the rise in blood glucose levels after meals.[6,12,14,15,20]

• Converted rice has a reduced gelatinization of starch and seems to be slower in breakdown during digestion. This results in a slower release of sugar into the bloodstream.

• Many vegetables are an excellent source of soluble fiber. Foods containing soluble fiber form a gel-like substance during digestion and seem to flatten the glucose response following digestion.[14,15]

Tasty Pot Roast p98

• This recipe provides a natural gravy. Adjust recipe by adding water or instant thickener during the last 15 minutes of cooking if you prefer a different consistency.

• Once cooked, cut meat against the grain for more tender results.

• Some supermarkets sell brisket in pieces, and these become even more tender when cooked. Cut off fat and place in medium-sized roaster and pour sauce over. Because pieces are smaller they may cook faster.

• Use lower temperatures to cook roasts. For a tender cut cook at 325°F (160°C) and 275°F (130°C) for medium tender cuts. Roasts today are leaner and have less marbling and fat covering them. Cooking them covered at a lower temperature for longer periods of time keeps the roast moister and decreases the shrinkage of the meat.

• Less tender cuts of beef (stewing beef or brisket) are best cooked in liquids to create a tender flavorful dish.

• When cooking any kind of tougher cut of meat, whether it is beef, pork, or chicken, try using wines and juices along with or instead of tinned soups. Also have fun with herbs and spices. Here are some suggestions:
—Over a stewing chicken try 1 can mushroom soup combined with 1/2 cup (125 ml) fresh orange juice, 1/2 cup (125 ml) chopped onion, 1 tbsp (15 ml) onion soup mix, 1 tsp (5 ml) ginger, and 1/2 tsp (2 ml) mace.
—Over tougher cuts of pork try: 1 can tomato soup combined with 1/2 cup (125 ml) apple juice

or red wine, 1 clove garlic crushed, 1/2 cup (125 ml) chopped onion, 1 tbsp (15 ml) soya sauce, 1 tbsp (15 ml) rosemary, 1 tsp (5 ml) basil.

These techniques allow you to enjoy meat dishes while decreasing overall salt and fat contents.

Tomato Sauce Lentils p100

• You may need to add extra water to some of these variations to prevent sticking.
• Read the labels on yogurt and other dairy products. The percentage butter fat (% B.F.) or milk fat (% M.F.) may vary considerably from one brand to another. Plain yogurt usually has about 1.5% M.F., fruit flavored has about 1.4% M.F., and low-fat yogurt has about .9% M.F. or less.
• When you use bouillon or tinned soups or sauces high in salt, you can omit any additional salt in the recipe.
• Lentils and other vegetable protein foods may fill you up quicker because they are high in fiber. You may also find that you get hungry quicker because they are low in fat. This is normal. Plan for a snack if this occurs.
• Lentils, a form of soluble fiber, slow down the digestive process and therefore the release of glucose to the bloodstream. This means that you will have a more controlled release of glucose into the bloodstream and a decrease in the swings of blood sugar.[7,12,14]
• If you use mainly legumes as the source of protein in your meals you may not be getting enough iron. To compensate for this, increase the amount of foods you eat that are high in vitamin C with that meal. This helps to get the maximum amount of iron from the plant source.
• You can use a cheaper white wine found at your liquor store. Remember the alcohol content is removed during the cooking process.
• You can store extra tomatoes in the refrigerator for a week or in the freezer for several months.

• Mixing plain yogurt with sour cream gives any garnish or dip a wonderful texture, flavor, and color with less fat.

Spaghetti Meat Sauce Pie p102

• You can replace fennel seed and hot peppers with any herbs or spices that you would normally add to lasagna.
• In Variation 3 you may have more sauce than can fit in a 10-inch (25-cm) pie plate. Use left over sauce on toast or over pasta along with a salad for a tasty lunch.
• Part-skim mozzarella cheese has a lovely stringy texture that melts beautifully on top of this pie. The stickier texture helps to keep the ingredients together. You don't notice the change in flavor even though the overall fat and salt content are decreased.
• When you gradually begin to add lentils to a meat dish you learn to enjoy their texture and flavor. Lentils tend to take on the flavor of the dish you are making.
• As you learn to cook with lower fat ingredients you may find that covered dishes retain more moisture. If you want to brown a dish, uncover for the last 10 minutes of cooking.
• Use the same technique to add lentils or other legumes to other sauces. This is a tasty high fiber option. In some recipes you may choose to replace some of the meat protein with legumes (vegetable proteins).
• Try this recipe with tomato or spinach noodles. They add interesting colors and flavors.
• You have slowly been increasing the total fiber content of this recipe by adding vegetables and whole wheat noodles. Anytime you increase the fiber in your diet it is important to do it slowly.
• Remember, vegetable proteins fill you up sooner due to their high fiber content. Their low fat content may make you hungry sooner. That is okay.

• People with diabetes will find that their blood sugars will remain more consistent if they include food choices that are higher in different forms of fiber-rich carbohydrates. Eating meals and snacks that include fiber-rich carbohydrate foods along with foods that contain protein and fat can help slow the rise in blood glucose levels that occurs naturally after food is eaten because a) fiber-rich carbohydrate foods are digested more slowly than carbohydrate foods that have little or no fiber, and b) food that contain protein or fat are digested more slowly than foods that are mostly carbohydrate. Combining some protein with carbohydrate food sources helps to slow the rise in blood glucose levels after meals.[6,12,14,15,20]

Crab-filled Crepes p104

• Variation 3 has extra cumin which seems to enhance the flavor of these crepes even with the decreased fat content. Normally decreasing the fat in a recipe will enhance the flavors. However, increasing the spice slightly does not overpower the flavors in this dish.
• You can use 1 tbsp (15 ml) dried parsley.
• Warming cream cheese in the microwave for a few seconds will soften it nicely.
• Cumin adds a unique delicious flavor to fish dishes. You can alter the flavor by replacing the cumin with basil, dill weed, or dill seed, or marjoram. These herbs all enhance crab flavor.
• You can toast almonds by quickly frying them in a pan on medium-high heat stirring constantly until browned, or in a medium oven (about 250°F or 180°C) on a cookie sheet. Stir frequently.
• Cauliflower or celery can replace the carrots or broccoli.
• Quark cheese has a similar flavor and texture to cream cheese yet is lower in fat and a better source of protein.
• As your taste buds appreciate lower fat foods, you may choose to use skim milk quark cheese

(or pureed 1% cottage cheese, *see* p23 for more information) if this recipe becomes too rich for you. 1% cottage cheese is an equivalent replacement in fat content for skim milk quark cheese.
• Many kinds of fish are an excellent lower-fat source of protein. Fats found in fish are high in omega-3 fatty acids. Including foods with this form of fat is thought to decrease cardiac and cancer risks.[10] For this reason it is a good idea to include a variety of protein foods in your weekly meals including fish.
• Carrots, broccoli, and cauliflower are all high in soluble fiber.
• Soluble fiber breaks down into a gel-like substance during digestion. This substance slows down the digestion of sugars in your system helping you to stay full longer, have a more constant supply of energy, and avoid big jumps in blood sugar levels. This seems to have a direct effect on keeping cholesterol and blood sugar levels in line.[1,12,14,15]

Vegetable Alfredo Sauce p106

• In many cases you can substitute yogurt for pureed cottage cheese, but in this recipe use cottage cheese for successful results and excellent flavor. *See* p23 for more information about cottage cheese.
• Evaporated milk in place of cream gives sauces the creamy texture with less fat content. If the brand of tinned evaporated milk you are using now is unsatisfactory, try another brand. Different brands differ in taste.
• This recipe has exciting colors and textures because of the variety of vegetables. You can alter these to include any vegetables that you enjoy. Just steam the vegetables until tender and add them as per the original recipe.
• This sauce in its final variation is an excellent combination of a variety of carbohydrates and proteins. It makes a delicious meatless meal.

Beef Stroganoff p108

• Even though the tomato paste is a small amount, do not omit. It gives this dish tangy flavor. *See p20 for tips on storing extra tomato paste.*

• Any beef that indicates that it is suitable for stir fry is a more tender cut, such as tenderloin or rib eye steak, loin tenderloin, inside round, and sirloin tip.

• If the sauce is not the desired consistency, add extra milk or water to thin it, or use an instant flour/thickener to thicken it.

• There is no legislation on the use of the word "light" on food product packaging. It could mean a lighter color or lighter overall weight of the package. When buying "light" products, read the label carefully to discover if the product actually has less fat content.

• Healthy Request soups are lower in salt, fat, and sometimes sugar contents. If they are not available at your grocery store, ask your grocer to order them.

• This dish is fairly saucy and is meant to be served over pasta or rice. You may choose to experiment with adding 1/2 to 1 cup (125 to 250 ml) cooked lentils or other legumes to add extra fiber and protein.

• You can use a slow cooker or crock pot in this recipe. Put all ingredients except the flour and sour cream (or pureed cottage cheese) into the slow cooker and cover. Cook this all day (8 hours or so) on a low setting in your slow cooker, or for 4 to 5 hours on a higher setting. About 15 minutes before serving mix sour cream (or equivalent) and flour and then whisk into crock pot or slow cooker. Turn the heat up to the highest setting and allow the mixture to thicken. Add additional water or use an instant thickener to create the desired consistency.

• You may choose to cook onions and garlic with no oil in a nonstick pan. This works if you stir frequently over medium heat.

• If you enjoy a peppery flavor, you can add 2 splashes of tabasco sauce and increase the pepper to 1/2 tsp (2 ml) in the sauce.

• Try different kinds of noodles under this sauce. Spinach, whole wheat, sweet red pepper, or tomato noodles create a nice flavor change.

• Red meats have been given a bad rap in the past. People who are choosing to eat healthier were once told to eat more fish and chicken and avoid beef because of the high fat content in the red meat. Good news! Beef and pork are leaner today than they were twenty years ago.

Peach Spice Chicken p110

• Using whole or fresh fruit to create your own spread rather than a commercial spread decreases the amount of sugar and preservatives added to this recipe. This spread has a wonderful flavor and is great on toast with peanut butter for breakfast. It is also a tasty topping over plain cheesecake, vanilla pudding, or ice cream.
—Use 4 peaches, peeled, pitted, and chopped. Place the fresh peaches in a bowl and sprinkle with 1/2 tsp (2 ml) ascorbic acid. Boil the peel and pits in 1 cup (250 ml) water with 1 whole clove, 1/4 tsp (1 ml) cinnamon, and 3 whole allspice. Boil until mixture is about 1/2 cup (125 ml) fluid. Remove allspice, peel, and pits. Add chopped peaches and cook for another 10 to 15 minutes on low heat, stirring frequently. The spread is now ready to use. Refrigerate any leftovers.

• In Variation 3 adding cornstarch helps to thicken the peach mixture when it is cooked.

• People with diabetes who want to make dishes that call for honey or brown sugar can use unsweetened fruit juices as substitutes. Fruit juices have more nutritional value than other sweetening agents and often improve the flavor of foods. It is important that when eating foods that are made of simple sugars (like fructose) that they are eaten after or with protein and complex carbohydrates to slow the release of sugar into the bloodstream.

Sweet & Sour Pork p112

• If you are using a tougher cut of pork you may find that you need to add 1 cup (250 ml) water to sauce and cook the dish covered for at least 1-1/2 hours. Another option is to cook the meat and sauce for 4 to 5 hours in a slow cooker also adding the extra water.

• Extra tomato paste can be stored in your refrigerator in a sealed container for about 2 weeks or in your freezer for several months. You can then easily access the tomato paste for other recipes and decrease waste. For more information, *see* p20.

• In Variation 3, adding honey to this recipe gives a mellow, sweet flavor, and adding garbanzo beans (a vegetable protein) adds extra texture, fiber, protein, and flavor.

• Garbanzo beans are also known as chick peas. If you use unprocessed ones, you will need to prepare them ahead of time, *see* p29 and information at the right. Try navy bean, lentils, white beans, kidney beans, or lima beans. Find the legumes your family enjoys the most.

• You may replace more and more of the pork meat with vegetable protein sources. This will gradually change this dish into a tasty alternative that is higher in fiber and lower in fat.

• Balancing animal sources of protein with vegetable proteins throughout your meal planning provides the nutrients you need to feel healthy and energized.

HOW TO PREPARE LEGUMES OR BEANS (except for lentils and split peas)—
1. Rinse legumes.
2. Soak overnight in 3 to 4 times as much water as the legumes.
3. Drain water.
4. Cover with same amount of water and bring to a boil.
5. Reduce the heat and let simmer until they are tender (about 20 to 30 minutes). Time varies for different beans.
6. Drain water and put into your favorite dish.

Quick method—
1. Rinse legumes.
2. Cover with cold water.
3. Bring to a boil and simmer for 2 minutes.
4. Cover tightly. Turn heat off and let sit for 1 hour.
5. Drain and use in your favorite recipe.

The repeated water change decreases the chance of abdominal discomfort and bloating often associated with eating dried beans and legumes.

WRITE DOWN THE TIPS THAT WORK FOR YOU—

—USE THESE TIPS IN YOUR FAMILY FAVORITES!

Why fluids important

Liquids or fluids are meant to quench the thirst and replenish the water stores in our bodies. These fluids come in many varieties, tastes, and textures. Some of the options we choose do a wonderful job of satisfying our thirst while others leave us with a greater thirst than before drinking. In this section some of the common beverages we enjoy are reviewed according to their ability to quench thirst, replenish the body's water stores, and satisfy taste. Variation changes will reflect the increase in water content as the goal for improving health in this section.

Facts about fluids

• We need fluids for a healthy body. Rehydration is the process of returning water to a system after it is lost. Dehydration refers to an inadequate amount of water in the body which can lead to an unhealthy body. Our body needs water because

1) Blood is mainly made up of water. Blood carries oxygen and nutrients to the brain. Too little water reduces the ability of blood to carry oxygen and nutrients to your brain. As a result you could get a headache, have decreased ability to concentrate, and feel dizzy.

2) Water helps to remove wastes from the body. Urine is mostly made up of water. Urine carries much of the waste from our body. Water is also important in keeping food moving through the intestinal tract. It helps to prevent constipation and aids in regular normal bowel movement.

3) Water, as a main component of blood, is necessary to maintain normal blood volume, Inadequate hydration may cause your heart to beat faster, flutter, or race in order to pump the lower amount of blood to muscles and extremities.

• The body requires 6 to 8 glasses of liquid a day to maintain normal body function.

• Once you are thirsty, your body is already partially dehydrated.

• Water is the best source of fluid to replenish the body's water stores. Some of the fluids we drink such as coffee, tea, cola drinks, and alcoholic beverages, actually dehydrate us.

• When your body is dehydrated it may send out hunger signals because there is water in food. Food will give us some extra fluid but it isn't the most efficient way to give the body fluids. If you are thirsty, drink first then decide if you are still hungry.

• Some people use fluids to quench hunger pangs. Fluids lead to temporary relief of hunger and a bloated full feeling but often results in uncontrollable hunger at a later time. Using fluid to mask hunger is a temporary solution that hides the fact that your body actually needs food to give it energy and sustenance.

What if you don't like water

Water is the best rehydrator available to us.[14] A rehydrator is a fluid that replaces the water that has been used up or lost from the body. However many of us do not naturally enjoy the flavor or color of water. We find it unappealing.

In order to start liking water you will need to make slow and gradual changes to add it to your fluid intake. The key is to make the switch gradually. If you make gradual shifts that incorporate more water

in your drinking patterns you will begin to enjoy the flavor and thirst quenching properties of water. When you enjoy something, you will want more of it.
Some suggestions on how to make more water part of your life
If you don't enjoy the flavor, taste, or color of water you may find these tips refreshing.

• Put about 3 or 4 thin slices of lemon or orange in your water and let it sit for about 1/2 to 1 hour in the refrigerator or on your counter before drinking. Serve over ice cubes for a refreshing thirst quencher with a fruity twist. For a quicker version, squeeze some lemon or orange juice on ice water and garnish with a fruit wedge.

• The temperature of water may affect the enjoyment level. If you don't enjoy cold water, try leaving some out on your counter for about one hour before drinking. If you prefer cold drinks, try refrigerating water in a sealed container to have it easily accessible.

• Try putting 1 to 2 cups (250 to 500 ml) of your favorite fruit juice in 6 to 8 cups (1.5 to 2 L) of water and refrigerate until cold. Serve over ice cubes with a slice of lemon or orange as a garnish.

• Add three times or more the amount of water suggested to your favorite fruit crystal drink. This option will quench your thirst more effectively than the regular concentration of drink crystal mixture.

• Invent your own drinks by adding a few drops of grenadine, black currant, or raspberry syrup in a glass of water and garnishing it with fruit and ice.

• Add a celery stick to your water. Let the

Fluids

flavor soak in for at least an hour and enjoy water with a different taste.

You are limited only by your imagination! Have fun with your drink choices. Try using favorite spices and extract flavorings for interest to your drinks. When using juices in drinks you may find that you need less sugar because of the natural sugar content found in fruit juices. Remember you are learning to enjoy drinks lower in sugar content by increasing the water content of the beverage. Enjoy the process. Make changes slowly. The bonus is that your newly acquired tastes can transfer to enjoying foods lower in sugar.

FOR BEST RESULTS—read through the entire recipe, each variation, and the TIPS on page 134 before preparing this drink.

Fruit spritzers, seltzers, or refreshers are appealing to the eye and the taste buds and are excellent thirst quencher options.

Favorite Fruit Drinks

Yields 4 cups (1 L)

Original Recipe

4 cups	favorite fruit juice, chilled	1 L
12	ice cubes	12
	several sections or small pieces of fruit for garnish	

1. Pour juice in a cooled pitcher. Pitcher and glasses can be cooled prior to adding the fruit juice by placing in the freezer for about 1 hour.
2. Place 3 ice cubes in each of 4 chilled glasses. Pour juice over ice cubes and garnish with fruit sections. Serve immediately.

VARIATION 1

3 cups	favorite fruit juice, chilled	750 ml
1 cup	water or	250 ml
	salt-free sparkling water, chilled	
12	ice cubes	12
	several sections or small pieces of fruit for garnish	

1. Add water to juice and prepare and serve as per the original recipe.

—NOTES—

• *If you use water or a salt-free sparkling water, the salt content will not increase in this drink. However, sparkling water contains sodium and will increase the salt content slightly.*

FOR BEST RESULTS—read through the entire recipe, each variation, and the TIPS on page 134 before preparing this drink.

This is a pretty drink served in a punch bowl with floating lemon slices on top.

Lemon, Lime, or Orange Ade

Yields 6 cups (1.5 L)

Original Recipe

6 cups	lemon, lime, or orange ade	1.5 L
4 to 6	orange, lemon, or lime slices for garnish	4 to 6

1. Pour lemon, lime, or orange ade over ice in tall cool glasses.
2. Garnish with fruit slices and serve immediately.

VARIATION 1

4 cups	lemon, lime, or orange ade	1 L
2 cups	salt-free sparkling water or mineral water	500 ml
4 to 6	orange, lemon, or lime slices for garnish	4 to 6

1. Mix water and juice in a large pitcher and prepare and serve as per the original recipe.

—NOTES—

• *This variation has less concentrated fruit flavor. The sharp flavors mellow a little. Add mint sprigs for a pretty and refreshing garnish.*

Guide to changes in salt, sugar, and water content using each variation.

	VARIATION 1	VARIATION 2	VARIATION 3
Salt			
Sugar	▼	▼▼	▼▼▼
Water	▲	▲▲	▲▲▲

123

VARIATION 2

2 cups	favorite fruit juice, chilled	500 ml
2 cups	water or	500 ml
	salt-free sparkling water, chilled	
12	ice cubes	12
	several sections or small pieces of fruit	
	for garnish	

1. Add water to juice and prepare and serve as per Variation 1.

—NOTES—

• *This variation has a lighter and more refreshing flavor. My family has found it much more thirst quenching than the previous variation.*

VARIATION 3

1 cup	favorite fruit juice, chilled	250 ml
3 cups	water or	750 ml
	salt-free sparkling water, chilled	
12	ice cubes	12
	several sections or small pieces of fruit	
	for garnish	

1. Add water to juice and prepare and serve as per Variation 1.

—NOTES—

• *This variation is delightfully refreshing and thirst quenching. If you choose, you can move farther to about 1/2 cup (125 ml) juice to 3-1/2 cups (875 ml) water.*

Guide to changes in salt, sugar, and water content using each variation.

	VARIATION 1	VARIATION 2	VARIATION 3
Salt			
Sugar	▼	▼▼	▼▼▼
Water	▲	▲▲	▲▲▲

VARIATION 2

3 cups	lemon, lime, or orange ade	750 ml
2 cups	salt-free sparkling water or	500 ml
	mineral water	
1 cup	water	250 ml
4 to 6	orange, lemon, or lime slices	4 to 6
	for garnish	

1. Mix both waters and juice in a large pitcher and prepare and serve as per Variation 1.

—NOTES—

• *Enjoy the refreshing quality of this drink. By adding more water and less juice, the drink is less sweet and more refreshing.*

VARIATION 3

2 cups	lemon, lime, or orange ade	500 ml
2 cups	salt-free sparkling water or	500 ml
	mineral water	
2 cup	water	500 ml
4 to 6	orange, lemon, or lime slices	4 to 6
	for garnish	

1. Mix both waters and juice in a large pitcher and allow fruit wedges to sit in the drink for about 10 to 20 minutes to mingle flavors. Prepare and serve as per Variation 1.

—NOTES—

• *Your taste buds will slowly adjust to the new flavors and consistencies of these drinks.*

FOR BEST RESULTS—read through the entire recipe, each variation, and the TIPS on page 134 before preparing this drink.

Try this delightfully tasty, colorful punch. If you prefer, exchange the juices listed with your favorite fruit flavors.

Cranberry Punch

Yields 8 cups (2 L)

Original Recipe

4 cups	cranberry juice	1 L
	(cran-raspberry, cran-apple, or cran-grape)	
2 cups	orange juice	500 ml
2 cups	ginger ale or 7-Up	500 ml

1. Mix orange and cranberry juices in a large pitcher.
2. Add ginger ale or 7-Up just before serving, so that the maximum fizz will remain in the drink.
3. Serve over ice cubes and garnish with orange slices.

VARIATION 1

3 cups	**cranberry juice**	**750 ml**
(cran-raspberry, cran-apple, or cran-grape)		
2 cups	orange juice	500 ml
2 cups	ginger ale or 7-Up	500 ml
1 cup	**water**	**250 ml**

1. Prepare as per original recipe adding ginger ale or 7-Up and water just before serving.

—NOTES—

• *Decreasing the overall juice content in this punch by adding water gives a slightly lighter fruit flavor.*

FOR BEST RESULTS—read through the entire recipe, each variation, and the TIPS on page 134 before preparing this drink.

If you do not enjoy sparkling water or find it too costly, try using fresh water or bottled spring water instead. The flavor is still wonderful but there is less fizz.

Tropical Refresher

Yields 6 to 7 cups (1.5 to 1.75 L)

Original Recipe

4 cups	unsweetened orange juice	1 L
1 cup	unsweetened pineapple juice	250 ml
5–6 drops	coconut extract	5–6 drops
1 cup	sparkling water	250 ml
5–6 cups	crushed ice	1.25–1.5 L
	pineapple spears and/or orange segments	
1 tbsp	coconut	15 ml

1. Mix orange and pineapple juice together with coconut extract.
2. Add sparkling water just before serving.
3. Pour over crushed ice, serve immediately.
4. Garnish with fruit and coconut.

VARIATION 1

3 cups	**unsweetened orange juice**	**750 ml**
1 cup	unsweetened pineapple juice	250 ml
5–6 drops	coconut extract	5–6 drops
1 cup	sparkling water	250 ml
1 cup	**water**	**250 ml**
5–6 cups	crushed ice	1.25–1.5 L
	pineapple spears and/or orange segments	
1 tbsp	coconut	15 ml

1. Prepare and serve as per original recipe. Add water when adding sparkling water.

—NOTES—

• *This variation has slightly less fruit flavor because of the added water.*

Guide to changes in salt, sugar, and water content using each variation.

	VARIATION 1	VARIATION 2	VARIATION 3
Salt	▼	▼▼	▼▼▼
Sugar	▼	▼▼	▼▼▼
Water	▲	▲▲	▲▲▲

VARIATION 2

2-1/2 cups	cranberry juice	625 ml
	(cran-raspberry, cran-apple, or cran-grape)	
1 cup	orange juice	250 ml
2 cups	ginger ale or 7-Up	500 ml
2-1/2 cups	water	625 ml

1. Prepare and serve as per Variation 1.

—NOTES—

• *This variation has less fruit juice and more water. The result is a less sweet, refreshing drink with the fruity flavor still very prominent.*

VARIATION 3

1-1/2 cups	cranberry juice	375 ml
	(cran-raspberry, cran-apple, or cran-grape)	
1 cup	orange juice	250 ml
2 cups	ginger ale or 7-Up	500 ml
3-1/2 cups	water	875 ml

1. Prepare and serve as per Variation 1.

—NOTES—

• *A very thirst quenching drink because of added water.*

• *Carbonated salt-free sparkling spring water with natural lemon-lime flavor can replace some or all of the water in drink recipes if you desire more "fizz." It will also heighten the flavor.*

Guide to changes in salt, sugar, and water content using each variation.

	VARIATION 1	VARIATION 2	VARIATION 3
Salt	▼	▼▼	▼▼▼
Sugar		▼	▼▼
Water	▲	▲▲	▲▲▲

VARIATION 2

2-1/4 cups	unsweetened orange juice	550 ml
3/4 cup	unsweetened pineapple juice	175 ml
3–4 drops	coconut extract	3–4 drops
1 cup	sparkling water	250 ml
2 cups	water	500 ml
5–6 cups	crushed ice	1.25–1.5 L
	pineapple spears and/or orange segments	
1 tbsp	coconut	15 ml

1. Prepare and serve as per Variation 1.

—NOTES—

• *As you decrease the fruit juice, decrease the coconut extract to keep it from overpowering the fruity flavors.*

VARIATION 3

1-1/2 cups	unsweetened orange juice	375 ml
1/2 cup	unsweetened pineapple juice	125 ml
3 drops	coconut extract	3 drops
1 cup	sparkling water	250 ml
3 cups	water	750 ml
5–6 cups	crushed ice	1.25–1.5 L
	pineapple spears and/or orange segments	
1 tbsp	coconut	15 ml

1. Prepare and serve as per Variation 1.

—NOTES—

• *Enjoy the fresher, lighter fruit flavor of this drink. Focus on how it feels in your mouth and how it quenches your thirst.*

Wine Sangria

Yields 7 to 8 cups (2 L) (more as ice melts)

Original Recipe

4–5 cups	ice cubes	1–1.25 L
1 cup	unsweetened white grape juice	250 ml
1/3 cup	lemonade frozen concentrate	75 ml
3–4 cups	white or red wine	.75–1 L
1 cup	mineral or sparkling water	250 ml
1 cup	fresh strawberries, sliced	250 ml
1	small orange, sliced	1
1	small lemon, sliced	1
1	small lime, sliced	1

1. Place ice in a large pitcher or punch bowl.
2. Mix grape juice with lemonade concentrate.
3. Pour wine, juice, and water over ice cubes.
4. Put fruit slices in the bowl or pitcher and stir in. Serve in tall glasses, including some fruit in each glass.

The Perfect Cup of Tea

Yields 2 cups (500 ml)

1. Warm the teapot by filling it with hot tap water. Let the water sit in the pot while you proceed.
2. Bring fresh cold water to a rolling boil.
3. Use 1 tea bag or 2 tsp (10 ml) of loose tea for every 2 cups (500 ml) of water.
4. Remove water from teapot. Put tea in warm teapot and pour boiling water over the tea.
5. Cover and brew for 3 to 5 minutes.
6. Remove tea bag or strain out tea leaves. Serve immediately.

Wine sangrias are a beautiful and delicious summer treat. The combined flavors of fruit and wine are a delightful drink.

VARIATION 1

4–5 cups	ice cubes	1–1.25 L
1 cup	unsweetened white grape juice	250 ml
1/3 cup	lemonade frozen concentrate	75 ml
3 cups	**white or red wine**	**750 ml**
2 cups	**mineral or sparkling water**	**500 ml**
1 cup	fresh strawberries, sliced	250 ml
1	small orange, sliced	1
1	small lemon, sliced	1
1	small lime, sliced	1

1. Prepare, mix, and serve as per the original recipe.

—NOTES—

• *This fruity drink is a favorite any time of year. By increasing the water content slightly and decreasing the wine content, you will enjoy a slightly fresher, less heavy flavor. This allows you to notice the fruity flavors more readily.*

• *Increasing the sparkling water, slightly increases the salt content of this drink. If you choose, you can keep the amount of sparkling water the same as the original recipe and add plain water. This will result in an overall decrease of salt content but the drink will have less "fizz."*

NOTES ON THE PERFECT CUP OF TEA—

• *For a warm and tasty option combine equal amounts of freshly brewed tea with warm apple or white grape juice. Add a bit of cinnamon and nutmeg (or cinnamon stick) to the tea while it is steeping for even more flavor.*

• *Try combining equal amounts of freshly brewed tea with warmed pineapple, grapefruit, or orange juice. Garnish with fresh lemon or orange slices.*

Guide to changes in salt, sugar, and water content using each variation.

	VARIATION 1	VARIATION 2	VARIATION 3
Salt	▲	▲▼	▲▼▼
Sugar		▼	▼▼
Water	▲	▲▲	▲▲▲

127

VARIATION 2

4–5 cups	ice cubes	1–1.25 L
3/4 cup	unsweetened white grape juice	175 ml
1/4 cup	lemonade frozen concentrate	50 ml
3 cups	white or red wine	750 ml
2 cups	mineral or sparkling water	500 ml
1 cup	water	250 ml
1 cup	fresh strawberries, sliced	250 ml
1	small orange, sliced	1
1	small lemon, sliced	1
1	small lime, sliced	1

1. Prepare, mix, and serve as per the original recipe.

—NOTES—

• *Decreasing the fruit juices and increasing the water content results in a drink that has less concentrated fruit flavors.*
• *This variation is less sweet and more refreshing than the previous variation. A delightful and satisfying flavor results.*

VARIATION 3

1/2 cup	unsweetened white grape juice	125 ml
2 tbsp	lemonade frozen concentrate	30 ml
2 cups	white or red wine	500 ml
2 cups	mineral or sparkling water	500 ml
2 cups	water	500 ml
1	small orange, sliced	1
1	small lemon, sliced	1
1	small lime, sliced	1
4–5 cups	ice cubes	1–1.25 L
1 cup	fresh strawberries, sliced	250 ml

1. Mix all of the ingredients except the ice and strawberries in a large pitcher.
2. Allow the fresh fruit to permeate the other fluids for about 1/2 hour.
3. Pour over ice, add strawberries, and serve as per the original recipe.

—NOTES—

• *Decreasing the fruit juices and wine content while increasing the water content makes this variation a lighter and more refreshing option.*
• *Allowing the fresh citrus fruits to sit in the fluids before serving allows their natural flavors to permeate the drink. You can use this technique for added flavor and color in any drink.*

• *Add cinnamon or other spice to your favorite fruit juice spritzer and microwave on high for about 1-1/2 minutes per glass. This will be more thirst quenching than a drink that includes tea, because tea is a dehydrator.*
• *Combine equal amounts of hot tea and warmed pineapple juice, along with a few crushed cardamom pods and a drop of coconut extract (optional). Very exotic.*

• *Combine 1/2 cup (125 ml) of freshly brewed tea with 1/2 cup (125 ml) vegetable cocktail juice and 1 tsp (5 ml) Worcestershire sauce.*
• *Try putting your favorite extracts into a cup of freshly brewed tea. Choose from 1/4 tsp (1 ml) vanilla, 1/4 tsp (1 ml) almond extract, 1/4 tsp (1 ml) butternut, 1 tsp (5 ml) grated orange or lemon peel.*

FOR BEST RESULTS—read through the entire recipe, each variation, and the TIPS on page 135 before preparing this drink.

Mixing tea with fruit drinks produces a lovely flavor and has less caffeine. You can enjoy this drink winter or summer. A great way to use leftover tea. Be sure tea bags are removed from the hot tea to prevent tannins from leaching and creating a bitter flavor.

Grape Soother

Yields 4 cups (1 L)

Original Recipe

1 cup	brewed tea, warm or cold	250 ml
3 cups	white or red grape juice	750 ml
2	sticks of cinnamon, **or**	2
2 tsp	cinnamon	10 ml

1. Combine tea, grape juice, and cinnamon in a microwave-safe bowl or pot. Warm until hot (4 to 6 minutes on high in the microwave).
2. Serve immediately in mugs. If desired you can place 1 cinnamon stick in each mug for garnish.

—NOTES—

• *If you use cinnamon powder it will sometimes form clumps which is not visually appealing.*

VARIATION 1

1 cup	brewed tea, warm or cold	250 ml
2-1/2 cups	**white or red grape juice**	**625 ml**
2	sticks of cinnamon, **or**	2
2 tsp	cinnamon	10 ml
1/2 cup	**water**	**125 ml**

1. Mix water with grape juice and tea before heating.
2. Prepare and serve as per original recipe.

—NOTES—

• *This variation has a lighter fruit flavor and isn't as sweet as the original recipe. The decrease in sweetness was not noticeable.*

FOR BEST RESULTS—read through the entire recipe, each variation, and the TIPS on page 135 before preparing this drink.

Nothing is quite as soothing as a warm cup of apple cider. Try serving cider with or instead of coffee or tea at your next winter party for a refreshing change.

Hot Apple Cider

Yields 4 cups (1 L)

Original Recipe

4 cups	unsweetened apple juice	1 L
2	cinnamon sticks, broken into pieces	2
3	whole allspice	3
2	whole cloves	2
1	crushed nutmeg	1
	whole cinnamon sticks for garnish	

1. Heat apple juice on stove top with spices until hot. You can put spices into a spice ball or cheese cloth bag for easy removal or strain loose spices.
2. Heat for 5 to 10 minutes without boiling to allow flavors to blend. Serve immediately in warm mugs garnished with a cinnamon stick.

VARIATION 1

3 cups	**unsweetened apple juice**	**750 ml**
1 cup	**water**	**250 ml**
2	cinnamon sticks, broken into pieces	2
3	whole allspice	3
2	whole cloves	2
1	crushed nutmeg	1
	whole cinnamon sticks for garnish	

1. Mix water with apple juice. Prepare and serve as per the original recipe.

—NOTES—

• *Decreasing the apple juice and adding water gives this drink a more "mellow" flavor.*

Guide to changes in salt, sugar, and water content using each variation.

	VARIATION 1	VARIATION 2	VARIATION 3
Salt	▼	▼▼	▼▼▼
Sugar	▼	▼▼	▼▼▼
Water	▲	▲▲	▲▲▲

VARIATION 2

1 cup	brewed tea, warm or cold	250 ml
2 cups	**white or red grape juice**	**500 ml**
2	sticks of cinnamon, **or**	2
2 tsp	cinnamon	10 ml
1 cup	**water**	**250 ml**

1. Prepare and serve as per Variation 1.

—NOTES—

• *There is still enough grape juice in this variation to give flavor and sweetness to make this a tasty drink. The warmth is soothing and the aroma and flavor are inviting.*

VARIATION 3

1 cup	brewed tea, warm or cold	250 ml
1 cup	**white or red grape juice**	**250 ml**
2	sticks of cinnamon, **or**	2
2 tsp	cinnamon	10 ml
2 cups	**water**	**500 ml**

1. Prepare and serve as per Variation 1.

—NOTES—

• *This variation has a much more subtle grape flavor but is still very tasty.*
• *We often prepare this delicious drink in one cup amounts without tea for a quick treat.* **See TIPS p135 for proportions.**

Guide to changes in salt, sugar, and water content using each variation.

	VARIATION 1	VARIATION 2	VARIATION 3
Salt	▼	▼▼	▼▼▼
Sugar	▼	▼▼	▼▼▼
Water	▲	▲▲	▲▲▲

VARIATION 2

2 cups	**unsweetened apple juice**	**500 ml**
2 cups	**water**	**500 ml**
2	cinnamon sticks, broken into pieces	2
3	whole allspice	3
2	whole cloves	2
1	crushed nutmeg	1
	whole cinnamon sticks for garnish	

1. Prepare and serve as per Variation 1.

—NOTES—

• *The increased water content makes this variation more thirst quenching and refreshing. The drink is a little less sweet but the apple flavor is still prominent.*

VARIATION 3

1 cup	**unsweetened apple juice**	**250 ml**
3 cups	**water**	**750 ml**
2	cinnamon sticks, broken into pieces	2
3	whole allspice	3
2	whole cloves	2
1	crushed nutmeg	1
	whole cinnamon sticks for garnish	

1. Prepare and serve as per Variation 1.

—NOTES—

• *This warm, spicy drink has a light apple flavor, a lighter color, and is less sweet. It quenches the thirst while warming hands and insides.*

Warm Orange Spice Drink

Yields 4 cups (1 L)

This drink is very soothing. A wonderful option for those cool days and evenings when a warm drink is the only thing that will hit the spot!

Original Recipe

3 cups	unsweetened orange juice	750 ml
1 cup	unsweetened pineapple juice	250 ml
1 tsp	mace or nutmeg	5 ml
1/4 tsp	vanilla or coconut extract	1 ml

1. Mix juices and spices in a microwave-safe bowl or a small saucepan.
2. Heat mixture until hot.
3. Add the extract and serve immediately.

—NOTES—

• *Ground spices may stick to the side of the cup. If you prefer, use crushed spices.*

VARIATION 1

2-1/3 cups	unsweetened orange juice	575 ml
2/3 cup	water	175 ml
1 cup	unsweetened pineapple juice	250 ml
1 tsp	mace or nutmeg	5 ml
1/4 tsp	vanilla or coconut extract	1 ml

1. Add water to juices. Prepare and serve as per original recipe.

—NOTES—

• *This drink has a rich golden color.*
• *Adding water to this variation while decreasing the fruit juice content, makes this drink refreshing yet flavorful.*

Warmed Kahlua & Milk

Yields 2-1/4 cup (550 ml)

Try your favorite liqueur with this recipe for a change in flavor.

Original Recipe

2 cups	whole milk	500 ml
1/4 cup	Kahlua liqueur	50 ml

1. Heat milk in the microwave or on the stove top. Once hot, add liqueur and serve in warm mugs.

—NOTES—

• *If using an element or flame on medium to heat milk, you will need to stir the milk and watch it carefully to prevent burning or scorching. An easier method is to use the microwave. Heat the milk on high for 1 to 2 minutes per cup or until hot.*
• *If desired, you can decrease the liqueur from 2 tbsp (30 ml) to 1 tbsp (15 ml) per cup of milk. This drink has a lower sugar content and a milder flavor.*

VARIATION 1

1 cup	2% milk	250 ml
1 cup	whole milk	250 ml
1/4 cup	Kahlua liqueur	50 ml

1. Prepare and serve as per the original recipe.

—NOTES—

• *This variation has a lower fat content than the original recipe because of the change to 2% milk. The flavor of the drink is a little lighter, not quite as creamy, but very tasty and enjoyable.*

Guide to changes in salt, sugar, and water content using each variation.	VARIATION 1	VARIATION 2	VARIATION 3
Salt	▼	▼▼	▼▼
Sugar	▼	▼▼	▼▼▼
Water	▲	▲▲	▲▲▲

VARIATION 2

2-1/3 cups	unsweetened orange juice	575 ml
1 cup	water	250 ml
2/3 cup	unsweetened pineapple juice	175 ml
1 tsp	mace or nutmeg	5 ml
1/4 tsp	vanilla or coconut extract	1 ml

1. Prepare and serve as per Variation 1.

—NOTES—
• *There is very little flavor difference in this variation—it is slightly less sweet. But it has enough fruit flavor remaining to satisfy your taste buds.*

VARIATION 3

1-2/3 cups	unsweetened orange juice	425 ml
2 cups	water	500 ml
1/3 cup	unsweetened pineapple juice	75 ml
1 tsp	mace or nutmeg	5 ml
1/8 tsp	vanilla or coconut extract	.5 ml

1. Prepare and serve as per Variation 1.

—NOTES—
• *The extract has been decreased so the flavor of the orange and pineapple juices are more noticeable. As the water increases the extract becomes more powerful.*
• *This variation has a lighter fruit flavor and is less sweet.*

Guide to changes in salt, sugar, fat, and water content using each variation.	VARIATION 1	VARIATION 2	VARIATION 3
Salt			
Sugar			
Fat	▼	▼▼	▼▼▼
Water			

VARIATION 2

2 cups	2% milk	500 ml
1/4 cup	Kahlua liqueur	50 ml

1. Prepare and serve as per the original recipe.

—NOTES—
• *The use of 2% milk instead of whole milk decreases the fat content in this variation. The flavor and texture change is minimal. This drink is a delicious soothing nighttime drink.*

VARIATION 3

1 cup	2% milk	250 ml
1 cup	1% or skim milk	250 ml
1/4 cup	Kahlua liqueur	50 ml

1. Prepare and serve as per the original recipe.

—NOTES—
• *The use of 1% or skim milk decreases the fat content in this variation, while still keeping some of the creamy body. This variation is thinner, having a more watery consistency. The flavor remains unchanged. In time you may choose to use only 1% milk.*

FOR BEST RESULTS—read through the entire recipe, each variation, and the TIPS on page 135 before preparing this drink.

Warmed Eggnog

Yields 4 cups (1 L)

Original Recipe

4 cups	commercial brand eggnog	1 L
	cinnamon and nutmeg for garnish	

1. Heat eggnog in microwave or on stove top until almost hot.
2. Serve immediately in warm mugs. Garnish with a sprinkling of cinnamon and nutmeg.

—NOTES—

• *If using an element or flame on medium to heat eggnog, you will need to stir and watch it carefully to prevent burning or scorching. An easier method is to use the microwave. Heat the eggnog on high for 1 to 2 minutes per cup or until hot.*

Eggnog is a favorite holiday drink. It is often served cold. Warming it intensifies the flavors making it a delicious treat. A perfect drink to warm you up after a cool afternoon or evening of fun.

VARIATION 1

3 cups light commercial brand eggnog		750 ml
1 cup	2% milk	250 ml
	cinnamon and nutmeg for garnish	

1. Combine milk with eggnog. Heat and serve as per original recipe.

—NOTES—

• *Commercial eggnog has a very strong, sweet flavor when served alone. Adding extra milk, while decreasing the eggnog and using the "light" version, gives you a lighter, appealing taste change. The flavors are more distinctive because of the decrease in fat content.*

FOR BEST RESULTS—read through the entire recipe, each variation, and the TIPS on page 135 before preparing this drink.

Milk & International Coffee

Yields 1 cup (250 ml)

Original Recipe

1 cup	whole milk	250 ml
1 tbsp	instant international coffee	15 ml
	(or according to directions on side of container)	

1. Heat milk in microwave or on stove top until hot but not boiling.
2. Stir in instant coffee and serve immediately.

—NOTES—

• *If using an element or flame on medium to heat milk, you will need to stir the milk and watch it carefully to prevent burning or scorching. An easier method is to use the microwave. Heat the milk on high for 1 to 2 minutes per cup or until hot.*

This warm flavorful beverage is high in calcium. Even those who don't like milk may reconsider. These mixes are usually added to boiling water. Using milk instead of water adds more nutritional value, flavor, and body to the drink.

VARIATION 1

1 cup	2% milk	250 ml
2 tsp	instant international coffee	10 ml

1. Decrease the amount of instant coffee by one-third depending on the directions on the side of the container.
2. Prepare and serve as per original recipe.

—NOTES—

• *Using lower fat milk gives this variation a lighter texture.*
• *The decrease in fat content (which masks flavor) enables us to decrease the amount of coffee flavoring without a noticeable taste change.*

Guide to changes in salt, sugar, fat, and water content using each variation.

	VARIATION 1	VARIATION 2	VARIATION 3
Salt	▼	▼▼	▼▼▼
Sugar	▼	▼▼	▼▼▼
Fat	▼	▼▼	▼▼▼
Water			

VARIATION 2

2 cups light commercial brand eggnog	500 ml
2 cups	2% milk	500 ml

cinnamon and nutmeg for garnish

1. Prepare and serve as per Variation 1.

—NOTES—

• *This variation has a lighter flavor and thinner texture due to the increase in milk and decrease in eggnog. The decrease in eggnog is not missed because heating eggnog heightens its flavor. This version has a less intense flavor and is not as sweet.*

VARIATION 3

1 cup	light commercial brand eggnog	250 ml
1 cup	2% milk	250 ml
2 cups	1% or skim milk	500 ml

sprinkling of cinnamon and nutmeg

1. Combine the spices with the milk and eggnog. Prepare and serve as per Variation 1.

—NOTES—

• *Adding the spices to the mixture before heating allows them to blend into the drink during the heating process. This heightens the flavor and the decrease in eggnog is less noticeable.*
• *The lower fat content allows you to taste the eggnog flavor more readily.*

Guide to changes in salt, sugar, fat, and water content using each variation.

	VARIATION 1	VARIATION 2	VARIATION 3
Salt			
Sugar	▼	▼▼	▼▼▼
Fat	▼	▼▼	▼▼▼
Water			

VARIATION 2

1 cup	1% milk	250 ml
1 tsp	instant international coffee	5 ml

1. Decrease the amount of instant coffee by two-thirds depending on the directions on the side of the container.
2. Prepare and serve as per original recipe.

—NOTES—

• *Decreasing the international coffee content decreases the sugar and hydrogenated oil content in this drink. The flavors in this drink are still delicious.*
• *The texture is lighter than the previous version.*

VARIATION 3

1 cup	1% or skim milk	250 ml
1/2 tsp	instant international coffee	2 ml

1. Decrease the amount of instant coffee by three-quarters depending on the directions on the side of the container.
2. Prepare and serve as per original recipe.

—NOTES—

• *Heating the milk seems to give even the lower fat milks a more creamy texture.*
• *You need only a little coffee flavor to accent the milk in this variation because of the lowered fat content of the milk.*

Tips

The following information for the recipes given in this section
will help you make choices and add variety to your meals.

Favorite Fruit Drinks p122

• Sparkling and mineral water contain some sodium (salt). By adding them to drinks and punches you add fizz as well as a slight increase in salt content. Some stores carry plain or lemon-lime flavored sparkling water in a salt-free version. Adding this to your favorite drink or punch will heighten the flavor, add fizz, and will not increase the salt content of the drink.

• Variation 3 contains mainly water with a little juice. The juice adds a zippy flavor and a little color to the water. It is a wonderful choice to use as a water replenisher when taking part in physical activity. I use it to fill my water bottle when exercising.

• Gradually discover the mixture of fruit juice and water that satisfies your taste buds. You will find the flavor and sweetness that you enjoy and have your thirst quenched as well.

• This recipe is tasty using one fruit juice. Experiment with using two juices together for a change in flavor. For example

    1 cup (250 ml) each orange juice and cranberry cocktail juice

    1 cup (250 ml) each apple juice and grape juice

• Have fun trying new combinations in each variation to disc over flavors that you enjoy and satisfy your taste.

Lemon, Lime, or Orange Ade p122

• Please refer to the first tip in Favorite Fruit Drinks above.

Cranberry Punch p124

• Carbonated sparkling water can be used in this punch along with or instead of water. For more information, *see* the first tip in Favorite Fruit Drinks above.

• There is plenty of sweet taste from the fruit juices and ginger ale even though the quantities have been reduced and water has been added.

• Try adding sparkling water in place of ginger ale or 7-Up to give a light refreshing taste without the added sweet flavors that can often mask fruit flavors.

• Variation 3 resembles flavored sparkling water with a little more fruit flavor and color than the commercial varieties.

• You may choose to decrease the overall juice content and increase the water content. As your taste buds begin to enjoy the taste and flavor of less fruit juice and more water, you may find pure juices too concentrated and not very thirst quenching or refreshing.

Tropical Refresher p124

• As you develop a preference for lighter and more thirst quenching drinks, try decreasing the fruit juice content a little more while increasing the water content.

• A friend who has been incorporating the HUGS philosophy of gradual change to her eating and activity patterns one summer evening on an outing she and some friends decided they were thirsty and stopped for a drink. They chose lemonade and looked forward to the thirst quenching drink. When the lemonade was served one sip of the drink caused their mouths to pucker with the sweet strong taste. The 10-year-old daughter announced that this drink was making her more thirsty! After discussing their dilemma for a few minutes, they decided to try a little experiment. They asked for extra glasses and water and diluted the lemonade. The result was a refreshing and positive flavor combination. They enjoyed the drinks more and felt more satisfied. The appealing drink they created quenched their thirst.

Wine Sangria p126

• If you are looking for some alternative ways to serve wine, try wine spritzers. Mix your favorite red or white wine with equal amounts of sparkling water. This is a refreshing change.
• Try adding mineral or sparkling water to your favorite beer or liqueur. The result is a lighter flavor that is easy to drink and lower in sugar.
•   A beer drink that is a favorite is a shandy. Mix beer with ginger ale or lemonade and garnish with fresh lemon or lime slices. Start with a mixture of 2/3 beer to 1/3 ginger ale or lemonade. Then move to a 1/2 and 1/2 concentration. As your taste buds learn to enjoy the changes, you may choose to add more juice, ginger ale, or water to this mixture to make it even more refreshing and thirst quenching.

The Perfect Cup of Tea p126

• After a few months of enjoying these creations, try brewing your tea for shorter periods of time. This will result in a liquid that has less caffeine content. You will find that you still enjoy the warm soothing flavors while decreasing your caffeine intake.
• When making changes to your favorite drinks, whether hot or cold, do it gradually. Like any food item that you are changing, you want to enjoy the process of change. If you find yourself craving the original ingredients, you are moving too quickly. Go back to the previous variation. There is no endpoint that is right for everyone. You must discover your own preferences.

Grape Soother p128

• Here is another hot, refreshing, easy to make, and more thirst quenching option because it omits the tea which is a dehydrator.

Add 1/4 cup grape juice to 3/4 cup water and 1/2 cinnamon stick. This tasty warm drink has no caffeine. You can warm this in a cup in the microwave for a quick treat.

Hot Apple Cider p128

• If you like, you can make more of this cider than you need. Store the brewed drink in a closed container in the refrigerator until you want to drink it. Then pour it into a mug and microwave on high about 1-1/2 minutes per cup or until hot.
• Apple juice has a very concentrated sweet flavor when served alone. Adding water gives this drink a more mellow flavor.
• This drink is ideal to take in a thermos on a winter activity outing. It quenches the thirst while warming the hands and insides.

Warmed Kahlua & Milk p130

• If you use an element or flame on medium to heat the milk, be careful not to burn or scorch the milk. An easier method of heating milk is in the microwave on high for 1 to 2 minutes per cup.

Warmed Eggnog p132

• Remember as you decrease the fat content in the milk you use, the flavor of the eggnog will be more intense because fat masks flavors.
• As your tastes change, in Variation 3 you may choose to use 3 cups (750 ml) 1% milk instead of mixing 2% and 1% milk.

Milk & International Coffee p132

• There are many international coffee flavors available. Choose the flavor that satisfies you most.
• Tune into the flavors and textures of this drink. Enjoy the subtle changes that occur as you decrease the amount of international coffee used.

**WRITE DOWN THE TIPS THAT WORK
FOR YOU—**

**—USE THESE TIPS IN YOUR FAMILY
FAVORITES!**

Desserts may conclude a meal and be enjoyed with tea and coffee any time of the day. Socializing over dessert is always a popular activity. But finding a dessert that is tasty and light is often a challenge.

Perhaps using artificial sweeteners will provide a lighter, healthier dessert? When you take out sugar and add artificial sweeteners to a food item, it is often replaced by fats to compensate for the loss in texture. If you look at the ingredients of low-calorie chocolate bars you will see glaring evidence of this fact. In order for the chocolate bar to have a smooth texture without added sugar, the fat is increased greatly. This is not a healthier option since fat consumption affects overall health and increases the risk for heart disease and cancer.

Another problem with using artificial sweeteners is that you don't learn to enjoy a less sweet taste. Replacing sugar with other sweeteners may reduce our energy intake but you haven't learned to enjoy foods that are lower in sugar content. Often after a few days or a few months of eating foods with artificial sweetener, you feel deprived and dissatisfied. You then return to the good old favorites to get the flavors and textures you enjoy.

The goal is to change your eating patterns and learn to enjoy foods that are lower in sugar and fat. With gradual changes to lower sweet and fat foods, you will no longer crave high-sugar, high-fat foods as frequently. You will enjoy and be satisfied with lower fat, lower sugar, and higher fiber foods.

Changes such as increasing protein content to replace fat content improves the

Desserts

nutritional value of the dessert, slows the digestive process which leaves you full longer, and gives you a more constant supply of energy throughout the day. People with diabetes find this beneficial because added protein keeps blood sugars more constant.

If you taste, savor, and enjoy the dessert you choose, you will often be satisfied with less. As you become aware that it is okay to eat desserts and become tuned into your internal hunger, needs, and wants, you may sometimes choose not to eat dessert because you no longer want it. When you learn to balance your eating patterns you may enjoy all kinds of exciting options and still be choosing healthier life-style patterns.

Special note Some recipes include suggestions for cooking with artificial sweeteners. People with diabetes may find that using some artificial sweeteners in desserts creates less blood sugar swings. See p148 for more information.

FOR BEST RESULTS—read through the entire recipe, each variation, and the TIPS on page 148 before preparing this dessert.

This creamy and delicious dessert is a family favorite. It is high in calcium and with the bananas it is an excellent source of potassium. It can also be put into a baked pie shell to make a banana cream pie. For a change, substitute 1 cup (250 ml) berries for the banana.

Aunt Marge's Banana Cream Pudding

Yields 2 cups (500 ml)

Variation 2 and 3 *yield about 1-3/4 cup (425 ml)*

Original Recipe

1 cup	2% milk	250 ml
1	egg	1
2 tbsp	all purpose flour	30 ml
1/4 cup	sugar	50 ml
3 tbsp	2% milk	45 ml
3/4 tsp	vanilla extract	3 ml
2	bananas	2
1 tbsp	lemon juice	15 ml
1/2 cup	whipping cream	125 ml
1/2 tsp	vanilla extract	2 ml
1 tbsp + 1-1/2 tsp	icing sugar	22 ml
	4 fresh mint sprigs for garnish	

1. Heat the milk in a microwave-safe bowl in the microwave for 1-1/2 minutes on high.
2. Separate the egg. Place egg white in a separate mixing bowl. Place egg yolk in a bowl and add flour, sugar, and 3 tbsp (45 ml) milk to make a sauce.
3. Pour egg mixture into warmed milk and whisk together. Heat this mixture in the microwave on high heat, stopping every minute to whisk mixture to prevent lumps. Heat until mixture starts to thicken to the consistency of runny yogurt (3 to 6 minutes).
4. While the milk/egg mixture is heating, beat egg white until stiff. Add egg white to heated milk mixture and whip the two together vigorously along with 3/4 tsp (3 ml) vanilla.
5. Cut bananas into thin slices, dip in lemon juice, and line the bottom of dessert serving bowls. Pour pudding over bananas. Allow to cool.
6. Before serving, whip cream until peaks form. Add vanilla and icing sugar and beat into whipped cream. Top desserts with whipped cream and mint sprigs.

VARIATION 1

1 cup	**1% milk**	**250 ml**
1	egg	1
2 tbsp	all purpose flour	30 ml
1/4 cup	sugar	50 ml
3 tbsp	**1% milk**	**45 ml**
3/4 tsp	vanilla extract	3 ml
2	bananas	2
1 tbsp	lemon juice	15 ml
1/3 cup	**whipping cream**	**75 ml**
1/2 tsp	vanilla extract	2 ml
1 tbsp	**icing sugar**	**15 ml**
	4 fresh mint sprigs for garnish	

1. Prepare and serve as per the original recipe.

—NOTES—

• *Stiffly beaten egg whites add to the fluffy, airy texture of this pudding. This dessert is a great alternative to any bought cooked pudding.*

• *Changing to 1% milk decreases the fat in this recipe without any flavor or texture change.*

• *Whipping cream is meant to be an accent to add flavor and texture. You need only a small amount. Sugar is decreased because the amount of whipping cream is decreased. These two changes lower the fat and sugar content in the recipe.*

• *Eggs and milk fats are agents that thicken foods. Eggs are the main thickening agent in this pudding. The change to 1% milk doesn't alter the consistency of this pudding.*

Guide to changes in sugar, protein, fat, and fiber content using each variation.

	VARIATION 1	VARIATION 2	VARIATION 3
Sugar	▼	▼▼	▼▼▼
Protein			
Fat	▼	▼▼	▼▼▼
Fiber		▲	▲

139

VARIATION 2

1 cup	1% milk	250 ml
1	egg	1
1 tbsp	**all purpose flour**	**15 ml**
1 tbsp	**oat bran**	**15 ml**
3 tbsp	**sugar**	**45 ml**
3 tbsp	1% milk	45 ml
1 tsp	**vanilla extract**	**5 ml**
2	bananas	2
1 tbsp	lemon juice	15 ml
1/4 cup	**whipping cream**	**50 ml**
1/2 tsp	vanilla extract	2 ml
1 tbsp	icing sugar	15 ml
	4 fresh mint sprigs for garnish	

1. Add oat bran to flour mixture. Prepare and serve as per original recipe. *Remember to cook pudding only until it starts to thicken. It will continue to thicken as it cools.*

—NOTES—

• *Oat bran is an excellent form of soluble fiber. It is almost flavorless and works well as a thickener.*
• *There are little flecks of oat bran in this variation. If you do not enjoy the added texture go back to 2 tbsp (30 ml) all purpose flour.*
• *Adding extra vanilla gives this pudding a delicious vanilla flavor. If you prefer another flavor extract such as coconut, try it in place of vanilla.*
• *The decrease in sugar makes the taste of the bananas more noticeable.*
• *You need only a small amount of whipping cream to enjoy it as an accent.*

VARIATION 3

1 cup	**skim milk**	**250 ml**
1	egg	1
1 tbsp	all purpose flour	15 ml
1 tbsp	oat bran	15 ml
2 tbsp	**sugar**	**30 ml**
3 tbsp	**skim milk**	**45 ml**
1 tsp	vanilla extract	5 ml
2	bananas	2
1 tbsp	lemon juice	15 ml
	omit whipping cream	
1/2 cup	**raspberries, or**	**125 ml**
1	**small banana, sliced**	**1**
1/2 tsp	vanilla extract	2 ml
1 tbsp	icing sugar	15 ml
	4 fresh mint sprigs for garnish	

1. Prepare as per Variation 2, using 2 bananas as outlined. Just before serving, top with the berries or additional banana slices and mint sprigs.

—NOTES—

• *Changing to skim milk decreases the fat content and makes the texture lighter and fluffier.*
• *Moving to a lower fat milk gives this pudding a slightly runnier consistency. You may need to increase the cooking time to thicken the dessert. See p148 for thickening formulas.*
• *Use the berries or banana as an accent on top of the pudding to replace the whipped cream. If you use berries, they will add lovely color.*
• *As the fat content of this dessert went down, less sweetening was required to get a sweet flavor.*
• *Coat bananas in lemon juice to prevent browning.*

FOR BEST RESULTS—read through the entire recipe, each variation, and the TIPS on page 148 before preparing this dessert.

This swirl chocolate and vanilla cheesecake is as pleasing to the eye as it is to the palate. Its rich creamy texture becomes a delightful fluffier texture through the variations. Serve it with pride at any festive occasion.

Marble Cheesecake

Yields 1—9-inch (23-cm) springform pan

Original Recipe

1 cup	graham cracker crumbs	250 ml
3 tbsp	sugar	45 ml
3 tbsp	butter or margarine, melted	45 ml
3 cups	cream cheese, softened	750 ml
3/4 cup	sugar	175 ml
1 tsp	lemon or vanilla extract	5 ml
3	eggs	3
1 oz	square unsweetened chocolate	30 g

1. Combine graham crumbs, 3 tbsp (45 ml) sugar, and butter in a bowl. Press mixture onto the bottom of a 9-in (23-cm) springform pan.
2. Bake at 350°F (180°C) for 10 minutes. Remove from oven and cool.
3. Combine cream cheese, remaining sugar, and vanilla in a mixing bowl. Mix at medium speed until well blended.
4. Add eggs, one at a time, mixing well after each addition. Once all eggs are added, whip until light and fluffy.
5. Melt chocolate. Add to 1 cup (250 ml) of cream cheese/egg batter in a separate bowl. Blend together. This is the chocolate batter.
6. Spoon plain batter and chocolate batter alternately over the crust. Cut through batters with a knife several times to create the marbled effect.
7. Bake at 450°F (230°C) for 10 minutes, then reduce oven temperature to 250°F (120°C) and continue baking for 30 to 40 minutes or until done (the cake no longer jiggles and feels somewhat firm when touched).
8. Loosen cake from rim of pan as soon as it is out of the oven; cool before removing rim.
9. Chill before serving.

VARIATION 1

1 cup	graham cracker crumbs	250 ml
2 tbsp	**sugar**	**30 ml**
2 tbsp	**butter or margarine, melted**	**30 ml**
3 cups	**light cream cheese, softened**	**750 ml**
3/4 cup	sugar	175 ml
1 tsp	lemon or vanilla extract	5 ml
3	eggs	3
1 oz	square unsweetened chocolate	30 g

1. Prepare crust as per original recipe.
2. Continue to prepare as per original recipe. When mixing the cream cheese and egg, make sure to whip the mixture until light and fluffy.
3. When baking cheesecake place a pan of water in the oven beside or under the cake. This increases moisture and prevents the cheesecake top from cracking during baking.
4. Bake at 450°F (230C) for 10 minutes, then at 250°F (120°C) for 50 to 60 minutes. Cooking time seems to increase slightly as the fat content decreases. Serve as per original recipe.

—NOTES—
- *The graham crumbs have their own sweet flavor. The decrease in sugar in the crust is not noticeable.*
- *The crust stuck together well even with the decrease in butter.*
- *Light cream cheese has less fat than regular cream cheese, with the same flavor and texture.*
- *As the fat decreases, this cheesecake requires a longer baking time to set.*

Guide to changes in sugar, protein, fat, and fiber content using each variation.

	VARIATION 1	VARIATION 2	VARIATION 3
Sugar	▼	▼	▼▼
Protein		▲	▲▲
Fat	▼	▼▼	▼▼▼
Fiber			

141

VARIATION 2

1 cup	graham cracker crumbs	250 ml
	omit sugar	
2 tbsp	butter or margarine, melted	30 ml
3 cups	**quark cheese**	**750 ml**
3	**eggs, separated**	**3**
3/4 cup	sugar	175 ml
1 tsp	lemon or vanilla extract	5 ml
3 tbsp	**unsweetened cocoa powder**	**45 ml**
	fresh or cooked fruit topping for garnish	

1. Prepare crust as per original recipe; omit sugar.
2. Put quark cheese in mixing bowl and whip until light and fluffy. Add egg yolks, one at a time, mixing well after each addition. Add sugar and lemon extract gradually to mixture, beating until well mixed and light and fluffy.
3. Remove 1 cup (250 ml) of cheese mixture and place in a separate bowl. Stir in cocoa until well blended.
4. In a clean bowl, beat egg whites until stiff. Fold into plain (not chocolate) cheese batter. Place in pan as per original recipe. Bake at 300°F (150°C) for 1-1/4 to 1-1/2 hours or until browned on top and toothpick comes out clean. When completely cool, remove springform pan outside ring and serve with topping. Do not loosen the rim before cooling.

—NOTES—
• *The graham crumbs have their own sweet flavor. The decrease in sugar in the crust is not noticeable.*
• *Quark cheese has a similar texture and flavor to cream cheese, is lower in fat, and slightly higher in protein.*
• *As the fat is decreased, this cheesecake requires a longer baking time to set.*
• *Separating the eggs and beating the egg whites gives this recipe a lighter, fluffier texture with greater moisture that compensates for the decrease in fat. The chocolate will now become a layer at the bottom.*

VARIATION 3

1 cup	graham cracker crumbs	250 ml
2 tbsp	butter or margarine, melted	30 ml
3 cups	**1% cottage cheese, pureed**	**750 ml**
3	eggs, separated	3
1/2 cup	**sugar**	**125 ml**
1 tsp	lemon or vanilla extract	5 ml
3 tbsp	unsweetened cocoa powder	45 ml
	fresh or cooked fruit topping for garnish	

1. Prepare crust as per Variation 2.
2. Beat pureed cottage cheese until light and fluffy.
3. Continue, bake, and serve as per Variation 2. Before serving, refrigerate the cheesecake until firm.

—NOTES—
• *Pureed cottage cheese has a similar texture and flavor to sour cream. Adding it to this recipe increases the protein and decreases the fat content. Cottage cheese has more moisture than quark cheese and may require a longer baking time.*
• *This variation has a fluffy souffle-like texture.*
• *Increasing the rich taste of the extract compensates for the decrease in sugar in the batter.*
• *You may substitute skim milk quark cheese for pureed cottage cheese in this variation. Skim milk quark cheese is lower in fat and higher in protein than cream cheese (Variation 1), and is lower in fat than regular quark cheese (Variation 2). The overall texture of the cheesecake is a little lighter.*

FOR BEST RESULTS—read through the entire recipe, each variation, and the TIPS on page 149 before preparing this dessert.

This carrot cake is dense and delicious. As you move through the variations there will be a thinner layer of frosting added. Less frosting accents the lovely flavors in the cake instead of masking them.

Carrot Cake

Yields 1—9-inch (23-cm) springform pan

Original Recipe

—CAKE—		
1-1/4 cup	oil	300 ml
1-1/2 cup	sugar	375 ml
3	eggs	3
2 cups	all purpose flour	500 ml
2 tsp	baking soda	10 ml
1/2 tsp	salt	2 ml
2-1/2 tsp	cinnamon	12 ml
1 tsp	ground cloves	5 ml
1/4 tsp	nutmeg	1 ml
8 oz	can crushed pineapple	237 ml
2 cups	carrots, grated	500 ml
1 cup	pecans, coarsely chopped	250 ml
—CREAM CHEESE FROSTING—		
1 cup	cream cheese	250 ml
1/2 cup	icing sugar	125 ml
1/2 tsp	white vanilla	2 ml

1. Preheat the oven to 350°F (175°C).
2. Beat oil, sugar, and eggs in a small mixing bowl until well blended.
3. Mix dry ingredients together in a large bowl.
4. Add egg mixture to dry ingredients and mix well.
5. Add pineapple, carrots, and pecans and mix well.
6. Pour batter into a greased and floured 9-in (23-cm) springform pan. Bake for 55 to 60 minutes or until toothpick inserted in center comes out clean.
7. While cake is cooling on a cooling rack, prepare the frosting.
8. Cream the cream cheese in a small bowl.
9. Add remainder of ingredients and blend well.
10. Cover cool cake with frosting.

—NOTES—
• *You may use dark vanilla in the frosting, however it will have a darker color.*

VARIATION 1

—CAKE—		
1 cup	**oil**	**250 ml**
1 cup	**loosely packed brown sugar**	**250 ml**
3	eggs	3
2 cups	all purpose flour	500 ml
2 tsp	baking soda	10 ml
1/2 tsp	salt	2 ml
2-1/2 tsp	cinnamon	12 ml
1 tsp	ground cloves	5 ml
1/4 tsp	nutmeg	1 ml
8 oz	can crushed pineapple	237 ml
2 cups	carrots, grated	500 ml
1 cup	pecans, coarsely chopped	250 ml
—CREAM CHEESE FROSTING—		
1 cup	**light cream cheese**	**250 ml**
1/3 cup	**icing sugar**	**75 ml**
1/2 tsp	white vanilla	2 ml

1. Prepare and bake as per the original recipe.

—NOTES—
• *Zucchini can be used in place of carrots for a flavor change.*
• *Brown sugar gives extra molasses flavor and added moisture to this variation.*
• *This variation is lower in fat and sugar content than the original recipe.*
• *The cake still remains moist and tasty because of the pineapple and carrot ingredients.*
• *Changing to light cream cheese is not noticeable in the flavor of the frosting.*

Guide to changes in sugar, protein, fat, and fiber content using each variation.	VARIATION 1	VARIATION 2	VARIATION 3
Sugar	▼	▼	▼▼
Protein	▲	▲	▲
Fat	▼	▼▼	▼▼▼
Fiber		▲	▲▲

143

VARIATION 2

—CAKE—

1 cup	oil	250 ml
1 cup	loosely packed brown sugar	250 ml
3	eggs	3
1 cup	**all purpose flour**	**250 ml**
2/3 cup	**whole wheat flour**	**150 ml**
2 tsp	baking soda	10 ml
1/2 tsp	salt	2 ml
2-1/2 tsp	cinnamon	12 ml
1 tsp	ground cloves	5 ml
1/4 tsp	nutmeg	1 ml
8 oz	can crushed pineapple	237 ml
2 cups	carrots, grated	500 ml
3/4 cup	**pecans, coarsely chopped**	**175 ml**

—CREAM CHEESE FROSTING—

1/2 cup	**light cream cheese**	**125 ml**
1/4 cup	**quark cheese**	**50 ml**
1/4 cup	**icing sugar**	**50 ml**
1/2 tsp	white vanilla	2 ml

1. Prepare and bake as per the original recipe. Add whole wheat flour when adding all purpose flour to dry ingredients.

—NOTES—

• *Replacing some white flour with whole wheat flour increases the fiber content of this dessert.*
• *You may choose to replace quark cheese with skyr cheese which is even lower in fat content. Using quark or skyr cheese increases the protein content.*
• *This variation is slightly heavier in texture than the original. The oil is left unchanged to allow your taste buds to enjoy the added fiber.*
• *Nuts are an accent in this cake. Decreasing them still gives you the flavor with less overall fat content.*
• *The total amount of frosting is decreased to emphasize it as an accent.*

VARIATION 3

—CAKE—

2/3 cup	**oil**	**150 ml**
2/3 cup	**honey**	**150 ml**
3	eggs	3
1 cup	all purpose flour	250 ml
2/3 cup	whole wheat flour	150 ml
2 tsp	baking soda	10 ml
	omit salt	
1 tbsp	**cinnamon**	**15 ml**
1 tsp	ground cloves	5 ml
1/4 tsp	nutmeg	1 ml
8 oz	can crushed pineapple	237 ml
2-1/2 cups	**carrots, grated**	**625 ml**
3/4 cup	pecans, coarsely chopped	175 ml

—CREAM CHEESE FROSTING—

2/3 cup	**quark cheese**	**150 ml**
3 tbsp	**icing sugar**	**45 ml**
1 tsp	**orange rind, grated**	**5 ml**
1/2 tsp	white vanilla	2 ml

1. Prepare and bake as per Variation 2. Add orange rind when adding vanilla to frosting.

—NOTES—

• *Honey is a more concentrated sugar than table sugars. You need less to get the same amount of sweet flavor. If you substitute honey equally for table sugars, you will be consuming more sugar than you were originally.*
• *Using honey and added vegetables adds moisture which makes the decrease in fat content less noticeable.*
• *Added vegetables increases the fiber content.*
• *The orange rind in the frosting and the cinnamon in the cake add lovely flavors to compensate for the lowered sugar content.*

Coconut Cream Pie

Yields filling for 1—9-inch (23-cm) pie

This pie is a delicious conclusion to a celebration meal. As you move through the variations you will notice that the pie has a lighter fluffier texture that is less filling. The decrease in fat heightens the tropical coconut flavor.

Original Recipe

2/3 cup	sugar	150 ml
1/2 tsp	salt	2 ml
2-1/2 tbsp	cornstarch	37 ml
1 tbsp	all purpose flour	15 ml
3 cups	whole milk	750 ml
3	egg yolks, slightly beaten	3
1 tbsp	butter	15 ml
1-1/2 tsp	vanilla	7 ml
3/4 cup	unsweetened shredded coconut	175 ml
9-inch	baked pie shell	23-cm
1 cup	whipping cream	250 ml

1. Mix sugar, salt, flour, and cornstarch in a heavy saucepan.
2. Stir milk into this saucepan gradually. Cook over moderate heat, stirring constantly until mixture thickens and boils.
3. Boil for 1 minute, stirring constantly.
4. Remove from heat. Stir a little of the hot mixture into the egg yolks and then blend egg yolk mixture into the hot mixture in the saucepan.
5. Return mixture to moderate heat and boil 1 minute more, stirring constantly.
6. Remove from heat and blend in butter and vanilla.
7. Cool filling, stirring occasionally. When cool, fold in coconut and pour into baked pie shell.
8. Whip cream and spread on pie.
9. Chill for two hours. Take pie out of refrigerator 20 minutes before serving to make the crust taste better.

—NOTES—
• *For pie crust variations, see p146.*

VARIATION 1

1/2 cup	sugar	125 ml
1/4 tsp	salt	1 ml
1/4 cup	cornstarch	50 ml
1 tbsp	all purpose flour	15 ml
3 cups	**2% milk**	**750 ml**
3	egg yolks, slightly beaten	3
1-1/2 tsp	**butter**	**7 ml**
1-1/2 tsp	vanilla	7 ml
3/4 cup	unsweetened shredded coconut	175 ml
9-inch	baked pie shell	23-cm
1/2 cup	**whipping cream**	**125 ml**

1. Prepare and serve as per the original recipe.

—NOTES—
• *By moving to a lower fat milk and decreasing the butter content this variation is lower in fat. Extra cornstarch is added to provide thickening power lost with the decreased fat. See p149 for more information.*
• *Even though sugar and salt are decreased in this variation, it tastes sweeter due to the lower fat content.*
• *The changes in this variation produce a lighter texture.*
• *Garnishing the pie with less whipped cream changes the focus of the whipped cream. Leftover whipping cream from the container can be refrigerated for several days or frozen (unwhipped) and used in other recipes at a later date.*

Left: Marble Cheesecake, Variation 3, p141; Warm Orange Spice Drink, Variation 1, p130;
Right: Grape Soother, Variation 2, p129; Carrot Cake, Variation 2, p143

Pizza on a Bun, Variation 3, p161;
served on Oma's Best Buns, Variation 3, p69 and bagels; Cranberry Punch, Variation 1, p124

Guide to changes in salt, sugar, fat, and fiber content using each variation.	VARIATION 1	VARIATION 2	VARIATION 3
	Salt ▼	Salt ▼	Salt ▼▼
	Sugar ▼	Sugar ▼	Sugar ▼▼
	Fat ▼	Fat ▼▼	Fat ▼▼▼
	Fiber	Fiber ▲	Fiber ▲

145

VARIATION 2

1/2 cup	sugar	125 ml
1/4 tsp	salt	1 ml
1/4 cup	cornstarch	50 ml
2 tbsp	**all purpose flour**	**30 ml**
3 cups	**1% milk**	**750 ml**
3	egg yolks, slightly beaten	3
1-1/2 tsp	**butter**	**7 ml**
1-1/2 tsp	vanilla	7 ml
3/4 cup	unsweetened shredded coconut	175 ml
9-inch	baked pie shell	23-cm
	omit whipping cream	
2 tbsp	**unsweetened shredded coconut**	**30 ml**

1. Mix as per the original recipe. *Note the filling may require less cooking time to make a nice consistency.*
2. When finished baking the pie crust, shut the oven off. Place 2 tbsp (30 ml) coconut on a cookie sheet and toast in the oven for a few minutes. Garnish pie with toasted coconut in place of whipped cream.

—NOTES—
* *This variation has a light fluffy texture.*
* *The fat content has been decreased by moving to 1% milk. Because of the decrease in fat content, the flour content needs to increase. The cornstarch was left the same in this variation.*
* *Using toasted coconut instead of whipped cream as a topping provides a nice garnish.*
* *The filling is not as high without the whipped cream topping. The crust can be formed lower up the sides of the pan to accommodate the decrease in filling.*

VARIATION 3

1/3 cup	sugar	75 ml
1/8 tsp	salt	.5 ml
5 tbsp	cornstarch	75 ml
2 tbsp	all purpose flour	30 ml
3 cups	skim milk	750 ml
3	egg yolks, slightly beaten	3
1-1/2 tsp	**butter**	**7 ml**
1-1/2 tsp	vanilla	7 ml
3/4 cup	unsweetened shredded coconut	175 ml
9-inch	baked pie shell	23-cm
2 tbsp	unsweetened shredded coconut	30 ml

1. Mix, prepare, and serve as per Variation 2.

—NOTES—
* *This variation is the lightest and fluffiest.*
* *The filling is definitely sweet enough to satisfy your sweet taste buds. The decrease in fat in this variation gives this pie a milder less sweet flavor that is very enjoyable.*
* *Moving to skim milk decreases the fat content in this variation. The cornstarch is increased slightly to replace the thickening power that was lost with the decrease in fat.*

The focus of a pie can be the filling rather than the crust. As you move to lower fat ingredients you will notice the gradual changes in texture of the crust. Enjoy!

Pie Crust

Yields 1— 9-inch (23-cm) pie crust, top and bottom, or 2—single layer 9-inch (23-cm) pie crusts

Original Recipe

2 cups	all purpose flour	500 ml
3/4 tsp	salt	4 ml
1 cup	shortening	250 ml
4 tbsp	cold water	60 ml

1. Mix flour and salt in a bowl.
2. Cut shortening into flour mixture and work it in with a pastry cutter or a fork until the mixture looks crumbly.
3. Add water to the dough 1 tbsp (15 ml) at a time until the dough holds together in a ball and doesn't fall apart when working with it. You may find you need to adjust the water amount.
4. Dough can be frozen at this point and brought out at another time to make fruit tarts or a pie shell after you have allowed it to thaw.
5. Roll into a thin layer, about 1/8 to 1/4 inch (3 to 6 mm) thickness. Place in the bottom of a pie plate. Crimp edges to sides of dish.
6. If you need a baked pie shell, bake at 400°F (200°C) for 8 to 10 minutes, pricking the bubbles with a fork at 4 minutes time.

VARIATION 1

2 cups	all purpose flour	500 ml
1/2 tsp	salt	2 ml
3/4 cup	shortening	175 ml
4–6 tbsp	cold water	60–90 ml

1. Prepare as per the original recipe.

—NOTES—

- *You will notice this variation requires a little more water than the original recipe.*
- *Decreasing the shortening lowers the fat content in this recipe. The result is a less rich, crisp, and flaky crust.*
- *With the decrease in fat you don't seem to need as much salt for flavor.*

	VARIATION 1		VARIATION 2		VARIATION 3	
Guide to changes in salt, protein, fat, and fiber content using each variation.	Salt	▼	Salt	▼	Salt	▼▼
	Protein		Protein		Protein	
	Fat	▼	Fat	▼▼	Fat	▼▼▼
	Fiber		Fiber		Fiber	

147

VARIATION 2

2 cups	all purpose flour	500 ml
1/2 tsp	salt	2 ml
1/2 cup	**shortening**	**125 ml**
5–7 tbsp	cold water	75–105 ml

1. Mix as per Variation 1.
2. Roll dough a little thinner, closer to the 1/8 inch (3 mm) thickness between two layers of wax paper. This makes it easier to keep the crust in one piece and you can roll it thinner.

—NOTES—

• *This variation is lower in fat because of the decrease in shortening.*
• *The crust is less flaky than in the last variation. It has more of a tea biscuit texture. It is very tasty.*
• *Rolling the pie crust a little thinner allows the accent of the pie to be in the filling. Instead of putting a full crust on top of your pie, try using lattice work. It is a very attractive way of decorating a pie and decreases the overall pastry content.*

VARIATION 3

2 cups	all purpose flour	500 ml
1/4 tsp	salt	1 ml
1/4 cup	shortening	50 ml
6–8 tbsp	cold water	90–120 ml

1. Mix as per Variation 2. It takes about 15 minutes to bake this crust so it browns.

—NOTES—

• *A lower fat content requires longer cooking time to brown crust. Less shortening also causes crusts to harden more quickly. It is better to eat the pie fresh.*
• *The crust has a more bread-like consistency.*
• *Because of the decrease of ingredients it needs to be rolled thinly to cover a similar area.*
• *Remember there is no right and wrong in eating. If you and your family find a variation too extreme for your taste enjoyment, return to the previous variation.*
• *You don't miss the lower salt content in this variation.*

Tips

Please read *The following information for the recipes given in this section will help you make choices and add variety to your meals.*

148 Author's Note: I am a person with diabetes and have found that using some artificial sweeteners in dessert products has allowed me to enjoy them with less blood sugar swings. The sweetener I use most frequently is aspartame. If I use it in microwave cooking there is little or no bitter aftertaste. The sweet flavor is decreased in the cooking process and I have learned to enjoy foods that are not as sweet. Many people prefer saccharin for baking. Experiment to find which is best for you.

It is essential to note that a person with diabetes can eat a traditional dessert that is sweetened with table or fruit sugars and not have large blood sugar swings. If the dessert is eaten in small amounts after a well balanced meal including both complex carbohydrates and protein, the digestion of the dessert is slowed to such an extent that blood sugar levels stay constant.

Aunt Marge's Banana Cream Pudding p138

• This dessert can easily be adapted for persons with diabetes. Replace the sugar with spoon for spoon aspartame. Microwave cooking is more satisfactory than stove top cooking when using artificial sweeteners. The bitter aftertaste is less. You can cook with aspartame as you would with sugar.

• Here are some approximate equivalent thickening ingredients for puddings when using skim or 1% milk:

for 1 cup (250 ml) liquid use
2 to 3 egg yolks, or
3 to 4 tbsp (45 to 60 ml) flour, or
2 tbsp (30 ml) cornstarch, or
4 tbsp (60 ml) oat bran, or
5 tsp (25 ml) tapioca

• Whipping cream is an accent that is often used on top of desserts. As you decrease the amount of whipping cream, tune into the textures and flavors which will be more noticeable.

• Try grated orange rind as a garnish instead of mint sprigs for a flavorful change.

• Leftover whipping cream will store in the refrigerator until the date indicated on the carton. It also freezes well for several months and can be thawed and used in baked and cooked goods.

• For a change, substitute 2 pieces of your favorite fruit for the banana.

Marble Cheesecake p140

• You may not be familiar with quark cheese. It is a soft, sharper tasting cheese that has a slightly thinner consistency than cream cheese. It is lower in fat and slightly higher in protein content than sour cream and cream cheese. In recipes for these products, it is a tasty substitute. Some stores will offer skim milk or low-fat quark cheese which has a fat content similar to 1% cottage cheese.

• Skyr cheese is lower in fat content than quark cheese but higher in fat than 1% cottage cheese. It is slightly more liquid than quark cheese but otherwise has similar qualities.

• For a more gradual transition from Variation 2 to Variation 3, try using half quark cheese and half skyr cheese. Be sure to adjust the cooking time to 1–3/4 hours due to the higher moisture content of skyr cheese.

• Chocolate squares are high in saturated fat. 1 oz (30 g) of unsweetened chocolate can be replaced with 3 tbsp (45 ml) of cocoa in any recipe calling for unsweetened chocolate baking squares. The chocolate is still a rich dark color and flavor.

- Separating eggs yolks and whites can give a dessert or cake added volume while decreasing the fat. Beat the egg whites until they are fluffy and fold them into cakes or desserts at the end of the mixing process. The result is a dessert with a lighter, fluffier, and moister texture.

Carrot Cake p142

- People with gardens who wish to preserve some of their extra carrots or zucchini can easily do so. Grate the vegetables finely, place into plastic bags, seal, and freeze. Grated carrots or zucchini make wonderful moistening additions to cakes, muffins, cookies, and breads. If you are using frozen grated vegetables you may find the batter becomes too moist. Either omit the pineapple juice or thaw the frozen vegetables and drain the liquid out.
- This cake is so moist that you may find it doesn't need frosting. Instead just sprinkle it with icing sugar using a doily to create a pattern for a very elegant look.
- This cake freezes well and tastes moist and fresh even after being frozen.
- Adding vegetables and whole wheat flour to the cake raises both the soluble and insoluble fiber content. The vegetable and oat bran soluble fiber becomes gel-like when digested and seems to have a direct effect on keeping cholesterol and blood sugar levels in line by slowing the digestion of starch and sugars in the intestines.[1,8,12,15] Including insoluble fiber (from the whole wheat flour) in your eating pattern gives you added roughage and helps you to become more regular. This is thought to decrease the risk for some bowl cancers.[10]
- *See* p78 for the formula for replacing white flour with whole wheat flour.
- A rough estimate of moving from sugar to honey to get the same amount of sweetness is:

    3/4 cup (175 ml) honey for every 1 cup (250 ml) sugar

- There seems to be a general paranoia about eggs. Many people believe eggs are the main culprit for raising cholesterol levels; however, the total amount of fat you eat is more significant. In this recipe you will have about 1/4 of an egg per serving.

Coconut Cream Pie p144

- Changing the fat content in some recipes results in a runnier product. This is because fat works as a thickening agent in recipes. To compensate for a decrease in fat content just increase the cornstarch or flour content in the recipe. *Warning* Too much thickener results in a product that is too tight and thick, noticeable by the fact that it thickens too quickly during the preparation process. Very minor changes in flour or cornstarch ingredients thicken the product while retaining moisture.
- Fat masks flavors. By decreasing the fat content in recipes, other flavors become more prominent. For this reason you can often decrease sugar contents along with fat contents without any noticeable change to the sweet flavors of a food. *The same principle applies to other foods.* If you make a clear soup creamy by adding milk or cream, you will find you need more salt, spice, or herbs to give the same amount of flavor. Conversely, when you use lower fat milks in cream soups you will often need less salt, herbs, or spices to heighten flavors. Cornstarch, flour, or oat bran may be needed to help thicken soups if you decrease the fat by using lower fat milks. Experiment with this technique to discover the flavor, textures, and tastes that you enjoy.

Pie Crust p146

- The focus of a pie can be the filling not the crust. The crusts are rolled thin in these variations. When a recipe calls for a top crust, try using lattice work or a crumb topping. This enhances the look of the pie, with less pastry needed.

Pie Crust *continued*

150

- A **crumb crust** that works well is
    1/2 cup (125 ml) oatmeal
    1 tsp (5 ml) cinnamon
    1 tbsp (15 ml) butter or margarine
    1 tbsp (15 ml) whole wheat flour
    1/4 cup (50 ml) brown sugar
Mix together and sprinkle over the pie before baking.

- Another option for crusts is using graham crumbs moistened with a small amount of butter or margarine. Try these proportions:
    1-1/4 cup (300 ml) graham cracker crumbs
    2 tbsp (30 ml) butter or margarine
Mix together. Spray an 8-inch (20-cm) pie plate with nonstick cooking spray. Put the crumb mixture in the pan and press down on the bottom and up the sides. Bake for about 10 minutes at 350°F (180°C) or until the crumbs are browning. Let cool before adding filling.

This crust works best for fillings that don't need to be baked after being put into the pie or for cheesecakes (either baked or unbaked).

Original Recipe

Here's your chance to work with these ideas and experiment with recipes that are your family favorites. Work through the process by setting up the original recipe and then choosing the changes you wish to make in each variation.

Guide to changes in salt, protein, fat, sugar, and fiber content using each variation.

VARIATION 1	VARIATION 2
Salt	Salt
Protein	Protein
Fat	Fat
Sugar	Sugar
Fiber	Fiber

VARIATION 1

—NOTES—

VARIATION 2

—NOTES—

VARIATION 3
Salt
Protein
Fat
Sugar
Fiber

VARIATION 3

—NOTES—

WRITE DOWN THE TIPS THAT WORK FOR YOU—

—USE THESE TIPS IN YOUR FAMILY FAVORITES!

Snacks are the little extras in life—the bites that tide us over to the next meal or help us make it through the night. Snacks come in many forms. They can be sweet or salty. Leftovers from other meals can become snacks. Sometimes snacks are fast foods and other times they are intricately prepared elaborate morsels. Snacks add spice and spontaneity to life. They can help to fuel our bodies for optimum energy levels.

As you learn to tune into your internal message systems you may find that your body is hungry more often than three times a day. This is okay. Researchers now suggest that many small snack meals are healthier for the body than three larger meals. The more constant availability of food gives a steadier amount of energy for the body and reduces the feast and famine response in the body. Learning when to snack by tuning into your body's hunger and fullness signals will keep your body from being famished, which sometimes leads to uncontrolled eating.

How do we know our bodies need a snack?
When did I last eat? Was it more than 3 or 4 hours ago? After several hours your body needs to be refueled.

Am I thirsty? To ensure adequate fluid balance, the body will send hunger messages when it is actually liquid that is required. Before eating, check out the effect of having something to drink. If this satisfies you, you were probably just thirsty. Do not use the dieting trick of masking hunger with liquids. Fluids are meant to rehydrate the body.

Am I feeling other symptoms of lowered blood sugar? If you experience headaches, shakiness, weakness, difficulty in concentration your body may be crying out for some energy foods. Don't ignore the body's hunger and fullness signals. Learn to listen to it and meet its needs.

Am I bored, tired, or upset? Often these feelings turn some people to food and others to smoking or drinking. Turning to these patterns can become destructive. Address the issues at hand and the hunger feelings may dissipate.

This section contains a variety of snack suggestions. When you have only an hour or two until meal time, a high carbohydrate snack can be satisfying. When a longer period between meals exists, go for the snack containing protein to sustain your energy levels.

Snacking is fun. It keeps life interesting and spontaneous. It is included in all parts of life and is part of the balance we all seek. We all need "time out" to rejuvenate mind, body, and soul, and replenish various energies that enable us to enjoy life to the fullest. Find balance in your life and it will become exciting and meaningful.

Snacks

FOR BEST RESULTS—read through the entire recipe, each variation, and the TIPS on page 166 before preparing this snack.

This delightful cookie is a family favorite. The oatmeal makes it chewy and the chocolate is yummy.

Double Chocolate Cookies

154

Yields 5 dozen

Original Recipe

1 cup	butter, softened	250 ml
1 cup	sugar	250 ml
1/2 cup	brown sugar, firmly packed	125 ml
1	egg	1
1/4 cup	water	50 ml
1 tsp	vanilla or almond extract	5 ml
1/2 tsp	baking soda	2 ml
1/3 cup	cocoa	75 ml
1/2 tsp	salt	2 ml
1-1/4 cup	all purpose flour	300 ml
3 cups	quick cooking oats	750 ml
2 cups	semisweet chocolate chips	500 ml

1. Cream butter, sugar, and egg in a large mixing bowl until fluffy.
2. Add water and vanilla and continue to beat well.
3. Add baking soda, salt, and cocoa continuing to beat the mixture well.
4. Add remaining ingredients in the order listed. Mix well.
5. Drop by rounded teaspoons full onto a greased cookie sheet, about 2 inches (5 cm) apart.
6. Bake at 375°F (190°C) for about 8 minutes or until almost no indentation remains when touched. It is better to just underbake these cookies because they stay softer when cooled. Over cooking will dry out the cookie.
7. Immediately remove from cookie sheet and cool on a cookie rack.
8. Once cooled, store in an airtight container to keep them as fresh as possible.

—NOTES—
• *These cookies freeze well.*

VARIATION 1

3/4 cup	**butter, softened**	**175 ml**
3/4 cup	**sugar**	**175 ml**
1/2 cup	brown sugar, **loosely packed**	125 ml
1	egg	1
1/4 cup	water	50 ml
1 tsp	vanilla or almond extract	5 ml
1/2 tsp	baking soda	2 ml
1/3 cup	cocoa	75 ml
1/2 tsp	salt	2 ml
1-1/4 cup	all purpose flour	300 ml
3 cups	quick cooking oats	750 ml
1-1/2 cups	**semisweet chocolate chips**	**375 ml**

1. Mix and bake as per the original recipe with the following alterations: use a nonstick cooking spray to grease the pans; flatten drop cookies to about 1/4 to 1/2 inch (.6 to 1.3 cm) thick with a fork or your hand before baking resulting in a flatter cookie; and bake only 6 to 8 minutes to keep cookies from drying out. *Cookies will not appear to be done, just firming up around the edges.*

—NOTES—
• *Decreasing the amount of butter and sugar in this recipe decreases the overall fat and sugar content. The flavor and texture are less rich for healthier eating.*
• *The cookies do not work well as drop cookies because of the decreased fat.*
• *The decrease in chocolate chips is not noticed. Many of the chips are left in the bottom of the bowl if you use a full 2 cups (500 ml).*

Guide to changes in salt, sugar, protein, fat, and fiber content using each variation.

	VARIATION 1	VARIATION 2	VARIATION 3
Salt		▼	▼▼
Sugar	▼	▼▼	▼▼▼
Protein		▲	▲▲
Fat	▼	▼▼	▼▼▼
Fiber	▼	▲	▲

155

VARIATION 2

2/3 cup	butter, softened	150 ml
2 tbsp	peanut butter	30 ml
1/2 cup	sugar	125 ml
1/2 cup	brown sugar	125 ml
1	egg	1
1/4 cup	water	50 ml
1 tsp	vanilla or almond extract	5 ml
1/2 tsp	baking soda	2 ml
1/3 cup	cocoa	75 ml
	a pinch of salt	
1 cup	all purpose flour	250 ml
3 tbsp	whole wheat flour	45 ml
3 cups	quick cooking oats	750 ml
1-1/2 cups	semisweet chocolate chips	375 ml

1. Mix and bake as per Variation 1. Add peanut butter to butter during the creaming process. Remember to use the flatten method and underbake these cookies.

—NOTES—
• Adding peanut butter while decreasing the butter content slightly decreases the fat content of these cookies while increasing the protein content. This makes them a more well balanced snack.
• The finished product has a wonderful nutty flavor mixed with the chocolate.
• Color and texture of the finished product doesn't seem to vary; however, you may notice that the dough is a little drier before baking.

VARIATION 3

1/2 cup	butter, softened	125 ml
1/4 cup	peanut butter	50 ml
1/2 cup	sugar	125 ml
1/3 cup	brown sugar	75 ml
1	egg	1
1/4 cup	water	50 ml
1 tsp	vanilla or almond extract	5 ml
1/2 tsp	baking soda	2 ml
1/3 cup	cocoa	75 ml
	omit salt	
3/4 cup	all purpose flour	175 ml
1/3 cup	whole wheat flour	75 ml
3 cups	quick cooking oats	750 ml
1 cup	semisweet chocolate chips	250 ml

1. Mix as per Variation 2. Bake cookies only 6 to 8 minutes or until the outsides look just done and the middle still looks soft. Lower fat cookies taste better and remain moister if you underbake them.

—NOTES—
• This variation is lower in fat and sugar and higher in protein content.
• Decreasing the chocolate chips lowers the fat and sugar content in these cookies.
• You may find that the cookies need to be made a little smaller to get the same number as in the original recipe.
• This cookie has a more festive speckled look because some of the oatmeal color stays light. Kids like the new look!
• The texture of the cookie is a little more crumbly. Freezing the cookies and taking them out about 10 minutes before serving eliminates the drier texture.

Strawberry Pops

156

Yields 3 cups (750 ml) or about 6 to 8 popsicles

Every parent looks for a quick and easy snack to give their kids. This popsicle takes only a few minutes to prepare and is high in calcium and vitamins. The tangy fruity taste is irresistible. It is a winner as an after school snack as well as a lovely dessert.

Original Recipe

| 3/4 cup | strawberry yogurt | 175 ml |
| 2 cups | frozen strawberries | 500 ml |

1. Combine all ingredients in a blender or food processor.
2. Cover and blend for 2 to 3 minutes.
3. Pour into 8—3 oz (85 ml) paper cups or popsicle holders.
4. When partially frozen insert sticks.
5. Freeze until solid.

VARIATION 1

| 3/4 cup | **light, strawberry yogurt** | **175 ml** |
| 2 cups | frozen strawberries | 500 ml |

1. Mix and freeze as per the original recipe.

—NOTES—

• *Strawberries can be blended either frozen or thawed.*
• *One package (10 oz or 284 ml) frozen strawberries is equal to about 2 cups (500 ml).*
• *If you have any leftover mixture, enjoy it as a tasty snack before freezing.*

—NOTES—

• *Read the labels on yogurt and other dairy products. The percentage milk fat (% M.F.) may vary considerably from one brand to another. Plain yogurt usually has about 1.5% M.F., fruit flavors usually have about 1.4% M.F., and low-fat yogurt about .9% M.F. or less. Use a low-fat yogurt or make your own yogurt with 1% or skim milk.*
• *People with diabetes can adapt this recipe by using aspartame sweetened yogurt and unsweetened strawberries.*

Strawberry Pops, Variation 2, p157

Favorite Fruit Drink (cranberry), Variation 1, p122;
Double Chocolate Cookies, Variation 3, p155; Soft Raisin Cookies, Variation 1, p162

Guide to changes in salt, sugar, fat, and fiber content using each variation.

	VARIATION 1	VARIATION 2	VARIATION 3
Salt			
Sugar		▼	▼
Fat	▼	▼	▼▼
Fiber			

157

VARIATION 2

3/4 cup	light, strawberry yogurt	175 ml
2 cups	**frozen strawberries, unsweetened**	**500 ml**

1. Mix and freeze as per the original recipe.

VARIATION 3

3/4 cup	**plain skim milk yogurt**	175 ml
1 tsp	**vanilla**	5 ml
1 tsp	**softened honey**	5 ml
2 cups	frozen strawberries, unsweetened	500 ml

1. Combine all ingredients in a blender or food processor including honey and vanilla. Honey can be softened by putting it in the microwave on high for a few seconds.
2. Cover and blend for 2 to 3 minutes.
3. Pour into 8 —3 oz (85 ml) paper cups or popsicle holders.
4. When partially frozen insert sticks.
5. Freeze until solid.

—NOTES—
• *This variation has a less sweet flavor.*
• *The strawberry flavor is more pronounced when there is less added sugar. The strawberries have enough of their own natural sweet flavor.*
• *The final result is a tangier lighter tasting popsicle or dessert with a bright fruity taste.*
• *You may notice a few icy crystals in the finished product because of the decreased fat and sugar contents.*

—NOTES—
• *Choosing to use skim milk plain yogurt decreases the amount of preservatives, sugar, and fat content in this recipe. You can then choose how sweet you want to make these snacks. 1 tsp (5 ml) orange juice concentrate instead of the honey is a lovely option and adds a nice orange flavor.*
• *Lowering the fat and sugar content with the same water content means the final product becomes more of an icy texture.*
• *This version has a tangy fruit flavor that has the texture of an icy commercial popsicle.*

These cheesy snacks are a great after-school snack as well as being a delicious finger food at a party. They freeze well, making them a convenient treat at any time of the day.

Cheese & Sesame Crisps

Yields 4 dozen

Original Recipe

2 cups	cheddar cheese, grated, loose	500 ml
2 cups	all purpose flour	500 ml
1 cup	butter or margarine, melted	250 ml
2 cups	rice crispies	500 ml
1 tbsp	onions, minced	15 ml
1 tbsp	sesame seeds	15 ml
1/4 tsp	seasoned salt	1 ml
3/4 tsp	dry mustard	3 ml
1/8 tsp	Worcestershire sauce	.5 ml

1. Place all ingredients into a bowl.
2. Mix together well, may need to use your hands.
3. Roll into small 1 inch (2.5 cm) balls.
4. Place on a greased cookie sheet, about 2-1/2 inches (6.3 cm) apart.
5. Press down with a fork to about 1/4 to 1/2 inch (.6 to 1.3 cm) thickness.
6. Bake at 350°F (180°C) for 12 to 15 minutes or until light brown.
7. Serve warm or cold.

—NOTES—
• *These crisps freeze well.*

VARIATION 1

2 cups	cheddar cheese, grated, loose	500 ml
2 cups	all purpose flour	500 ml
3/4 cup	**butter or margarine, melted**	**175 ml**
1/4 cup	**plain yogurt**	**50 ml**
2 cups	rice crispies	500 ml
1 tbsp	onions, minced	15 ml
1 tbsp	sesame seeds	15 ml
1/4 tsp	seasoned salt	1 ml
3/4 tsp	dry mustard	3 ml
1/8 tsp	Worcestershire sauce	.5 ml

1. Mix and bake as per the original recipe. You may find that these brown in 10 to 12 minutes due to the decrease in fat content.

—NOTES—
• *If you do not like the sharp taste of cheddar cheese, replace it with mozzarella cheese. The color of the crisps will change but the flavor is still wonderful.*
• *The butter has been decreased to lower the overall fat content in this recipe.*
• *The texture and flavor doesn't really change with this variation; however, you may find that it is more difficult to incorporate all the rice crispies without mashing some.*

Guide to changes in salt, protein, fat, and fiber content using each variation.

	VARIATION 1	VARIATION 2	VARIATION 3
Salt		▼	▼▼
Protein	▲	▲	▲▼
Fat	▼	▼▼	▼▼▼
Fiber		▲	▲▲

VARIATION 2

1 cup	cheddar cheese, grated, loose	250 ml
1 cup	part-skim mozzarella cheese, grated, loose	250 ml
1-1/2 cups	all purpose flour	375 ml
1/3 cup	whole wheat flour	75 ml
3/4 cup	butter or margarine, melted	175 ml
1/4 cup	plain yogurt	50 ml
2 cups	rice crispies	500 ml
1 tbsp	onions, minced	15 ml
1 tbsp	sesame seeds	15 ml
1/4 tsp	seasoned salt	1 ml
1/2 tsp	dry mustard	2 ml
1/8 tsp	Worcestershire sauce	.5 ml

1. Mix and bake as per Variation 1.

—NOTES—

• *Cheddar cheese is quite high in fat and salt. Moving toward using part-skim mozzarella cheese lowers the overall fat and salt content in this recipe. The part-skim mozzarella adds an additional stringy texture to the snacks that is a bonus to these chewy snacks.*
• *The color of this variation is a lighter orange.*
• *As the fat in these crisps decrease, you need less seasonings to give the flavor. Therefore the dry mustard was decreased.*
• *This variation is higher in fiber because of the added whole wheat flour.*

VARIATION 3

1/4 cup	pureed 1% cottage cheese omit cheddar cheese	50 ml
1-1/2 cup	part-skim mozzarella cheese, grated, loose	375 ml
1 cup	all purpose flour	250 ml
2/3 cup	whole wheat flour	150 ml
3/4 cup	butter or margarine, melted	175 ml
1/4 cup	plain yogurt	50 ml
2 cups	rice crispies	500 ml
1 tbsp	onions, minced	15 ml
1 tbsp	sesame seeds	15 ml
1/8 tsp	seasoned salt	.5 ml
1/2 tsp	dry mustard	2 ml
1/8 tsp	Worcestershire sauce	.5 ml

1. Add pureed cottage cheese to the bowl before mixing together.
2. Prepare and bake as per Variation 1.

—NOTES—

• *Cottage cheese is lower in fat and salt than cheddar cheese or part-skim mozzarella cheese. Using it in this recipe gives a protein option lower in fat.*
• *Omitting the cheddar cheese and moving to part-skim mozzarella alone decreases the fat and salt content in this variation. It also changes the color of these snacks to a creamy color with a crispy texture.*
• *Moving to more whole wheat flour increases the insoluble fiber content in this recipe.*
• *This variation has decreased the total amount of protein content slightly.*

Pizza on a Bun

Yields 7 to 8 cups (1.75 to 2 L) pizza mix
Variation 1 yields 6 to 7 cups (1.5 to 1.75 L)
Variation 2 yields 5 cups (1.25 L)
Variation 3 yields 6 cups (1.5 L)

This tasty mixture is a favorite party snack. It is easy to prepare and stores well so you can mix it up ahead of time. Serve on your favorite bun, bagel, or toast for a delicious well rounded snack. Serve it with a salad for a quick lunch option. This recipe adapts well to most pizza ingredients.

Original Recipe

1	onion, finely chopped	1
2 cups	pepperoni, finely cubed	500 ml
2 tbsp	oil	30 ml
10 oz	canned mushrooms with juice	284 ml
1	green pepper, finely chopped	1
1 lb	mozzarella cheese, grated	500 g
10 oz	can tomato soup	284 ml
1 tsp	oregano	5 ml
3/4 tsp	Italian seasoning	3 ml
1/8 tsp	Worcestershire sauce	.5 ml
1/8 tsp	tabasco sauce	.5 ml
10 to 12	buns, halved	10 to 12

1. Fry onions and pepperoni in oil in a heavy saucepan. Continue to fry until onions are translucent.
2. Add mushrooms and green peppers to the saucepan and fry 1 minute more.
3. Remove from heat, drain, and cool.
4. Place cooled meat and onion mixture in a mixing bowl and add the remainder of the ingredients.
5. Stir until everything is mixed together.
6. Spread on half a bun of your choice.
7. Broil in oven until the sauce is brown and bubbly.
8. Serve warm.

—NOTES—
• *1 lb (500 g) of cheese is equal to 4 cups (1 L) cheese.*
• *This pizza sauce mix can be stored in the refrigerator for 1 week or the freezer for 3 to 4 months.*

VARIATION 1

1	onion, finely chopped	1
1-1/2 cups	**pepperoni, finely cubed**	**375 ml**
	omit oil	
10 oz	canned mushrooms with juice	284 ml
1	green pepper, finely chopped	1
1 lb	mozzarella cheese, grated	500 g
10 oz	can tomato soup	284 ml
1 tsp	oregano	5 ml
3/4 tsp	Italian seasoning	3 ml
1/8 tsp	Worcestershire sauce	.5 ml
1/8 tsp	tabasco sauce	.5 ml
10 to 12	buns, halved	10 to 12

1. Cook onions and pepperoni in a nonstick pan sprayed with nonstick cooking spray.
2. Prepare as per the original recipe.

—NOTES—
• *Using less pepperoni decreases the fat and protein content in this recipe. It also lowers the salt content.*
• *Using a nonstick frying pan allows you to cook the vegetables and pepperoni without added fat.*
• *Pepperoni is an accent flavor. The decrease is not noticeable as the flavor is still retained.*

Guide to changes in salt, protein, fat, and fiber content using each variation.	**VARIATION 1**	**VARIATION 2**	**VARIATION 3**
	Salt ▼	Salt ▼▼	Salt ▼▼▼
	Protein ▼	Protein ▼▼	Protein ▼▼▼
	Fat ▼	Fat ▼▼	Fat ▼▼▼
	Fiber	Fiber	Fiber ▲

161

VARIATION 2

1	onion, finely chopped	1
1 cup	**pepperoni, finely cubed**	**250 ml**
10 oz	canned mushrooms with juice	284 ml
1	green pepper, finely chopped	1
1 lb	mozzarella cheese, grated	500 g
10 oz	**can "Healthy Request" tomato soup**	**284 ml**
1 tsp	oregano	5 ml
3/4 tsp	Italian seasoning	3 ml
1/8 tsp	Worcestershire sauce	.5 ml
1/8 tsp	tabasco sauce	.5 ml
10 to 12	buns, halved	10 to 12

1. Prepare as per Variation 1.

—NOTES—

• *This variation has reduced the pepperoni content farther. This in turn decreases the fat, protein, and salt content in this recipe.*
• *Moving toward less meat slowly begins to move this recipe toward a healthier balance between carbohydrates and protein.*
• *Serve the pizza bun mix on whole wheat buns or bagels to provide an appetizing texture and flavor to the snack. These breads are made with whole grains and provide more fiber than white buns.*
• *Healthy Request soups are lower in salt and some are lower in fat than regular canned soups. There doesn't seem to be any flavor change with this change.*

VARIATION 3

1	onion, finely chopped	1
1 cup	pepperoni, finely cubed	250 ml
1 cup	**prepared chick peas chopped or sliced**	**250 ml**
10 oz	canned mushrooms with juice	284 ml
1	green pepper, finely chopped	1
1 lb	**part-skim mozzarella cheese, grated**	**500 g**
10 oz	can "Healthy Request" tomato soup	284 ml
1 tsp	oregano	5 ml
3/4 tsp	Italian seasoning	3 ml
1/8 tsp	Worcestershire sauce	.5 ml
1/8 tsp	tabasco sauce	.5 ml
10 to 12	buns, halved	10 to 12

1. Prepare as per Variation 1, adding chick peas to the mixture when adding tomato soup.

—NOTES—

• *Part-skim mozzarella cheese has a lovely flavor with a lower fat and salt content than regular mozzarella. The cheese is also slightly stringier in texture.*
• *Adding chick peas (also known as garbanzo beans) to this recipe adds extra fiber, complex carbohydrates, and vegetable protein.*
• *Chopping chick peas up makes them look like mushrooms so people who don't enjoy legumes will hardly notice the change.*
• *As you move to lower fat ingredients in the recipe, you may find the flavor improves when you prepare the mix a day in advance. This allows the flavors to have a chance to mingle.*
• *Decreasing the fat content makes the spices more apparent. This is a delicious variation.*

FOR BEST RESULTS—read through the entire recipe, each variation, and the TIPS on page 167 before preparing this snack.

Soft Raisin Cookies

Yields 6 dozen
Variation 2 and 3 *yields about 5 dozen*

Cookies are a favorite snack for most families. These cookies are soft and flavorful. In these variations you will enjoy a delicious snack that becomes lower in fat and higher in fiber content. If you have a favorite cookie, try using the ideas suggested here to modify your recipe.

Original Recipe

2 cups	raisins	500 ml
1 cup	boiling water	250 ml
1 cup	shortening	250 ml
2 cups	sugar	500 ml
3	eggs	3
1 tsp	vanilla	5 ml
3-1/2 cups	all purpose flour	875 ml
1 tsp	baking powder	5 ml
1 tsp	baking soda	5 ml
1 tsp	salt	5 ml
1/4 tsp	cloves	1 ml
1/4 tsp	nutmeg	1 ml
1/2 tsp	cinnamon	2 ml

1. Put raisins in a small saucepan. Pour boiling water over raisins and place over high heat until the mixture boils.
2. Cover and reduce heat to low and cook for 5 minutes.
3. Cool this mixture.
4. Cream shortening and sugar.
5. Add eggs and vanilla and beat until fluffy.
6. Add cooled raisins along with any remaining water to creamed mixture and mix well.
7. Sift dry ingredients together including the spices.
8. Slowly add dry ingredients to the wet ingredients.
9. Drop by heaping teaspoons onto a greased cookie sheet.
10. Bake at 350 °F (180°C) for 10 to 12 minutes or until cookies are a light golden brown.

—NOTES—
• *These cookies freeze very well.*

VARIATION 1

1-1/2 cups	raisins	375 ml
1 cup	boiling water	250 ml
3/4 cup	**shortening**	**175 ml**
1-3/4 cups	**sugar**	**425 ml**
3	eggs	3
1 tsp	vanilla	5 ml
3-1/2 cups	all purpose flour	875 ml
1 tsp	baking powder	5 ml
1 tsp	baking soda	5 ml
1 tsp	salt	5 ml
1/4 tsp	cloves	1 ml
1/4 tsp	nutmeg	1 ml
1/2 tsp	cinnamon	2 ml

1. Mix, prepare, and bake as per the original recipe.

—NOTES—
• *If you chop the raisins into smaller pieces you can use less while still adding flavor and color. Depending on preference you may enjoy the texture of biting into fewer juicy whole raisins or having raisin pieces in every bite.*
• *Raisins are a wonderful source of iron and fiber, however, they are also high in concentrated fruit sugars. By decreasing them a little you have decreased the sweet content without changing the flavor or texture. You still get a raisin or two in every bite.*
• *Decreasing the shortening is hardly noticed in this recipe and decreases the overall fat content. The cookies are still chewy and delicious.*
• *The change in sugar content is not noticeable.*

Guide to changes in salt, sugar, fat, and fiber content using each variation.

	VARIATION 1	VARIATION 2	VARIATION 3
Salt		▼	▼▼
Sugar	▼	▼▼	▼▼
Fat	▼	▼	▼▼
Fiber		▲	▲

VARIATION 2

1-1/2 cups	raisins	375 ml
1 cup	boiling water	250 ml
3/4 cup	shortening	175 ml
1-1/2 cups	**sugar**	**375 ml**
3	eggs	3
1 tsp	vanilla	5 ml
3 cups	**all purpose flour**	**750 ml**
1/3 cup	**whole wheat flour**	**75 ml**
1 tsp	baking powder	5 ml
1 tsp	baking soda	5 ml
1/2 tsp	**salt**	**2 ml**
1/4 tsp	cloves	1 ml
1/4 tsp	nutmeg	1 ml
1/2 tsp	cinnamon	2 ml

1. Mix and bake as per Variation 1 with the following exception: sift all dry ingredients **except** the whole wheat flour. Add whole wheat flour after sifting dry ingredients and stir together.

—NOTES—

• *This variation is lower in sugar. The raisins and spices give these cookies a wonderful sweet taste so you don't notice the decreased sugar.*

• *Whole wheat flour is added to replace some of the all purpose flour. This step increases the fiber content in these cookies giving them moe texture and making them a hearty snack.*

• *The fat in this variation is left unchanged so that you can learn to enjoy the added flavor and texture of the fiber.*

• *Storing cookies in a sealed container helps to keep them from drying out. This becomes more important as the fat content is decreased.*

VARIATION 3

1-1/2 cups	raisins	375 ml
1 cup	boiling water	250 ml
2/3 cup	**shortening**	**150 ml**
1 cup	**sugar**	**250 ml**
3/4 cup	**unsweetened applesauce**	**175 ml**
3	eggs	3
1 tsp	vanilla	5 ml
3 cups	all purpose flour	750 ml
1/3 cup	whole wheat flour	75 ml
1 tsp	baking powder	5 ml
1 tsp	baking soda	5 ml
	omit salt	
1/4 tsp	cloves	1 ml
1/4 tsp	nutmeg	1 ml
1/2 tsp	cinnamon	2 ml

1. Add applesauce to wet ingredients after the shortening and sugar are creamed. Follow instructions as per Variation 2.

—NOTES—

• *Adding unsweetened applesauce adds extra moisture and sweetness to this recipe. This means that you don't notice the decrease in sugar and fat.*

• *The baking soda seems to have a salty enough taste that we can omit the table salt.*

FOR BEST RESULTS—read through the entire yogurt and yogurt cheese recipes and the TIPS on p168 before preparing this snack.

Yogurt or yogurt cheese are tasty low-fat additions to many recipes. They can be used alone as a snack, as an accent in a main dish, or as a dessert with fruit. They can be used in place of or in combination with higher fat products such as sour cream, butter, oil, or cream cheese. There seems to be no end to the uses of yogurt.

164

Yogurt

Yields approximately 8 cups (2 L)

The Process

Supplies you need

—Milk/yogurt thermometer (available at health food stores)
—Container that can be sterilized and has a sealing lid
—Yogurt starter (yogurt culture or plain yogurt)
—An insulated cooler that fits snugly around the yogurt container or an insulated wrap (*see* TIPS p168)

8 cups	milk (any kind)	4 L
1/2 cup	powdered milk	125 ml
2 tsp	unflavored gelatin (optional)	10 ml
1/4 cup	plain yogurt, **or**	50 ml
1 packet	yogurt culture	1 packet

1. Sterilize all cooking utensils and containers by pouring boiling water over them.
2. Mix milk, powdered milk, and gelatin (optional) in a microwave-safe bowl or in the top of a double boiler.
3. Heat milk mixture using either the microwave or double boiler to 180°F (82°C).
4. Once it has reached this temperature, put the bowl into a cold water bath (being careful not to get water into the milk) and cool to 118°F (48°C).
5. Once the mixture has cooled, add the yogurt starter (plain yogurt or yogurt culture) and mix.
6. Pour into sterilized yogurt container. Quickly cover container and place in insulated cooler or wrap, cover, and incubate the milk until it has curdled (approximately 4 to 8 hours). *The milk must stay between 106° and 110°F (41° and 43°C) in order to incubate properly.*
7. The yogurt is ready when it has thickened.
8. Remove 1/4 cup (50 ml) yogurt off the top of the fresh yogurt and place in a small sterilized jar with lid to use as a starter for the next batch.
9. Refrigerate the remaining yogurt until you use it.
Note *If making yogurt cheese, omit the gelatin.*

MAKING AN INSULATED WRAP

You need thick foam rubber (at least 1-in or 2.5-cm thick) and plastic that will cover this foam rubber (a plastic bag works well). Cut the foam rubber into 3 pieces: one piece to form the bottom of the container, one longer piece to wrap snugly around the yogurt container, and a third to act as a lid that will slide snugly into the cylinder over the container. Wrap each piece of foam with plastic and tape securely. Put the wrapped pieces together using tape to make a snug basket for the yogurt container. This helps keep the heat in and is easier to clean if it gets dirty.

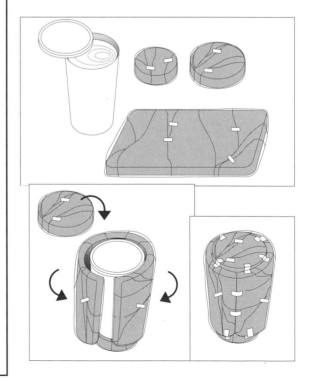

IF THE YOGURT DOESN'T TURN OUT, SOME POSSIBLE REASONS:

1. Your utensils were not properly sterilized

If the utensils aren't completely clean it can bring foreign bacteria into the yogurt mixture that may keep the yogurt from curdling.

What to try—Make sure that you are starting with clean containers and utensils. Then pour boiling water over everything that will come in contact with the yogurt mixture. Be sure that the surface that you lay your utensils on is clean and sterile as well.

2. Your yogurt got too cold or hot during the curdling time

If there was a draft where you stored your yogurt or your insulation around the container wasn't complete, the yogurt mixture may have cooled down too quickly and not had enough time to incubate at the right temperature.

What to try—Try storing your yogurt in your oven or under a blanket to prevent drafts from contacting the container. Avoid standing your container near windows or doors where drafts are more prevalent. Make sure that your insulated container is tightly wrapped, with no places for drafts to enter.

3. The yogurt starter you used was ineffective

If your yogurt starter was old or contaminated, you may end up with a yogurt that won't curdle.

What to try—Try buying and using some new culture at your local health food store in the refrigerator section. Don't allow this culture to get too warm on the way home from the store (i.e. don't put it on the dash of your car in the sun or in a pocket right next to your body because heat may decrease the efficacy of the yogurt culture). Or try buying a fresh container of plain yogurt from your local grocery store and use the first 1/4 cup (50 ml) of this container to act as a starter for a new batch of yogurt.

Yogurt Cheese
Yields 1-1/2 cups (375 ml)

The Recipe

3 cups	unflavored low-fat natural yogurt (no gelatin added)	750 ml
1	medium size strainer	1
	cheesecloth, or	
2	coffee filters	2

1. Line the strainer with cheesecloth or coffee filters.
2. Place strainer in another bowl to catch moisture that drips through cheesecloth or coffee filters.
3. Put yogurt in strainer and cover with plastic wrap.
4. Allow yogurt to set for 3 hours (soft yogurt cheese) or from 8 to 10 hours (firm yogurt cheese) or overnight.
5. Discard liquid under strainer.
6. Place yogurt cheese into a clean container with a lid. and store in refrigerator. Yogurt cheese keeps about one week.

Some ideas for using yogurt cheese

• In an herb cheese spread for putting on crackers. Use 1 cup (250 ml) of **firm** yogurt cheese with 1 clove garlic (minced) and 1/4 to 1/2 tsp (1 to 2 ml) each of two herbs such as rosemary and basil or dill weed and chives.

• In a dessert topping to replace whipped cream. Use 1 cup (250 ml) **soft** yogurt cheese with 2 tbsp (30 ml) of a sweetening agent such as sugar, honey, or aspartame, 1 tsp (5 ml) vanilla or almond extract, and 1 tsp (5 ml) lemon or orange rind.

• In dressings or dips in place of mayonnaise or sour cream.

• In hollandaise sauce in place of butter and/or cream.

• On top of potatoes in place of or mixed with sour cream.

• In stroganoff in place of or mixed with sour cream to add a lovely tangy flavor.

Please read

Tips
*The following information for the recipes given in this section
will help you make choices and add variety to your meals.*

Double Chocolate Cookies p154

• Vanilla, almond, and lemon extracts all provide a sweet flavor and can be increased in a recipe when decreasing sugar for desserts, muffins, cookies, and breads.

• You can even decrease the amount of chocolate chips to 3/4 cup (175 ml) and still have plenty of chips in each cookie to give the chocolate texture and flavor. This further decreases the fat and sugar content in these cookies.

• Using smaller-sized chips gives each cookie an accent flavor that is very satisfying.

• Oatmeal is an excellent form of soluble fiber. Soluble fiber becomes a gel-like substance when digested and seems to have an effect on slowing blood glucose absorption and lowering cholesterol levels.[14,15] The protein in peanut butter mixed with the oatmeal makes this cookie a good snack choice.

• You may choose to increase the amount of whole wheat flour in this recipe and decrease the all purpose flour. *See* p78 for replacement formula.
Special note People with diabetes can replace the sugar in this recipe with artificial sweetener like aspartame or brown sugar replacements. The baking process decreases the sweetness somewhat if you use aspartame, and the cookie is still tasty. Using sugar replacements gives a slightly bitter aftertaste. Using sugar replacements produces cookies that are a little drier in texture than those using sugar. Freezing the cookies seems to compensate for the dryness. The additional protein of the peanut butter along with the fat in these cookies slows the absorption of glucose in the bloodstream. The combination of carbohydrates and protein in these cookies makes it a good snack option for people with diabetes.

• Placing an apple in your cookie container can help to keep cookies or other bread products moist. Don't place the apple in the freezer with your baking because it just freezes and serves no purpose.

Strawberry Pops p156

• Strawberries are high in vitamin C. Vitamin C is thought to play an important role in cancer prevention. Vitamin C is destroyed in the cooking process. Fresh frozen fruits are not cooked so using them in this recipe maintains the high vitamin C content. The yogurt and milk are a great source of calcium. Together these ingredients make a wonderful snack option.

• If you choose to use this recipe as a dessert item in a bowl you may want to freeze it in a metal pan that is the right size to make this mixture about 1/2-inch (1-cm) thick. Stir the mixture every half hour or so until the mixture is the consistency of ice cream. Serve in dessert bowls garnished with fresh strawberries. This makes an irresistible fruity summer dessert.

• If you are working with a child or adult who is having trouble eating a well-balanced diet, another variation to this recipe is to cut the plain yogurt in half and add 1/2 cup (125 ml) pureed 1% cottage cheese. This doesn't change the flavor very much and increases the protein content in this snack.

Cheese & Sesame Crisps p158

• When you want to change your own recipe to include more whole wheat flour try the following formula:

**1 cup (250 ml) all purpose flour =
2/3 cup (150 ml) whole wheat flour**

• Things to remember when you are increasing

fiber content:

Increase your fiber intake gradually so that you will enjoy the shift in flavors and textures.

Doing it gradually helps your body to get used to the change to more fiber and minimizes the effects of bloating and stomach discomfort.

Drink plenty of fluids, especially with insoluble fiber, so that it will be able to perform its function of regularity.

• Whole wheat fiber is an insoluble form of fiber. Increasing the total fiber content in your diet has many benefits such as improved bowel regularity, a longer feeling of fullness, and a reduction in the risks of some cancers such as colon and rectal cancers.

Pizza on a Bun p160

Special technique tip When using herbs, try whole leaf herbs and rub them between your hands over the other ingredients. This helps extract the lovely flavors of the herbs.

• If you choose to use whole tomatoes and blend them to make the sauce, this will lower the sugar, salt, and other preservatives in this recipe. A much more tomato-flavored sauce also results.

• For people who don't enjoy the flavor of processed meat or find they cannot eat it, use 1 lb (500 g) of extra lean ground beef prepared in the microwave (*see* Hearty Hamburger Soup, p36 for instructions). Or you can use leftover meat or chicken on your pizza.

• Another option is to increase the onion, green pepper, and chick pea content and make it a meatless snack or meal choice. If you choose to do this you may also want to increase the herbs in this recipe to enhance the flavors. This may be necessary because some of the flavors of pizza come from the fat and spices found in processed meats. Some herbs you might like to try are basil, thyme, oregano, and rosemary.

• Canned chick peas can be stored in an airtight container in the refrigerator for several weeks and then used in any salad or sauce you are preparing the next week.

• If your local grocery store does not carry Healthy Request soups, ask your grocer if they will bring them in for you. These soups have a long shelf life and make them a lower risk product. Many consumers are looking for healthier choice foods and these products are often a good selling item.

Soft Raisin Cookies p162

• You can substitute a soft margarine or butter for shortening in this recipe. It is a matter of preference.

• *See* p78 for the formula to replace all purpose flour with whole wheat flour.

• Whole wheat fiber is an insoluble fiber. Increasing it in your diet can improve your bowel regularity, decrease your risks for certain cancers, and help to satisfy your hunger.

• Things to remember when you are increasing fiber content:

Increase your fiber intake gradually so that you will enjoy the shift in flavors and textures.

Doing it gradually helps your body to get used to the change to more fiber and minimizes the effects of bloating and stomach discomfort.

Drink plenty of fluids, especially with insoluble fiber, so that it will be able to perform its function of regularity.

• Molasses and/or honey can be used to replace sugar in sweetening foods. Molasses gives the cookies a distinctive flavor and dark color. Both honey and molasses give these cookies an added soft texture when used in place of sugar. You will need less honey as it is a more concentrated form of sugar. Try 3/4 cup (175 ml) honey for each 1 cup (250 ml) white sugar. Molasses is less sweet than honey and can be replaced cup for cup in the recipe.

Yogurt p164

• You can buy yogurt with varying percentages of milk fat (% M.F.). It is important to read the labels because the % M.F. may vary greatly from brand to brand and yet the taste may be similar. Plain yogurt has about 1.5% M.F., fruit flavored yogurt has about 1.4% M.F., and frozen yogurt has about 6.3% M.F. If you are looking for low-fat yogurt, find the containers that have about .9% M.F. or less.

• Making your own yogurt is quite a bit cheaper and you can use skim milk to make it. Skim milk doesn't alter the taste very much and is much lower in fat, making it a healthier choice yet retaining all the taste.

• If you decide to make your own yogurt, you may decide to invest in a yogurt maker. They are readily available in health food stores, but you can find them at garage sales and in some department stores, as well. The method outlined at the left, however, works equally as well.

• Make sure your starter yogurt is fresh. Remove 1/4 cup (50 ml) of yogurt from the container *before* using purchased yogurt for some other purpose. Also be sure that the ingredients on the container list bacteria culture or yogurt culture. Yogurt that has inactivated cultures will not work.

• Skim milk gives a runnier yogurt because there is less fat or milk solids in this milk. To compensate for this, add a little more unflavored gelatin or another 1/2 cup (125 ml) powdered milk. Adding 2 tsp (10 ml) unflavored gelatin to the skim milk mixture is enough to get a yogurt with a nice consistency.

• Many people like to stir in 1 to 2 tsp (5 to 10 ml) vanilla extract once the yogurt has curdled. This is especially nice if you are using the yogurt for fruit and dessert recipes.

• You must refrigerate the yogurt until you use it. It can last in the refrigerator for up to 2 months. It depends on how may times you use it and take it out of the refrigerator, and if the utensils you use to remove the yogurt each time are clean.

Yogurt Cheese p165

• It is important to use yogurt that contains no gelatin or thickeners.

• Use clean equipment to make and store this cheese. The yogurt cheese will grow mold more quickly if you use utensils or containers that aren't clean.

• Yogurt cheese is easy to make and has a tangy flavor like cream cheese, quark cheese, or sour cream, and is significantly lower in fat than these products. It can be used in place of or in combination with these products for a tasty lower fat option.

• Soft yogurt cheese (3-hour stage) can be used in place of sour cream, whipping cream, or mayonnaise in recipes.

• Firm yogurt cheese (8 to 10 hour stage or overnight) can be used in place of cream cheese or quark cheese.

WRITE DOWN THE TIPS THAT WORK FOR YOU—

Congratulations! By now you will have tried some or all of the ideas in this book. You now have the tools you need to "tailor your tastes" to reflect healthier eating choices. We challenge you to take these ideas, tips, and techniques, and transfer them to your own kitchen. Use them in your favorite recipes so that your family can enjoy the process toward healthier eating. Take time out with your family to enjoy the process of preparing and eating meals. The rewards are well worth the time and effort.

Remember, make changes gradually. There is no "right" place for you to be in the process of healthier eating. Find the tastes and textures that satisfy you. Make changes and stick with them for several months before making new changes. Enjoy the new tastes, flavors, and textures you are experiencing on your journey to healthier eating. Enjoyable eating is an important part of healthy living. Have fun!

—USE THESE TIPS IN YOUR FAMILY FAVORITES!

TASTE AND APPETITE ANALYSIS 2

1 Never
2 Rarely
3 Sometimes
4 Often
5 Very Often
6 Always

☐ I eat at least three meals a day.

☐ Foods that are good for you taste good.

☐ I find it easy to make changes in recipes.

☐ Healthy meals are easy to prepare.

☐ I eat fewer fatty foods.

☐ I eat snacks between meals if I am hungry.

☐ It is easy to find ingredients to make healthier meals.

☐ I change recipes to decrease the energy and/or fat content.

☐ I enjoy the taste of lower fat foods.

☐ I enjoy foods that have a crisp, crunchy, or chewy texture.

☐ I enjoy experimenting with my regular recipes.

☐ I start my day with breakfast.

☐ I eat more potatoes, rice, pasta, and legumes than meat at my meals.

☐ I read labels to help me make choices to suit my taste preferences.

☐ When I finish eating, I feel satisfied and energized.

☐ I use herbs to add taste to a meal.

☐ **TOTAL** Add **4** to the total to determine your percentage.
   (Compare this score with the same quiz at the end of the book)

Make copies of your completed Analyses (pp19 and 170) and mail to
IIUGS International Inc., Box 102A, RR#3, Portage la Prairie, Manitoba,
Canada R1N 3A3. We will send you a free newsletter.

References

1. Anderson, J. W., Gustafson, N. J., "Hypocholesterolemic effects of oat and bean products," *Journal of the American Dietetic Association*, Vol. 48, No. 3 (suppl.), Sept. 1988, pp749–753.
2. *Nourishing our Children's Future, A Resource Manual for Health Professionals*, Canadian Dietetic Association, 480 University Ave., Ste 601, Toronto, Ont., M5G 1V2, 1994.
3. Cunnane, S. C., Ganguli, S., Menard, C., Liede, A.C., Hamadeh, M. J., Chen, Z., Wolver, T. M. S., and Jenkins, D. J. A., "High x-linolenic acid flaxseed; Some nutritional properties in humans," *British Journal of Nutrition*, Vol. 69, 1993, pp1–11.
4. Dawson, A., "Flax Touted As Latest Health Food," *The Manitoba Co-operator*, Box 9800, Winnipeg, MB, R3C 3K7, Mar. 31, 1988.
5. *50th Annual Flax Institute of United States*, The Flax Institute of USA, Box 5051, University Station, North Dakota State University, Fargo, ND, 58105, Jan. 1986.
6. Franz, M. J., "Avoiding Sugar: Does Research Support Traditional Beliefs?," *The Diabetes Educator*, Vol. 19, No. 2, Mar./Apr. 1993, pp144–150.
7. Jaret, P., "Things Go Better with Beans," *HEALTH*, Oct. 1993, p32.
8. Jenkins, D. J., Wolever, T. M., Rao, A. V., Hegele, R. A., Mitchell, S. J., Ransom, T. P., Boctor, D. L., Spadafora, P. J., Jenkins, A. L., Mehling, C., et al., "Effect on blood lipids of very high intakes of fiber in diets low in saturated fat and cholesterol," *New England Journal of Medicine*, Vol. 329, No. 1, July 1993, pp21–26.
9. Joint Working Group of the Canadian Pediatric Society of Health Canada, *Nutrition Recommendations Update . . . Dietary Fat and Children*, Health and Welfare, Canada, De L'èglantine St., Tunney's Pasture, Ottawa, Ont., K1A 0K9,1993.
10. Lindsay, A., Smart Cooking, *Quick and Tasty Recipes for Healthy Living*, Macmillan Canada, Toronto, Ontario, 1986.
11. McIntosh, D., *Flaxseed—New uses?*, Flax Growers Western Canada, Box 832, Regina, Sask.
12. Nishimune, T., Yakushiji, T., Sumimoto, T., Taguchi, S., Konishi, Y, Nakahara, S., Ichikawa, T., Kunita, N., "Glycemic response and fiber content of some foods," *American Journal of Clinical Nutrition.*, Vol. 54, No. 2, Aug. 1991, pp414–419.
13. *Advantages of Consuming Flax*, Omega-Life, Inc., Paul Stitt, P.O. Box 730, Manotowic, Wisc., 54420.

14. Omichinski, L., *You Count, Calories Don't*, Tamos Books Inc., Winnipeg, MB, 1993.

Eat when pleasantly hungry. Waiting till blood sugar level has dropped too low causes overeating and nibbling.

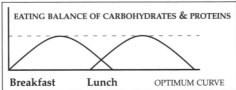

EATING BALANCE OF CARBOHYDRATES & PROTEINS

Breakfast   Lunch   OPTIMUM CURVE

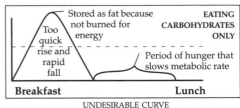

Stored as fat because not burned for energy   EATING CARBOHYDRATES ONLY

Too quick rise and rapid fall

Period of hunger that slows metabolic rate

Breakfast   Lunch

UNDESIRABLE CURVE

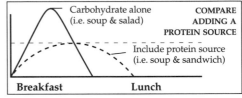

Carbohydrate alone (i.e. soup & salad)   COMPARE ADDING A PROTEIN SOURCE

Include protein source (i.e. soup & sandwich)

Breakfast   Lunch

Additional notes—Milk does contain some protein but it is also very high in carbohydrate. Due to its liquid form and the fact that it is lower in protein content than those mentioned under "protein," it is not as satisfying to be used as "holding over" power. For this reason, it is found under the carbohydrate section.

—Those vegetables that you pull from the ground such as carrots, parsnips, beets, and turnips as well as corn, squash, and peas are the starchy ones. The other vegetables can be used as a filler. They contain the vitamins and minerals, and are not considered part of the carbohydrate component of the meal due to high-water content with very little carbohydrate content. Include both complex and simple carbohydrates at each meal.

15. Riccardi, G., Rivellese, A. A., "Effects of dietary fiber and carbohydrate on glucose and lipoprotein metabolism in diabetic patients," *Diabetes-Care*, Vol. 14, No. 12, Dec. 1991, pp1115–1125.

16. Scott, N., "Nutrition expert says flax could be major health food," *The Leader Post*, 1964 Park St., Regina, Sask., S4P 3G4, Mar. 8, 1991.

17. Stecyk, T., "New medicinal roles being found for flax," *The Western Producer*, Box 2500, Saskatoon, Sask., S7K 2C4, July 26, 1990, p60.

18. Stitt, P., "Nutritional importance of flax," *Flax Growers Newsletter*, P.O. Box 832, Regina, Sask., S4P 3B1, Nov. 1986, pp13–14.

19. *Advantages of Omega-3 Concentrate Over Fish Oil*, The Essential Nutrient Research Company (ENRECO), Paul Stitt, P.O. Box 730, Manitowic, Wisc., 54420.

20. Wang, S. R., Chase, P., Garg, S. K., Hoops, S. L., Harris, M. A., "The effect of sugar cereal with and without a mixed meal on Glycemic Response in Children with Diabetes," *Journal of Pediatric Gastroenterology and Nutrition*, Vol. 13, No. 2, 1991, pp155–160.

21. Whyte, J. L., McArthur, R., Topping, D., Nestel, P., "Oat bran lowers plasma cholesterol levels in mildly hypercholesterolemic men," *Journal of the American Dietetic Association*, Vol. 92, No. 4, Apr. 1992, pp446–449.

22. Wrick, L. L., Robertson, J. B., et al., "The influence of dietary fiber source on human intestine transit and stool output," *Journal of Nutrition*, Vol. 113, 1983, pp1464–1479.

Order form

HUGS Resources for the non-diet life-style . . . .

The hallmark of HUGS is versatility.
Group, individual, and professional support combinations emerge from our resources.

☐ **Teens & Diets—No Weigh: Building the road to healthier living.** Free Information package.
• A refreshing new program that aims to prevent the onset of a diet life-style and build healthier living patterns relevant to the teen life-style. Emphasizes skill building around self-esteem, assertiveness, critical thinking, hands-on cooking, non-diet nutrition concepts, and physical activity. Self-training facilitator guide with 8 complete lesson plans; participant support material package includes uniquely designed teen journal, parent guide, and *Tailoring Your Tastes* cookbook.

* ☐ **HUGS Fun Fitness Video*** ea $24.95 (includes a message about weight and dieting)
• Gentle, physical activity—If other exercise tapes have left you feeling that fitness is not for you, you'll appreciate our gentle and fun approach to activity. Relaxed participants have been filmed in a natural, outdoor setting. You can enjoy moving at a level that leaves you feeling energized, not exhausted, Experience our refreshing new approach. Gain the desire to be more active.

* ☐ **HUGS Audio Tapes*** set $41.95 (includes daily affirmation plan for lifelong better health)
• Stop dieting and start living—Set of 3 tapes provide new perspectives on life leading to increased confidence about making decisions that are best for your situation. Learn how to use positive language, relax, and be more assertive as you take your focus off weight.

☐ **HUGS Club News** Annual subscription (4 issues) CANADA $15 (Can$) plus GST;
USA $15 (US$); OVERSEAS $25 (Can$)
• Includes group discussion features—A support network of news, articles, inspiration, and motivation designed to keep the reader off the diet roller coaster and linked with others who have chosen the non-diet life-style.

☐ **HUGS Journal Analysis** 7-day analysis $60
• A personal counseling session—Find out how your activity and eating are affecting your energy levels and outlook on life.

☐ **HUGS Classes** 10 weeks • Call 1-800-565-4847 to see if classes are available in your area.

☐ **HUGS at Home** $199 (includes indexed binder guide, *You Count, Calories Don't*, HUGS Fitness Video & Audio Tapes, HUGS Club News subscription, and a Journal Analysis)
• Here's the answer when HUGS classes aren't available in your area.

☐ **HUGS Facilitator Kit** for program delivery Complete information package $5
• Our international network of licensees is growing constantly. The information package explains the HUGS approach and how HUGS resources can be used in the community, in fitness facilities, in hospitals, in clinics, in workplaces, and in educational institutions. HUGS self-training kit equips the facilitator to deliver cost recovery programs and/or develop an independent business.

* ☐ *You Count, Calories Don't** ea $19.95 (Can$); $14.95 (US$)

* ☐ *Tailoring Your Tastes** ea $19.95 (Can$); $14.95 (US$)

* Add $5.00 Cdn per item for shipping & handling—Add $10 shipping charge for orders outside North America; for air mail, add $20 shipping charge

---

Please send this form with payment to:

HUGS International Inc.
Box 102A, RR#3
Portage la Prairie, MB
Canada R1N 3A3

Fax orders
(204) 428-5072

Toll free orders
1-800-565-4847
(Canada and USA)

e mail address:
lomichin@portage.net

☐ **Yes, I'd like to purchase the HUGS resources checked off above.**

Name _____
Street address _____
City, Prov/State _____
Postal Code/Zip _____
Phone (H) _____ (W) _____
Cheque enclosed ☐
Visa No _____
Mastercard No. _____
Expiry date _____ Signature _____

Total Cost (all items) _____
Shipping Charges
(No. * items X $5.00) _____
Sub-total _____
PST (MB) _____
GST (Canada) _____
Total $ _____